World Histories of Crime, Culture and Violence

Series Editors

Marianna Muravyeva
University of Tampere
Tampere, Finland

Raisa Maria Toivo
University of Tampere
Tampere, Finland

Palgrave's World Histories of Crime, Culture and Violence seeks to publish research monographs, collections of scholarly essays, multi-authored books, and Palgrave Pivots addressing themes and issues of interdisciplinary histories of crime, criminal justice, criminal policy, culture and violence globally and on a wide chronological scale (from the ancient to the modern period). It focuses on interdisciplinary studies, historically contextualized, across various cultures and spaces employing a wide range of methodologies and conceptual frameworks.

More information about this series at
http://www.springer.com/series/14383

Kerstin von Lingen
Editor

Debating Collaboration and Complicity in War Crimes Trials in Asia, 1945–1956

palgrave
macmillan

Editor
Kerstin von Lingen
Heidelberg University
Heidelberg, Germany

World Histories of Crime, Culture and Violence
ISBN 978-3-319-53140-3 ISBN 978-3-319-53141-0 (eBook)
DOI 10.1007/978-3-319-53141-0

Library of Congress Control Number: 2017948957

Cover image: Bakoenasee, TIMOR 1945-10-11. Four Natives suspected to have collaborated with the Japanese. Adjutant de Bree (Netherlands Indies Civil Administration/ NICA) and Captain Hilmer-Smith (Australia/ Timforce) are standing to the right. (PHOTOGRAPHER SGT K. B. DAVIS)
Courtesy of Australian War Memorial (AWM, 120175)

Printed on acid-free paper

This Palgrave Macmillan imprint is published by Springer Nature
The registered company is Springer International Publishing AG
The registered company address is: Gewerbestrasse 11, 6330 Cham, Switzerland

Contents

List of Contributors

CHEAH Wui Ling has been Assistant Professor at the Faculty of Law of the National University of Singapore since 2007. She was educated at the National University of Singapore (LL.B., LL.M.), Harvard Law School (LL.M.), European University Institute and Oxford University (D.Phil). She is a qualified lawyer (called to the New York Bar) and holds a diploma in arbitration (Queen Mary University of London). Prior to entering academia, she served as a Legal Officer at INTERPOL's Office of Legal Affairs (Lyon, France). Her teaching experience includes periods at the Centre for Transnational Legal Studies (London, UK), Oxford University (UK), Université Jean Moulin Lyon 3 (France) and the Royal University of Law and Economics (Cambodia). Her work has been published in journals such as the *Harvard Human Rights Journal*, *Journal of International Criminal Justice* and *International Journal of Law in Context*. Currently, she is working on a book project on the Singapore war crimes trials. She is also co-founder of the Singapore War Crimes Trials Web Portal (http://www.singaporewarcrimestrials.com/).

Deokhyo Choi is a research professor at the Research Institute of Korean Studies, Korea University. He received his Ph.D. in History from Cornell University in August 2013. His Ph.D. dissertation, "Crucible of the Post-Empire: Decolonization, Race, and Cold War Politics in U.S.-Japan-Korea Relations, 1945–1952," won the International Convention of Asia Scholars (ICAS) Best Dissertation Prize 2015 in the Humanities. He has published numerous articles in English, Japanese, and Korean. His recent articles include. "Writing the

'Empire' Back into the History of Postwar Japan" (*International Journal of Korean History*, February 2017) and "'Mindful of the Enslavement': The Cairo Declaration, Korean Independence, and the Ambiguity of the Liberation of Koreans in Defeated Japan" (*The Significance and Effects of the Cairo Declaration*, 2014). *The research leading to these results received funding from the European Research Council under the European Union's Seventh Framework Programme (FP7/2007–2013)/ERC grant agreement n°* 313382.

Robert Cribb is Professor of Asian History at the Australian National University, Canberra. His research focuses on Indonesian history, with special attention to violence, national identity, and environmental politics. His recent publications include *Historical Atlas of Northeast Asia 1590–2010* (New York: Columbia University Press, 2014, with Li Narangoa). He recently completed (with Sandra Wilson, Beatrice Trefalt, and Dean Aszkielowicz) *Japanese War Criminals: The Politics of Justice After the Second World War* (New York: Columbia University Press, 2017).

Arnaud Doglia is currently a postdoctoral research fellow in the Department of East Asian Studies at the University of Geneva, Switzerland. He is interested in contemporary Japan and East Asia. He received his MA (East Asian studies) and his PhD (Japanese studies) from the University of Geneva. His first book, published by Peter Lang, is entitled *Japanese Biological Warfare, 1880–2011: Historical Realities and the Anatomy of Memory* (2016). His current research, Japanese Medical Atrocities: Narratives of Reconversion of Former War Criminals in Postwar Japan, seeks to analyze in depth the network of scientists and physicians who participated in medical experiments up to 1945, equally discussing their profile, reconversion, and responsibility. Other topics of interest include the birth of bioethics in Japan, Japanese war crimes and their memories in East Asia, World War II and Cold War atrocities, and social history and popular culture during the Allied occupation and in postwar Japan. *The research leading to these results has received funding from the European Research Council under the European Union's Seventh Framework Programme (FP7/2007–2013) /ERC grant agreement n° [313382]. This chapter was published in the context of Project 100011_169861 (Le Japon et l'Asie de l'Est face à la Seconde Guerre mondiale), funded by the Swiss National Science Foundation.*

Barak Kushner teaches modern Japanese history in the Faculty of Asian & Middle Eastern Studies at Cambridge University. He was awarded a 2012–2013 British Academy Mid-Career Fellowship which he used to complete his third book entitled *Men to Devils, Devils to Men: Japanese War Crimes and Chinese Justice* (Harvard University Press, 2015). In 2013 he launched a 5-year European Research Council funded project, "The Dissolution of the Japanese Empire and the Struggle for Legitimacy in Postwar East Asia, 1945–1965." Kushner's second book, *Slurp! A culinary and social history of ramen – Japan's favorite noodle soup* (Brill, 2012), analyzed food and history within Sino-Japan relations and was awarded the 2013 Sophie Coe Prize for Food History. *The Thought War – Japanese Imperial Propaganda* (Hawaii 2006), Kushner's first book, delved into the history of wartime Japanese propaganda. He was a 2008 Abe Fellow and conducted research concerning "Cold War Propaganda in East Asia and Historical Memory." Previously, Kushner worked in the US Department of State as a political officer in East Asian affairs and taught Chinese and Japanese history at Davidson College in North Carolina, USA. As a scholar he has written on wartime Japanese and Chinese propaganda, Japanese media, Sino-Japanese relations, Asian comedy, food history, BC class war crimes, and the Cold War. (For more see www.barakkushner.net)

Konrad M. Lawson has a broad interest in the aftermaths of modern war, and most of his research has been on the continuities and transformations of the 1940s transwar period. His first book manuscript explores the relationship between war crimes and treason in retribution against the military and police collaborators who helped maintain Japan's wartime occupations in East and Southeast Asia up until its defeat in 1945. Other topics of interest are the global history of political retribution, early post-WWII Scandinavia, decolonization in East and Southeast Asia, the colonial and postcolonial histories of Korea and Taiwan, Sino-Japanese cultural and political relations, and the transnational history of encounters and interactions with and within Asia.

Kerstin Von Lingen is a historian and researcher at the Cluster of Excellence "Asia and Europe in a Global Context" at Heidelberg University. Since 2013, she has led an independent research project entitled "Transcultural Justice: Legal Flows and the Emergence of International Justice within the East Asian War Crimes Trials, 1946–1954," supervising four doctoral dissertations on the Soviet, Chinese, Dutch, and French war crimes trial policies in Asia. Her many publications include two monographs in English, *Kesselring's Last Battle: War*

Crimes Trials and Cold War Politics, 1945–1960 (Lawrence: University of Kansas Press, 2009) and *Allen Dulles, the OSS and Nazi War Criminals: The Dynamics of Selective Prosecution* (Cambridge: Cambridge University Press, 2013), as well as the (co)edited volumes *War Crimes Trials in the Wake of Decolonization and Cold War in Asia, 1945–1956: Justice in Times of Turmoil*, Palgrave 2016, as well as the multi-authored volumes *Kriegserfahrung und nationale Identität in Europa* [War Experience and National Identity in Europe after 1945] (Paderborn: Schoeningh, 2009) and (with Klaus Gestwa) *Zwangsarbeit als Kriegsressource in Europa und Asien* [Forced Labor as a Resource of War: European and Asian Perspectives) (Paderborn: Schoeningh 2014).

Sandra Wilson is a Professor at the School of Arts and a Fellow of the Asia Research Centre at Murdoch University, Australia. She received her BA (Hons) in History and her Master's in Japanese Studies at the University of Western Australia, and her D.Phil. in Modern Japanese History at Oxford University. Her research interests include the history of Japanese nationalism, post-1945 Chinese and Japanese films about the Second World War, and war crimes and war criminals in the Asian theatre after the Second World War. Her publications include *The Manchurian Crisis and Japanese Society, 1931–33*, London, Routledge, 2002, and, with Robert Cribb, Beatrice Trefalt and Dean Aszkielowicz, *Japanese War Criminals: the Politics of Justice After the Second World War*, New York, Columbia University Press, 2017.

Esther Zwinkels is a researcher at the Netherlands Institute of Military History in The Hague. At Leiden University she is finishing her PhD thesis, which deals with investigations and trials of collaboration and war crimes cases after the Second World War in the Dutch East Indies. Her publications include "Containing 'potentially subversive' subjects: the internment of supporters of the National Socialist Movement in the Dutch East Indies, 1940–1946" in*Incarceration and Regime Change: European Prisons during and after the Second World War* ed. Christian G. De Vito, Ralf Futselaar, and Helen Grevers (New York: Berghahn, 2016) and *Het Overakker-complot. Indisch verzet tegen de Japanse bezetter op Sumatra 1942–1945* (Houten: Spectrum, 2011). This research is supported by the Netherlands Organisation for Scientific Research (NWO) as part of the research project "Recognition and Retribution. Transitional justice in the Dutch East Indies after the Second World War". The author would like to thank Petra Groen and the editors of this volume for comments on earlier drafts.

List of Tables

War Crimes Trials in Asia: Collaboration and Complicity in the Aftermath of War

Kerstin von Lingen and Robert Cribb

In the years following the Second World War in Asia, the victorious Allied powers undertook an immense program of war crimes trials, charging Japanese political and military leaders, military personnel, and associated civilians with crimes against peace and with breaches of the laws and customs of war. The actions that were prosecuted included massacre, murder, torture, ill treatment, and withholding of food and medicine.

This volume draws on papers presented at the conference "Rethinking Justice? Decolonization, Cold War and Asian War Crimes Trials" held at Heidelberg University, 26–29 October 2014. For this chapter, we also draw on the results of intensive discussions with 2014's visiting fellows Sandra Wilson and Kirsten Sellars to the Research Group "Transcultural Justice" on Asian war crimes trials, Milinda Banerjee, Lisette Schouten, Anja Bihler, Ann-Sophie Schoepfel, and Valentyna Polunina, at the Cluster of Excellence "Asia and Europe in a Global Context" at Heidelberg University, whom we would like to thank for their valuable input.

K. von Lingen (✉)
Cluster of Excellence "Asia and Europe in a Global Context", Heidelberg University, Heidelberg, Germany
e-mail: lingen@asia-europe.uni-heidelberg.de

R. Cribb
Australian National University, Canberra, Australia
e-mail: robert.cribb@anu.edu.au

K. von Lingen (ed.), *Debating Collaboration and Complicity in War Crimes Trials in Asia, 1945–1956*, World Histories of Crime, Culture and Violence, DOI 10.1007/978-3-319-53141-0_1

The vast majority of trials were conducted in the immediate aftermath of war by individual Allied powers according to their own legislation and regulations. Only the International Military Tribunal for the Far East (IMTFE), which convened in Tokyo from 1946 to 1948 to hear the prosecution of Japan's most senior leaders, took place formally under an international charter. All the trials, however – both the IMTFE and the national trials – drew their legal basis from developments in international law that had taken shape during the nineteenth and early twentieth centuries.

The trend of those developments was to limit the absolute sovereignty of the state in humanitarian matters and to assert the primacy of international norms, regardless of formal state-sanctioned legality. The war crimes trials in Asia, along with their counterparts in Europe, represented a watershed moment in this transition because they marked the demise of an old political-legal order based on legal pluralism and (implicitly) cultural relativism and the advent of a new, putatively universalist legal order.

Yet universality evaded the trials process in two important respects. First, they were tightly bound to the issue of treason, which was not universalist at all but rather was embedded in the notion that each individual owes loyality to a specific state. This link arose because occupation forces everywhere engaged in cooperative relationships with local people and institutes. The distinction, however, between innocuous engagement, which amounted to no more than sustaining daily life, and collaboration, which actively assisted the enemy, was nowhere clear or certain. Second, the trials evaded universality because they were constrained both temporally and by nationality. The timing of an atrocity was crucial in whether it could be considered a war crime; also crucial was the nationality of perpetrators and victims. In the end, these limits led to profound dissatisfaction with the trials process, despite its vast scale and ambitious intentions.

The war crimes trials that followed the Second World War in Asia represented an attempt to implement international humanitarian law relating to war and to expand its scope so as to provide new protections for civilians in occupied territories. This expansion was conceived in Europe, where the inhabitants of independent nation-states under Axis occupation had been subjected to terrible treatment. Applied to Asia, international humanitarian law encountered a colonial order that, though in many cases fatally wounded by the war, still ran according to very different principles of international order. This order was premised on human difference and inequality, with formal legal distinctions between metropoles and their colonies and formalized systems of racial and ethnic classification. The majority of colonial polities were subordinate to distant Western sovereign powers while being nonetheless politically and legally distinct from the metropolitan polities. Internally, too, colonies were marked by legal pluralism, which gave different legal rights to different ethnic groups. Differences in legal rights and responsibilities lay at the heart of this racial and ethnic differentiation. The new international order, by contrast, did away with formal hierarchy, ushering in a world of nominally equal nation-states, all of them constrained by international law and norms. Within the newly sovereign states, the principle of ethnic hierarchy was diminished, though not eliminated, by new norms of citizenship. Indonesia and Malaysia, for example, made a formal distinction between citizens of indigenous and foreign descent, but the legal implications of this distinction were much weaker than in the colonial period. The ideological contestation between the American and Soviet blocs split the new international order, masking the fact that both communism and liberal capitalism asserted the fundamental equality of humans and the international responsibilities of states. In the period of transition, however, the ambiguous national status of colonized peoples proved deeply disruptive to the universalism of international humanitarian law. In this context, the trials of Japanese defendants for war crimes, defined by the international community, served as critically significant sites for producing new visions of justice and political legitimation.

The issue of collaboration became one of the most contested elements in the legal reckoning that took place after the Second World War. As Timothy Brook states, collaboration "superimposes a moral map over the political landscape it ventures to describe."[1] In the colonial context, the term achieved an extra dimension, and there were different implications in the category of collaboration in the different theaters of war. In Europe, "collaboration" targeted the wrong choice of war-time alliances and divided each nation into good and bad actors in time of war. In many postwar European trials, especially in the West, "collaboration" meant the active choice to side with the occupying Nazi power.[2] Many collaborators did not act solely out of political opportunism but had genuine faith in a new fascist world order. Before the war, they had often been leaders or members of established nationalist or even fascist movements in their home countries.[3] After the war, these attempts were identified all over Europe as treason and an offense to national honor; collaborators were severely punished. In military circles, treason is considered the highest of all crimes, for it is considered both a "crime against the nation" and a betrayal of one's comrades.[4] In practice, treason was thus considered the most severe form of collaboration.

Other treason trials in Europe had to do with regime change and the birth of a communist state and, thus, gave new governments the chance to veil their attempts at retribution against old elites by presenting a narrative of purging wrong wartime choices. As Istvàn Deák underlines, there were two factors in collaboration trials: the "desire to place the blame on specific individuals for what had been, in reality, a large scale popular accommodation with the enemy, and the perceived need to eliminate, or at least reduce, the influence of social, political, and ethnic groups that might stand in the way of the creation of a new society and state." The result was "an enormous demographic unheaval."[5] In Germany, the speedy release of convicted war criminals proved devastating in terms of memory politics as well as for the overall narrative since it nourished a view in some parts of society that German officers had been "unjustly" sentenced.[6] However, early on, German politics opted, under gentle Allied pressure, for an official line of recognizing war guilt and paying compensation to victims or their families.[7] For the most part, German *Vergangenheitspolitik* (the politics of coming to terms with the past) then settled in the late 1970s on a ritualized acknowledgment of the Holocaust as a unique crime. Following that acknowledgment came the establishments of new memorials, remembrance days, and even the curious "belated trials" of former Auschwitz camp guards in the spring of 2015, seventy years after the end of the war. This political choice of reconciliation with the burden of the past enabled Germany over the decades following the Second World War to be recognized again as a partner in international affairs and, by the end of the Cold War, to return to the center stage of European politics.[8] This strategy was attentively observed by Asian countries as a possible example but, for various reasons, never fully copied. However, all these facets influenced the narrative of war time behavior substantially.

Some parts of Asia resembled Europe in the pattern of reckoning with collaboration. In China, as in Europe, collaboration with Japan often arose out of prewar political convictions, blended with opportunism.[9] Wang Jingwei, leader of the collaborationist Reorganized National Government of the Republic of China, had been before the war a prominent leader of the ruling Guomindang in the Republic of China. He was drawn to work with Japan partly because he was being edged out of power by Chiang Kai-shek, partly because of his strong hostility to the West and partly by reason of his conviction that Japan was likely to prevail militarily. As in Europe, too, the postwar regime took harsh revenge on collaborators, putting 25,000 so-called traitorous Chinese (*Hanjian*) on trial and sentencing many of them to death.[10] Wang died before the war's end, but the Guomindang had his tomb blown up with TNT and his body burned as postmortem punishment.[11] Deokhyo Choi's chapter in this volume describes a similar situation in Korea. Koreans made no demands for the prosecution of their former Japanese rulers. They focused, rather, on the issue of Korean collaboration with Japan, which was in many respects a proxy for the bitter internal struggle between Korean communists and anti-communists.

Collaboration and Complicity as a Legal Problem

The law of occupation is a part of the law of war. It implies the establishment of authority over a foreign territory and, thus, touches on the problem of sovereignty.[12] The Hague Convention of 1899, ratified in 1907,[13] imposed two types of obligations on an army that seizes control of enemy territory during war: the obligation to protect the life and property of the inhabitants and the obligation to respect the sovereign rights of the ousted government.[14] The expectation under the Hague Convention was that adjustments in the sovereignty over territory would be made in postwar peace settlements, not unilaterally during the conflict. Often called *belligerent occupation* (as seen as a byproduct of hostilities), this regime is temporary and has ramifications for the population affected. According to this law, the occupying power is bound to respect and maintain the political and other institutions that exist in that territory and is responsible for the maintenance of public order and civil life in the territory under its control.[15] The price of this protection was that the inhabitants of occupied territories were expected to go about their daily lives without in any way resisting or hampering the occupation. However, nearly all conflicts of the twentieth century demonstrated the emptiness of these rules. Most occupants implemented the law of occupation in a way that promoted their own interests, often at the expense of the occupied. In turn, most outside or exile governments refused to acknowledge the validity of acts that the occupant had enacted.[16] Exiled governments consistently asserted their claim to the allegiance of citizens in occupied territories, and they celebrated and encouraged acts of resistance and insubordination.[17]

The Geneva Convention of 1949 both shifted the focus of international law from governments to individuals and broadened its scope. In actual conflicts, the presumption is made that the protection of human rights does not cease in cases of international armed conflicts.[18] However, this understanding of occupation was mainly the fruit of the developments of international law during and after the Second World War and the growth of legal experience in dealing with its outcome in court. Tribunals needed to scrutinize the degree of abuse of sovereign rights by the occupier and its behavior toward the local population.[19] The entanglement between pressure exerted by occupiers to render service and voluntary collaboration with the enemy became, thus, a contested field of both legal and political battles in the immediate postwar period.

Decolonization as the Background of Trials on Collaboration

In Southeast Asia, however, and by extension in India, the situation was made more complicated by the issue of decolonization. According to the definition of Prasenjit Duara, "Decolonization refers to the process whereby colonial powers transferred institutional and legal control over their territories and dependencies to indigenously based, formally sovereign, nation states."[20] This transfer of power and legal control led to changing norms of legality and political legitimacy. Since the war crimes trials took place in this context, they were affected by contestations between European colonial powers, the United States, the Soviet Union, and anticolonial nationalists in Southeast and South Asia. At the start of the war, India and most of Southeast Asia were ruled by Western colonial powers. Nationalist movements had emerged in most colonies, though they varied greatly in strength and in the degree of consensus they were able to muster concerning the kind of independence they wanted to achieve. All of these nationalist movements drew inspiration from Japan's early success in modernizing and industrializing and from Japan's military victories against Russia in the early twentieth century. Japan's subsequent imperial expansion in Korea and China had aroused misgivings among some nationalists in the Asian colonies, but others continued to find Japan inspiring. In particular, Japan's wartime slogan "Asia for the Asiatics" and the willingness of Japanese authorities to sponsor nationally based client states in Manchuria, Mongolia, and, later, Burma and the Philippines, as well as less certain promises of independence for India and Indonesia, led some local leaders to see Japan as a champion of self-determination rather than as its enemy. Regardless of Japan's intentions, moreover, the wartime occupation enormously weakened European colonial authority. European colonial armies were defeated, colonial rulers were driven out or interned, the elaborate structures of colonial authority and privilege were swept aside, and the Japanese authorities gave material assistance to sympathetic nationalist groups. Even though Japan was eventually defeated, the Japanese interlude made colonial rule unsustainable in its antebellum form in most of the region.

With the exception of the Portuguese, whose tiny, undeveloped colony in East Timor was untroubled by nationalism, all the colonial powers in Southeast Asia responded to this new situation with a strategy of carrot and stick. To win over those sections of the nationalist movements they regarded as moderate, the colonial powers promised – and delivered – political reforms that would have been dramatic and transformative had they been implemented before the war. Their aim was to move toward forms of independence that would preserve colonial economic and strategic interests as far as possible. At the same time, they used military force against so-called extremists who demanded more thoroughgoing change. The balance between political concessions and military force varied greatly among the colonial powers. Broadly speaking, the United States and Britain made earlier and more extensive concessions and achieved relatively peaceful transitions to independence in the Philippines in 1946, India and Pakistan in 1947, and Burma in 1948. The Netherlands and France, by contrast, made fewer concessions and were drawn into protracted, destructive wars ending in negotiated transfers of sovereignty in 1949 and 1954.

In these circumstances, the status of colonial subjects who had worked with the Japanese authorities became a critical issue with two dimensions. First, did they have the same obligation as metropolitan citizens to remain loyal to the colonial power? Official lawyers were in no doubt that they did, but the fact that nationalist movements had long argued for breaking ties with the metropole and the fact that the metropole was now proceeding to implement that break put the formal legal position into doubt. CHEAH Wui Ling in this volume draws attention to the legal anomalies arising from this question in Singapore. She discusses prosecutions in which the facts were not significantly in dispute but in which the liability for prosecution depended on the status of the victim. The expansion of war crimes law to protect civilians in occupied territories exposed the lack of protection available to the civilian subjects of belligerent powers. In specific terms, anyone who had accepted Japanese protection – as some Indians were believed to have done – thereby lost the protection of war crimes law.

Second, in collaborating with the Japanese authorities, did they commit treason against their own people? By virtue of collaboration, the nationalist leaders Ba Maw and Aung San in Burma, José P. Laurel in the Philippines, Sukarno in Indonesia, and Subhas Chandra Bose in India were all implicated in Japanese oppression. To varying degrees, prewar anticolonial nationalist movements denounced compatriots who collaborated with the colonial authorities, but they seldom did so with any great vitriol. In the aftermath of the war, Western observers were inclined to equate these men with European collaborators with the Nazis,[21] but local opinion so strongly regarded them as patriots that the colonial powers never felt entirely confident in proceeding to collaboration trials. All those who had worked with the Japanese authorities could argue plausibly that they had treated the occupation authorities as a means to the end of national self-determination. Indeed, virtually everyone who worked with the occupation authorities could plead force of circumstance or noble motive. Placing collaborators on trial might have had a potential declarative function in postwar colonial strategy by tainting those who had collaborated with Japan, but the tactic was risky because defendants could easily present themselves as victims and because a trial might easily become a platform for denouncing the colonial power's failure to defend its subjects.[22]

Esther Zwinkels shows in her analysis of Dutch trials of alleged collaborators in Indonesia that the colonial government pursued a mixed agenda, attempting both to punish collaboration during the occupation years and to win support of Indonesia for a postwar order aligned with Dutch interests by showing some tolerance for wartime misdemeanors. A relatively high number of collaborator trials was the result. It is telling that in most jurisdictions, treason trials of local people who had collaborated with Japanese forces were conducted more promptly than the war crimes trials of Japanese.

The Dimension of Time

Contemporary thinking in international law admits no statute of limitations for crimes against humanity. European governments prosecute aged surviving staff of Nazi death camps; an International Crimes Tribunal in

Bangladesh arraigns men accused of genocide during the 1971 liberation war; a hybrid court in Cambodia prosecutes surviving leaders of the Khmer Rouge regime that committed its worst atrocities in 1975–1979. Outside the courtroom, there are demands for moral reckoning for even earlier crimes, such as the Nanjing Massacre of 1937, the Herero genocide in Namibia in the early twentieth century, and the Atlantic slave trade of the nineteenth century and earlier.

The legal staff who ran the trials in Asia after the Second World War, however, worked under the constant pressure of time. They were aware not only that the task of assembling persuasive cases against defendants was growing more difficult with time but also that the world outside the courtroom was changing. As Japan moved from being a defeated enemy to being a likely Cold War partner of the West, the pressure to reckon with the crimes of wartime diminished. In 1948 the U.S. government and the Occupation authorities in Japan decided not to proceed with a second round of IMTFE trials, even though the potential defendants were conveniently available in detention in Tokyo's Sugamo Prison. In the late 1940s and early 1950s, the British and other prosecuting authorities made similar decisions to wind up their trial processes for the sake of facilitating Japan's rehabilitation. Konrad Lawson's chapter in this volume illustrates the complex legal, political, and moral issues that arose in considering whether to grant amnesty to Filipino leaders who had collaborated with the Japanese forces. This effort to clear the moral ground for a new postwar order in East Asia influenced the position of the Japanese already convicted of war crimes. The formal position that they were individual perpetrators bearing responsibility for the specific crimes that they had committed increasingly gave way to a perception, especially in Japan, that they were scapegoats unreasonably being punished for a nation whose guilt was now being forgiven by the prosecuting powers in the interest of Cold War realities.[23]

This sensitivity to time was as embedded in the legal basis for the trials as much as it was set within their political context. International law on war crimes was universal geographically but not temporally. It applied to actions carried out in wartime only. Crucially, moreover, its scope was constricted by the belligerent status of both perpetrators and victims. This constriction arose because the legal basis for the war crimes trials after the Second World War rested on four distinct foundations that, though connected, were not yet integrated.

The first foundation of the postwar trials was a series of agreements, generally known as the Geneva Conventions, which prescribed humane treatment for prisoners of war. These conventions mandated the provision of proper accommodation, food, and other care for prisoners of war, as well as requiring prompt repatriation upon the conclusion of hostilities. The second foundation was a series of agreements, generally called The Hague Conventions, prescribing humane conduct in war. These agreements included regulations covering the declaration of war and the correct behavior of neutrals, as well as prohibiting weapons judged to be inhumane, such as poison gas and expanding bullets. The third foundation was the 1928 General Treaty for Renunciation of War as an Instrument of National Policy (often known as the Kellogg–Briand Pact), which was understood as prohibiting aggressive war.

Finally, the fourth foundation upon which the postwar prosecutions rested was the wartime work of the United Nations War Crimes Commission (UNWCC), which had carefully developed an extended legal basis for prosecuting crimes against peace and war crimes against civilians.[24] Prior to the Second World War, international law was widely believed to give little protection to the civilian inhabitants of occupied territories. They were believed to be legitimately subject to many forms of harsh, occupation discipline. Atrocities such as the 1937 massacre of Chinese civilians in the Chinese capital of Nanjing by Japanese military forces were widely condemned as barbarous, but there was no legal basis for considering them to be criminal and no mechanism for bringing perpetrators to justice. After the First World War, a German Court at Leipzig until 1922 brought 17 defendants to trial of twelve charges of war crimes against enemy civilians, prisoners of war and enemy shipping. Ten of the defendants were found guilty, seven were acquitted, but in none of the cases which involved solely crimes against civilians was a guilty verdict reached. Thus, these verdicts did not strengthen the protections of civilians in occupied territories.[25]

The UNWCC's extension of the basis for prosecuting wartime misconduct under international law derived from the work of a Commission on Responsibilities established as part of the process leading to the 1919 Treaty of Versailles. That commission produced a list of thirty-two actions that it believed should in future constitute war crimes. The list included murder, torture, rape, deliberate starvation, forced conscription, forced prostitution, looting, confiscation, and currency debasement.[26] It reflected the ambition of the Versailles planners to establish new international standards for behavior in times of war, though they were careful to ground these standards in legal and philosophical precedent. In effect, armies of occupation were henceforth to be held to much higher standards of behavior toward the inhabitants of occupied territories than had ever previously been the case. The list, however, was not endorsed as part of the Versailles Treaty or in any subsequent international agreement. In the first half of the 1920s, international law specialists devoted considerable attention to ideas for an International War Crimes Court, but the idea had lost traction by 1925. In 1934 a meeting of the International Committee of the Red Cross in Tokyo adopted a "Draft International Convention on the Condition and Protection of Civilians of Enemy Nationality who are on Territory belonging to or occupied by a Belligerent,"[27] but this document also failed to win international support, and the question of giving formal legal protection to civilians largely disappeared from the international agenda until the scale of Nazi atrocities in German-occupied Europe became apparent after 1939.[28] The UNWCC then returned to the Versailles list, interpreting it as a statement of international customary law concerning war crimes that could become the basis for prosecuting perpetrators once they were apprehended.

The four different legal foundations were complementary in many respects – covering the treatment of prisoners of war, the proper conduct of war, recourse to aggressive war, and treatment of civilians in occupied territories. The humane extension of the legal definition of war crimes to include atrocities against civilians, however, unexpectedly created a new form of distinction between war crimes and acts that were not war crimes, based partly on the status of the perpetrators and victims. As a general principle, Western law criminalizes particular acts carried out with criminal intent, regardless of who the perpetrator may be.[29] National law is limited by national borders, whereas international law is universal. War crimes law applied in Asia in the aftermath of the Second World War, however, stopped significantly short of universality in four key respects. First, it did not impinge on the legality of actions carried out for military necessity. This understanding meant that actions against enemy territory were generally not considered to be war crimes. Thus, the firebombing of Tokyo and the dropping of atomic bombs on Hiroshima and Nagasaki were not formally criminal. Second, under war crimes law, authorities could not commit war crimes against their own citizens. Such atrocities were considered to be crimes against humanity rather than war crimes, but this category of misdemeanor was still only weakly developed in international law, and there were almost no prosecutions on such charges in the Asia-Pacific theater after the Second World War.[30] Third, war crimes, defined as acts of war that could not be justified by military necessity, could not be committed by noncombatants and, therefore, not by the inhabitants of occupied territories. For these perpetrators, only domestic criminal laws, including potentially laws on treason, were applicable. And fourth, the possibility of arraigning defendants from the Allied side was excluded from planning, not only because it was assumed culturally that the Allied side had not been guilty but also as a prerogative of victory. War crimes, in effect, could be committed only against people whom one had an obligation to protect, most notably prisoners of war and the inhabitants of occupied territories. The wartime allies fighting Japan were not technically in occupation of any territory until the commencement of the occupation of Japan after the end of hostilities; partly because of the savagery of the war, moreover, they held relatively few prisoners of war. They were thus intrinsically less vulnerable to accusations of war crimes under the new standards being set by the trials. Both the IMTFE and the national courts formally excluded any Japanese defense that employed the principle of *tu quoque* ("you did it too"). In other words, although the war crimes trials in Asia and the Pacific were presented as giving universal law and shared human values priority over national law and national sovereignty, the application of war crimes law accentuated national distinctions.

Thus, the war crimes trials process that followed the Second World War in Asia was intended to deal narrowly with the consequences of atrocities carried out by aggressors in the course of warfare. The restriction of the practical definition of war crimes to atrocities carried out by aggressors left Koreans in a deeply ambiguous position. Koreans were Japanese colonial subjects. Japan had forcibly annexed the previously independent country in 1910, but Allied planners limited the war crimes investigation process after the Second World War to the period from 1928. In the eyes of the prosecutors, Koreans were thus Japanese subjects and had none of the protections enjoyed under international law by the inhabitants of occupied territories. Japan's efforts to erase Korean culture,[31] therefore, as well as the brutal treatment of Korean laborers and the recruitment of Korean women for enforced prostitution, were not addressed by Allied courts, even though these actions would have constituted war crimes had the status of Koreans been considered differently in international law. Koreans might have been protected by the new concept of crimes against humanity, which paid no attention to the national status of victims, but that concept was barely formed and seldom used in the Asian context. Neither the United States nor the Soviet Union in their respective occupation zones in postwar Korea saw any political value in prosecuting Japanese for their actions in Korea or against Koreans outside the country. As noted earlier, Koreans themselves expressed little interest in the prosecution of Japanese in the immediate aftermath of the war.

The logic of treating Korea as part of Japan for war crimes purposes meant that Koreans serving with the Japanese military forces were as liable as Japanese to be prosecuted for war crimes if the evidence could be found. And indeed, many Koreans had served as guards in Japanese prisoner-of-war camps, and a number were prosecuted for the ill treatment of their charges. Since the 1990s, a perception has developed that one element in the Cold War exoneration of Japan was an Allied tactic of placing an undue burden of guilt on Koreans in Japanese service.[32] Sandra Wilson's chapter in this volume shows conclusively that this perception is mistaken. As a category, Koreans were treated less severely than the Japanese officers who commanded them.

The consequence of this national and temporal unevenness in defining Japanese war crimes was a tangle of bitter moral inconsistencies, which is partly teased out in the chapters of Barak Kushner and Arnaud Doglia. Many Japanese authorities seized upon the selective prosecution of Japanese accused to dismiss the trials as victors' justice and to assert that Japanese soldiers had done nothing but their duty to the nation, nothing that exceeded the normal violence of warfare. Minear, writing in 1971, characterized the postwar trials (specifically the IMTFE) as "victors' justice," implying that the vengeful Allies had gone too far in their prosecutions.[33] By the early 1990s, by contrast, perturbed by the accusation of one-sidedness, Western, Chinese and Korean commentators sometimes emphasized the most barbarous elements in Japanese wartime behavior, especially the Nanjing Massacre, the Rape of Manila, the work of Unit 731, and the harsh treatment of laborers on the Thailand–Burma Railway and other wartime strategic projects. Rather than implying that more men had been found guilty than was proper, they stressed the crimes that had not been punished and the perpetrators who had escaped prosecution. Over time, thus, the calculated decision of prosecuting governments in the late 1940s and early 1950s that enough was enough, that the trials should cease, and that any moral claims arising from crimes that had not been under prosecution could be allowed to lapse was reinterpreted as a failure of will.

Conclusion

Conceived as an intensely moral search for justice, the trials aligned both with and against the interests of the Western powers, who were trying to reconfigure their colonial presence in the region. They aligned both with and against the aim of the United States and its allies to win hearts and minds in the struggle against communism, and they aligned both with and against the interests of colonized peoples struggling for independence. In consequence, Japan was punished both too much and too little by the trials process, which contributed to the somehow distorted memory of that period that this volume tries to readdress.

When assessing the part played by war crimes trials in the framework of decolonization, and in view of the Allied strategy versus collaboration, four features seem discernible. First, the Allies were required to administer war crimes trials, and although there was no direct political advantage in holding them, there would have been serious disadvantages in failing to conduct them. Second, the trials were an indirect means of discrediting the most anti-Western groups who had generally been pro-Japanese. For political reasons, these groups could not be prosecuted, so trying Japanese war criminals was a way to remind the local community that these groups had betrayed their own people. Third, they offered an assurance to metropolitan publics that the transition to independence in Southeast Asia was not a second defeat by Japan but rather a natural culmination of the civilizing mission. This is especially true with regard to the U.S. and British strategies. Finally, the trials provided a means of tainting Japan with the memory of the war as a way to hamper the return of Japanese economic interests to the region.

New issues have the capacity to shake up political orders. In the first half of the twentieth century, class politics that transcended national borders disrupted assumptions about the loyalties of ordinary people. In the second half of the century, environmental and gender issues did the same. In the middle of the century, the war crimes trial program of the victorious Allies introduced a new and unexpected set of considerations into the politics of decolonization and Cold War in Asia. War Crimes trials against the Japanese, in this regard, were meant as a conclusion of the business of war by judicial means. Japan had already been defeated, but the trials were meant to confirm that the victory of the West was not just a matter of superior force but also a moral victory of good over evil and served to establish the terms for future partnerships, owing to the legal assessment of "loyal behavior" in war time.

Notes

1. Timothy Brook, *Collaboration: Japanese Agents and Local Elites in Wartime China* (Cambridge, MA: Harvard University Press 2005), 5.
2. Tony Judt, *Postwar: A History of Europe since 1945* (New York: Penguin, 2005). For an overview with national case studies, see Norbert Frei (ed.), *Transnationale Vergangenheitspolitik: Der Umgang mit deutschen Kriegsverbrechern in Europa nach dem Zweiten Weltkrieg* (Göttingen: Wallstein, 2006); Richard Ned Lebow, Wulf Kansteiner, and Claudio Fogu (eds), *The Politics of Memory in Postwar Europe* (Durham, NC: Duke University Press, 2006).
3. See Gerhard Hirschfeld, *Nazi Rule and Dutch Collaboration: The Netherlands under German Occupation 1940–1945* (Oxford: Berg, 1988); Gregor Joseph Kranjc, *To Walk with the Devil: Slovene Collaboration and Axis Occupation, 1941–1945* (Toronto: University of Toronto Press, 2013).
4. Konrad M. Lawson, "Wartime Atrocities and the Politics of Treason in the Ruins of the Japanese Empire, 1937–1953" (PhD thesis, Harvard University, 2012), 22.
5. István Deák, Jan T. Gross, and Tony Judt (eds), *The Politics of Retribution in Europe: World War II and Its Aftermath* (Princeton, NJ: Princeton University Press, 2000), 3.
6. Norbert Frei, *Adenauer's Germany and the Nazi Past: The Politics of Amnesty and Integration* (New York: Columbia University Press, 2002).
7. Norbert Frei, José Brunne, and Constantin Goschler (eds), *Die Praxis der Wiedergutmachung: Geschichte, Erfahrung und Wirkung in Deutschland und Israel* (Göttingen: Wallstein, 2009); Hans Günther Hockerts, Claudia Moisel, and Tobias Winstel (eds), *Grenzen der Wiedergutmachung: Die Entschädigung für NS-Verfolgte in West- und Osteuropa 1945–2000* (Göttingen: Wallstein, 2006).
8. Kerstin von Lingen, "Germany as a Role Model? Coming to Terms with Nazi War Deeds, 1945–2015," in: Barak Kushner and Sherzod Muminov (eds), *The Dismantling of Japan's Empire in East Asia: Deimperialization, Postwar Legitimation and Imperial Afterlife* (Abingdon, UK: Routledge, 2017).

9. Timothy Brook, *Collaboration: Japanese Agents and Local Elites in Wartime China* (Cambridge, MA: Harvard University Press 2005); and a general overview by Barak Kushner, *Men to Devils, Devils to Men: Japanese War Crimes and Chinese Justice* (Cambridge, MA: Harvard University Press, 2015).
10. Xia Yun, "Traitors to the Chinese Race (Hanjian): Political and Cultural Campaigns Against Collaborators during the Sino-Japanese War of 1937–1945" (PhD diss., University of Oregon, 2010); Lo Jiu-jung, "Trials of the Taiwanese as Hanjian or War Criminals and the Postwar Search for Taiwanese Identity", in *Constructing Nationhood in Modern East Asia*, ed. Chow Kai-wing et al. (Ann Arbor: University of Michigan Press, 2001), 279–316; Margherita Zanasi, "Globalizing Hanjian: The Suzhou Trials and the Post-World War II Discourse on Collaboration", *American Historical Review* 113 (2008): 731–751.
11. Gerald E. Bunker, *The Peace Conspiracy: Wang Ching-wei and the China War, 1937–1941* (Cambridge MA: Harvard University Press, 1972), 285.
12. Eyal Benvinisti, *The International Law of Occupation* (Princeton NJ: Princeton University Press 1993, 2nd edition, 2012), 3.
13. Convention (II) with Respect to the Laws and Customs of War on Land and its annex: Regulations concerning the Laws and Customs of War on Land. The Hague, 29 July 1899; Convention (IV) respecting the Laws and Customs of War on Land and its annex: Regulations concerning the Laws and Customs of War on Land. The Hague, 18 October 1907.
14. Eyal Benvenisti, "The Origins of the Concept of Belligerent Occupation," in: *Law and History Review* Vol. 26, No. 3, *Law, War, and History* (Fall, 2008), 621–648, here 622.
15. Eyal, Benvenisti, "Occupation and Territorial Administration," in: Rain Livoja andTimothy McCormack (eds), The *Routledge Handbook for Armed Conflict*, 2016, 435–454, here 436.
16. Benvenisti, Occupation and Territorial Administration, 437.
17. The Issue had been debated since the French-Spanish War in 1808 and again during the Brussels Conference of 1874, which ultimately rejected the right of the occupied to defy the invader (*franc-tireurs*), see Benvenisti, "Origins of the Concept," 628.
18. See here Theodor Meron, *Human Rights in International Law: Legal and Political Issues* (Oxford: Clarendon, 1985); Jean S. Pictet, *Humanitarian Law and the Protection of War Victims* (Leiden: Sijthoff 1975).
19. Benvenisti, Occupation and Territorial Administration, 454.
20. Prasenjit Duara, "Introduction: The Decolonization of Asia and Africa in the 20th Century," in: Prasenjit Duara (ed), *Decolonization: Perspectives from Now and Then* (London: Routledge 2004), 1–18, here 2.

21. See, for instance, "Soekarno is Quisling like Laurel and Bamaw, says 'Washington Post'," *Cairns Post* (Australia), 31 October 1945, 3.
22. Paul Kratoska, "The Second World War and Nation-Building in Southeast Asia," in: Franz Knipping, Piyanāt Bunnāk, and Vimolvan Phatharodom (eds), *Europe and Southeast Asia in the Contemporary World: Mutual Influences and Comparisons* (Baden-Baden: Nomos, 1999), 125.
23. Sandra Wilson, Robert Cribb, Beatrice Trefalt, and Dean Aszkielowicz, *Japanese War Criminals: The Politics of Justice after the Second World War* (New York: Columbia University Press, forthcoming).
24. United Nations War Crimes Commission, *History of the United Nations War Crimes Commission and the Development of the Laws of War* (London: HMSO, 1948).
25. Gary Jonathan Bass, *Stay the Hand of Vengeance* (Princeton NJ: Princeton University Press, 2000), 58–105; Jürgen Matthäus, "The Lessons of Leipzig: Punishing German War Criminals after the First World War," in: Patricia Heberer and Jürgen Matthäus (eds), *Atrocities on Trial* (Lincoln NE: University of Nebraska Press, 2008), 3–23. Fifteen other German soldiers were tried for crimes against prisoners of war and at sea. Gerd Hankel, *Die Leipziger Prozesse. Deutsche Kriegsverbrechen und ihre strafrechtliche Verfolgung nach dem Ersten Weltkrieg* (Hamburg: Hamburger Edition, 2003), 103.
26. "Commission on the Responsibility of the Authors of the War and on Enforcement of Penalties," *American Journal of International Law* 14, no. 1/2 (1920), 95–154.
27. XVth International Conference of the Red Cross, Draft International Convention on the Condition and Protection of Civilians of enemy nationality who are on territory belonging to or occupied by a belligerent (Tokyo, 1934), https://www.icrc.org/ihl/INTRO/320?OpenDocument (accessed 28 Nov. 2016).
28. Daniel Marc Segesser and Myriam Gessler, "Rafael Lemkin and the International Debate on the Punishment of War Crimes (1919–1948)," in: Dominik J. Schaller and Jürgen Zimmerer, eds, *The Origins of Genocide: Raphael Lemkin as a Historian of Mass Violence* (London: Routledge, 2009), 11–12.
29. For an early discussion of this doctrine, see Walter Wheeler Cook, "Act, Intention, and Motive in the Criminal Law," *Yale Law Journal* 26, no. 8 (1917), 646 [645–663].
30. The sole exception was General Sakai Takashi, who faced charges of war crimes, crimes against peace, and crimes against humanity in a court convened by the Republic of China. See "Trial of Takashi Sakai," in United Nations War Crimes Commission, *Law Reports of Trials of War Criminals, XIV* (London: HMSO, 1949), 1–7.

31. Mark Caprio, *Japanese Assimilation Policies in Colonial Korea, 1910–1945* (Seattle: University of Washington Press, 2009).
32. See especially Gavan McCormack, "Apportioning the Blame: Australian Trials for Railway Crimes," in: Gavan McCormack and Hank Nelson (eds), *The Burma-Thailand Railway: Memory and History* (St Leonards, NSW: Allen & Unwin, 1993), 85–115.
33. Richard H. Minear, *Victors' Justice: The Tokyo War Crimes Trial* (Princeton, NJ: Princeton University Press, 1971).

Kerstin Von Lingen is a historian and researcher at the Cluster of Excellence "Asia and Europe in a Global Context" at Heidelberg University. Since 2013, she has led an independent research project entitled "Transcultural Justice: Legal Flows and the Emergence of International Justice within the East Asian War Crimes Trials, 1946–1954," supervising four doctoral dissertations on the Soviet, Chinese, Dutch, and French war crimes trial policies in Asia. Her many publications include two monographs in English, *Kesselring's Last Battle: War Crimes Trials and Cold War Politics, 1945–1960* (Lawrence: University of Kansas Press, 2009) and *Allen Dulles, the OSS and Nazi War Criminals: The Dynamics of Selective Prosecution* (Cambridge: Cambridge University Press, 2013), as well as the (co)edited volumes *War Crimes Trials in the Wake of Decolonization and Cold War in Asia, 1945–1956: Justice in Times of Turmoil*, Palgrave 2016, as well as the multi-authored volumes *Kriegserfahrung und nationale Identität in Europa* [War Experience and National Identity in Europe after 1945] (Paderborn: Schoeningh, 2009) and (with Klaus Gestwa) *Zwangsarbeit als Kriegsressource in Europa und Asien* [Forced Labor as a Resource of War: European and Asian Perspectives) (Paderborn: Schoeningh 2014).

Robert Cribb is Professor of Asian History at the Australian National University, Canberra. His research focuses on Indonesian history, with special attention to violence, national identity, and environmental politics. His recent publications include *Historical Atlas of Northeast Asia 1590–2010* (New York: Columbia University Press, 2014, with Li Narangoa). He recently completed (with Sandra Wilson, Beatrice Trefalt, and Dean Aszkielowicz) *Japanese War Criminals: The Politics of Justice After the Second World War* (New York: Columbia University Press, 2017).

Koreans in the Trials of Japanese War Crimes Suspects

Sandra Wilson

About 240,000 Korean men took part on the Japanese side during the Second World War, about half as soldiers and half as civilian auxiliary personnel (*gunzoku*).[1] Korea had been colonised by Japan in 1910, and Koreans participated in the Japanese war effort as imperial subjects, rather than as inhabitants of an occupied region. As soldiers, Koreans fought in battle against the Allies on many fronts; as civilians contracted to serve with the Japanese military, they supported and supplied the war effort and released Japanese troops for service on the front line. Of the roughly 120,000 Korean civilian employees, about 2.5% were members of the so-called Noguchi Unit, recruited to work as guards at camps housing Allied prisoners of war (POWs) and internees, mostly on the Burma–Thailand Railway, in Singapore and in Java.[2] When the war ended and Allied governments began to round up suspected war criminals, field commanders were instructed to treat suspects of Korean and Taiwanese ethnicity as Japanese, as far as war crimes were concerned.[3] Staff of POW camps, along with members of the Japanese military police (*Kenpeitai*), were specially targeted for apprehension, investigation and possible trial[4]; thus, Korean Guards were vulnerable to arrest. Although the guards constituted a small minority of Koreans serving on the Japanese side,

S. Wilson (✉)
School of Arts, Murdoch University, Murdoch, Australia
e-mail: s.wilson@murdoch.edu.au

K. von Lingen (ed.), *Debating Collaboration and Complicity in War Crimes Trials in Asia, 1945–1956*, World Histories of Crime, Culture and Violence, DOI 10.1007/978-3-319-53141-0_2

they made up the overwhelming majority of the Koreans who were eventually tried as 'Japanese' war criminals. Overall, 148 Koreans were convicted and sentenced as war criminals in the Allied trials from 1945 onwards. Three of them were enlisted soldiers (of whom one had commanded a POW camp in the Philippines); another sixteen were interpreters sentenced by the Nationalist Chinese authorities. The remaining 129 were camp guards, thirty-five of whom had worked at camps along the notorious Burma–Thailand Railway.[5]

In writings about the Allied trials of Japanese suspects, two alternative views of the Korean Guards are prominent. Contemporary comments by POWs and Allied officials, and later popular works focusing on former Allied POWs, often describe the Korean Guards, with whom the prisoners came into daily contact, as the captives' 'worst tormentors'.[6] As an official British telegram tersely observed in early 1946, 'Have reason to believe some of these people [Koreans in the Japanese forces] amongst the worst of the guards over our prisoners during occupation'.[7] An Australian former POW on the Burma–Thailand Railway told a veterans' group in 1948 that 'The Japanese were gentlemen compared with the Korean guards.'[8] By contrast, the noted historians Gavan McCormack and Utsumi Aiko, amongst others, portray the Korean Guards as victims. They were more or less forced into service in the Japanese military according to McCormack and Utsumi, and once there, they were allegedly routinely mistreated. McCormack goes so far as to state that in a military where recruits were 'deliberately bashed and brutalised as part of their training', Koreans, considered 'inferior to the lowest private Japanese soldier', were 'as much alienated, victimised and exploited as, on the other side, were the POWs and the Asian labourers' in the Burma–Thailand Railway camps.[9]

In this view, the Koreans were further victimised by the Allies at the end of the war. The Allies, according to Utsumi, 'ignored the issue of Japanese colonialism'.[10] The implication appears to be that the Allied authorities should have excused Koreans and Taiwanese for alleged war crimes, or at least exercised a significant degree of leniency towards them, because of their colonial status and thus, presumably, their diminished responsibility for Japan's wartime actions; but they did not do so. Treatment of Koreans is also regarded as a manifestation of a broader problem in the Allied conduct of war crimes trials. The Allies, according to both McCormack and Utsumi, let those who were truly responsible for war crimes – the emperor and senior Japanese military officers and planners – escape prosecution, or they gave senior officers light sentences and wrought their vengeance instead upon the most junior personnel, who included a significant number of Korean Guards. Utsumi writes:

> These trials [of ordinary military personnel] ... resulted in the conviction of thousands of low ranking Japanese soldiers and civilian personnel in direct interaction with allied POWs, as well as Korean personnel who faced charges by their former prisoners. While the high command for the most part was untouched, many of those with least authority were executed and others served long prison sentences.[11]

In her major 2008 study of Korean war criminals, Utsumi concludes that poor treatment of Allied POWs resulted partly from the fact that the Japanese government did not have coherent guidelines on how to deal with the prisoners and that it was Koreans and Taiwanese who bore the burden of the authorities' policy failure in the subsequent war crimes trials.[12] Commenting on the Australian trials for offences committed along the Burma–Thailand Railway, McCormack makes the same assertion: 'it was the lowest ranks of the Japanese system, specifically the Korean guards, upon whom the heaviest retribution was visited'.[13]

Utsumi and McCormack proceed mainly on the basis of case studies, piecing the stories together from official records, memoirs and interviews. Descriptions of the experiences of individual guards are absorbing and, in human terms, deeply compelling. Such individual stories, however, cannot be taken to represent the general experience of Korean Guards; moreover, the individual stories recounted by historians were often produced decades after the events in question, with the benefit of hindsight, detached from their original context and in the light of recent political and ideological preoccupations, especially a concern with the historical wrongs perceived to have been inflicted by Japan on Korea. By contrast, examination of the broader, contemporary documentary evidence on war criminals contradicts the arguments made famous by Utsumi, McCormack and others.

Statistical analysis of the available data on apprehension, investigation, prosecution, sentencing and release of suspected and convicted war criminals shows conclusively that Koreans were not over-represented among war criminals and that they did not suffer the heaviest penalties. Lists of prison populations, trial transcripts and records of sentencing outcomes and sentence reviews are available in abundance in the military, political and diplomatic records in the British, Dutch, Australian and Japanese archives. Utsumi has used this material extensively, and her work contains much valuable information not only on her specific case studies but more generally on the recruitment of the Korean Guards, their distribution among prison camps in Southeast Asia and their subsequent service with the Japanese military. In the main, however, she and McCormack have chosen to pursue individual stories rather than to examine broad trends. Because of their deep sympathy with the Korean experience of Japanese colonial oppression, and a consciousness of the discrimination Korean soldiers continued to suffer after the war, Utsumi and McCormack appear to have become advocates for the former guards; they may have chosen to concentrate on individual stories not only because those stories are accessible but also in order to make a stronger impact on the reader.[14] Broad data relevant to the choice of defendants, sentencing outcomes and clemency reviews, in particular, have been insufficiently explored. To understand the situation of the Korean Guards, it is crucial not only to recount specific life histories, but also to pay close attention to the raw material in the archives in order to establish the underlying statistics that relate to the guards as a group. It is necessary not only to tell the story of individual lives but also to count up the numbers.

Most important, the archival data as a whole show that the Allied authorities did not target junior personnel but, rather, sought out the middle ranks, as well as the most senior officers they could convincingly prosecute. The greatest burden of war crimes prosecutions fell neither on the most junior nor the most senior but on non-commissioned officers (lance-corporal and above) and junior officers (lieutenant, captain and major).[15] Soldiers in these ranks did not make policy, but they did give day-to-day orders, including orders in camps that directly affected the welfare of POWs and internees. The most junior members of the Imperial Japanese Army were the three ranks of privates: private second class (*nitōhei*), private first class (*ittōhei*) and superior private (*jōtōhei*, equivalent to corporal in the U.S. Marine Corps).[16] Korean Guards, as civilians, did not have a formal place in the hierarchy of enlisted men, but in practice they were among the lowest-ranking military personnel. Broadly, as Warner notes, 'the authority conferred by one rank over another was vastly greater [in the Imperial Japanese Army] than in the British or American armies'.[17] Subordinate military personnel in general, and Korean Guards specifically, were under-represented, not over-represented, in Allied prosecutions of Japanese war crimes suspects. If prosecuted and convicted, they usually did not receive the heaviest sentences, and often benefited from sentence reductions at the initial stage. Then, when the Allies began to consider more general clemency in the 1950s, Koreans and other junior personnel were again likely to have their sentences reduced, on the grounds that their responsibility for criminal acts was not as great as that of more senior personnel. Throughout the war crimes trials process, in other words, there is strong evidence that investigators, prosecutors and clemency officials paid serious attention to rank and accepted that, by and large, senior and middle-ranking personnel bore the largest responsibility for war crimes.

Of the 242,341 Koreans who served with the Japanese military during the war, according to official statistics, 3,016 were prison guards.[18] In February–March 1942, Japanese military authorities, already critically short of manpower, were overwhelmed when they suddenly found themselves with 250,000–300,000 prisoners after the Japanese conquest of Singapore and Java. The Army Ministry then decided that POWs would be used as labour in Japan and other parts of the empire and that detention camps would be opened to house them. Prisoners in camps within the home islands would be guarded by Japanese servicemen, but guards for camps located elsewhere would be recruited in Korea and Taiwan.[19] The policy of using colonial subjects as guards freed Japanese soldiers for front-line duties; Hayashi notes that it was also intended as propaganda, on the assumption it would undermine the high status of white people in Korean and Taiwanese eyes and would display Japanese power.[20]

Conscription for military service had not yet been introduced in the Japanese colonies, so many capable young men were available. In May 1942, the Korean government-general announced it would accept applications for thousands of new positions as camp guards, as part of a more general recruitment of Korean civilians to perform a wide range of tasks in the Japanese military.[21] Contracts were to be for two years and, although civilian auxiliary employees stood so low in the pecking order that they had to salute even a second-class private, the pay was surprisingly good. While still in Taiwan or Korea, the civilian recruit would earn 30 yen per month; the pay rose to 50 yen when overseas. By contrast, a second-class private received 6 yen per month. At 1943 rates, Utsumi notes, 50 yen was the same pay as an army sergeant (*gunsō*) received. Civilian auxiliary employees could also be promoted after one year of service if they passed extra examinations. Some civilian employees earned 100 yen per month.[22]

Korean men responded well to the call for applications. The issue of their motivation is tangled and is closely associated with the question of whether or not the guards should be considered primarily as victims. Though she acknowledges in her Japanese-language work that motives were diverse,[23] Utsumi emphasises duress. In one of her English-language essays, she claims that young men from the colonies were 'conscripted' as POW guards.[24] As Palmer notes, however, 'Conscription [of labour rather than soldiers] was not widely employed in Korea until 1944, and even then it was largely limited to freezing workers to their positions.'[25] Some accounts recorded from the 1990s onwards by former guards similarly emphasise coercion. Social and institutional pressure to sign up was intense in some cases, especially as quotas for recruitment were set for each district. Kim Wan-gun (Kanekado Kankon), Utsumi's major case study, was subjected to great pressure from a Japanese policeman to enlist[26]; others were coerced by fellow Koreans, who might have been police, recruiters or heads of patriotic units.[27] Kidnapping and trickery were used in some cases.[28] Another factor was that alternative employment might be scarce or unattractive. A former guard recalled that the prospective job as a guard seemed better than being forced to work in a Japanese coal mine.[29] In May 1942, the same month that recruitment of guards began, a decree was issued stating that conscription of Korean men for military service would begin in 1943. Takahashi concludes that the threat of conscription induced people to volunteer as guards.[30] Palmer makes the same point about volunteer labour service more generally: unlike Japanese men, Korean men were exempt from conscription into the military if they volunteered for labour service (including work as guards), and in any case, wages were lower in the military.[31]

Despite the evidence of social pressure and limited choices, it is likely that many men chose voluntarily to apply, because the apparent terms of employment were positively attractive. Though actual rates of pay varied, some civilian employees of the military earned three times the average Korean salary or more; for skilled positions, there was competition amongst applicants.[32] The high rate of pay seemed to promise significant social mobility at the expiration of the contract: after two years of service, one could expect to live on the same level as the Japanese occupiers in Korea.[33] The former guard who did not want to go to the Japanese coal mines added that the pay for guards was good, the contract was only for two years, and it represented a chance to travel.[34] In later recollections, however, the choice to apply voluntarily is sometimes downplayed. The account by Yi Hak-Nae

(Hiromura Kakurai), given in a 1991 speech in Canberra and later translated for publication by McCormack, contains a confusing mixture of comments on why he applied to become a guard:

> I thought that I would learn something from such work, the pay was not bad and I could avoid military service by the 2 year contract; so I signed up. On the surface it was voluntary, but there was a quota for my district, and in effect we were impressed.... As I said earlier, the Japanese government compulsorily pressed us into service.[35]

Palmer is doubtless accurate in his assessment that recruitment of Korean civilians for the Japanese military relied on 'an interplay of cooperation, coercion, and inducement between the colonial government and Koreans'.[36]

Before leaving Korea, applicants who had passed the screening process received two months' training from Colonel Noguchi Yuzuru, a career army officer.[37] In August 1942 they left the port of Busan, later to be dispersed to serve under the command of Japanese non-commissioned officers (NCOs) and junior officers in POW camps in Thailand, Malaya and Java. As can be seen from Table 1, Korean Guards far outnumbered Japanese servicemen in the camps in these regions: 804 of the 840 personnel originally allocated to POW camps in both Malaya and Thailand were Korean civilian employees. I Gil (Kasayama Yoshikichi) was one of about thirty Korean Guards at a POW camp in Java. According to his later recollection, they served under a Japanese lance corporal, a sergeant and an officer, usually a lieutenant.[38]

Japanese forces were frequently moved around during the Second World War, and it is clear that the guards were no exception. POWs themselves were sent from Changi Prison in Singapore, from Java and elsewhere to

Table 1 POW camp personnel (according to a report dated 28 August 1942)

Rank/location of camps	*1st/2nd Lieut.*	*Sgt (Cpl)*	*Subtotal (Japanese)*	*Civilian (Korean)*	*Total*
Thailand	9	27	36	804	840
Malaya	9	27	36	804	840
Java	16	47	63	1,408	1,471
Total	34	101	135	3,016	3,151

Source: Utsumi Aiko, *Kimu wa naze sabakareta no ka: Chōsenjin BC-kyū senpan no kiseki* (Tōkyō: Asahi Shinbun Shuppan, 2008), 97

camps along the Burma–Thailand Railway and to other places of work, and guards were needed to supervise them. Utsumi calculates that a total of 17,700 prisoners were sent from Java to Thailand and Burma in the three months between November 1942 and February 1943. In April 1943, another 6,600 prisoners were sent from Java to the Netherlands Indies islands of Ambon, Haruku, Seram and Flores.[39] Presumably, large numbers of the 1,408 Koreans originally assigned to Java were sent to the same destinations as the prisoners. Sixty Korean Guards, for example, including Kim Wan-gun (Kanekado Kankon), whose case is described by Utsumi, and I Gil (Kasayama Yoshikichi), were dispatched to the small island of Haruku, east of Ambon, to guard 2,070 POWs sent there to build a Japanese airfield.[40] The Burma–Thailand Railway was a major destination for Korean Guards. At one stage, POWs and Asian labourers along the railway were supervised by 40 Japanese officers, 85 Japanese non-commissioned officers and 1,280 Korean Guards.[41] Thus, more than one-third of the Noguchi Unit served along the railway at one point.

In assessing whether Korean Guards and junior military personnel in general were disproportionately punished, the first issue is how many people were brought to trial, from among the many thousands of suspects initially apprehended from the POWs and surrendered personnel in Allied custody at the end of the war. After Japan's defeat, camp personnel were included in the categories specifically earmarked for apprehension as war crimes suspects. The great majority of the Korean suspects were apprehended by the Netherlands, Britain and Australia, as these were the countries responsible for trials for offences committed in Java and on the Burma–Thailand Railway. At one point, of the 3,000 suspects housed in Changi Prison in Singapore, 2,000 had been incarcerated for possible prosecution for crimes committed on the railway.[42] Many Korean Guards must have been among them, given the large number of guards who served along the railway. Yet Korean Guards were not prosecuted in any great numbers: the total of 129 guards convicted represents only 4.3% of the 3,016 in the Noguchi Unit. Doubtless this figure is higher than the percentage of ordinary soldiers convicted as war criminals, but considering that prison camps were specifically targeted, it is a very low number (Table 2).

In terms of selection of defendants, the example of British trials in Southeast Asia reveals what appears to be the standard pattern. In total, 920 defendants received verdicts from the British authorities in 306 trials, across 20 trial locations, of which the most important were Singapore, Hong Kong and Rangoon (Table 3). Junior personnel make up a very

Table 2 Koreans (including non-guards) convicted in Allied war crimes trials in the Pacific theatre, 1945–1951

Prosecuting country	*USA*	*UK*	*Australia*	*Netherlands*	*France*	*Philippines*	*China*	*Total*
Total war criminals convicted	1,453	978	949	1,038	230	169	883	5,700
Koreans	3	49	12	68	0	0	16	148

Adapted from Utsumi Aiko, *Kimu wa naze sabakareta no ka: Chōsenjin BC-kyū senpan no kiseki* (Tōkyō: Asahi Shinbun Shuppan, 2008), 7

Table 3 Outcome of British trials in Southeast Asia

Rank		*Total number tried*	*Death sentence at original sentencing*	*Life sentence at original sentencing*	*Defined sentences at original sentencing (average length)*	*Acquittal*	*Death sentence commuted at confirmation*	*Prison sentence reduced at confirmation*
Senior officers (Lt-Col and above)		48	24	3	16 (11.7 years)	5	0	1
Junior officers (Lt, Capt, Major)		218	87	19	76 (8.25 years)	36	7	6
NCOs and WOs		401	116	22	213 (7.9 years)	50	7	8
Private		33	4	0	18 (7.7 years)	11	1	2
Guard/Korean		64	11	10	40 (9.0 years)	3	5	12
Civilian	Interpreter	28	10	1	12 (7.8 years)	5	0	3
	'Civilian'	81	18	5	49 (7.3 years)	9	11	6
	Unspecified	38	8	5	23 (11.1 years)	2	2	2
Total		**911**	278	65		121	33	40

Totals have been calculated from the slightly incomplete card indexes in TNA, WO 357/3 and WO 357/5. The actual number of verdicts delivered by British courts was 920. Note that the number of Korean Guards convicted (61) does not match Utsumi's figure (49) cited earlier. One reason is probably that when defendants were prosecuted in two trials, they are counted twice here.

small proportion of those charged. The great majority of the defendants were NCOs, warrant officers (WOs) or higher: together, these groups account for 73% of defendants, with NCOs/WOs alone covering 44%. Privates accounted for only thirty-three defendants, or 4%, and Korean Guards for sixty-four defendants, or 7%. Korean Guards outnumbered private soldiers because all of them worked at prison camps, which were singled out by the Allied authorities, whereas private soldiers were spread out across the front lines and elsewhere. The very small number of the most junior soldiers who were charged means that investigations against the remainder were not pursued, whereas middle-ranking and senior officers were targeted in much greater numbers. In one high-profile Burma–Thailand Railway case, heard in Singapore in 1946, the charge explicitly referred to the beating of prisoners by Koreans, but no Korean personnel were arraigned.[43]

Similar trends are evident elsewhere, with some variations. In Hong Kong, Australian courts convicted forty-two defendants. Only two were privates and one was listed as a Korean Guard (and one was unspecified). In Australian tribunals in Singapore, a higher number of Korean Guards – fifteen of the sixty-two defendants (24%) – were tried, doubtless because crimes on the Burma–Thailand Railway were prosecuted in Singapore. In addition, one of the five civilian interpreters convicted in Singapore is known to have been Korean. The Philippine and French governments did not try Korean Guards but convicted a low number of privates: 27 out of 155 who received a verdict in the Philippines (18%) and 19 out of 231 (8%) in French military courts. More than one-third of those convicted in the Philippine trials were junior officers (captains and lieutenants).[44] The same pattern – preferring higher-ranking servicemen, in a tacit or explicit recognition that junior soldiers and civilian auxiliaries had limited capacity to refuse the orders of their seniors or generally to make independent decisions – recurs throughout each stage of the war crimes trial process, across the national tribunals.

Trials of Koreans mostly took place in the Netherlands Indies and Singapore. If Korean Guards were considered to have mistreated prisoners wilfully and excessively, they were sometimes severely punished upon conviction. Over all of the Allied trials, twenty-three Korean Guards were executed.[45] Kaneoka Kiko (Kaneoka Kiyoshi) was hanged at Changi for ill-treatment of British, Australian and Dutch POWs on Ambon and at sea, resulting in the death of one of them. He was said to have 'behaved throughout with a vicious brutality' and to have run a 'reign of terror' in the camp: 'Everything possible to have made the Prisoners [sic] lives a misery appears to have been done by this man.'[46] It was said of Kobayashi Torao, a Korean prosecuted in the Palembang Guard case, that 'His beatings and savagery were such as to drive men to the grave.'[47] Toyoyama Kisei, whose original death sentence for inhumane treatment of prisoners was commuted, was described as 'notoriously the worst Korean guard in F Force', a force of British and Australian POWs working on the Burma–Thailand Railway. His brutality 'went beyond all limits'. It was also claimed that he and his fellow defendant Lieutenant Fukuda Tsuneo, commandant of Lower Songkurai Camp, shared responsibility for the deaths from malnutrition, starvation and overwork of over a hundred Australian POWs.[48]

Koreans who were found guilty of war crimes did not generally, however, receive the highest penalties, except in extreme cases such as those just described. The war crimes trials process recognised that the personnel who directly committed acts of brutality in the camps or provided inadequate food or medical care were not necessarily those who should be held most responsible, because up to a point they were carrying out orders which they could not realistically oppose or refuse, and food and medicine were in short supply. The large Palembang Guard case, in which sixteen of the twenty-four defendants were Korean Guards at a POW camp in Sumatra, resulted in five executions. Though all the non-guards were hanged – a captain, two lieutenants and three sergeants – Kobayashi Torao, mentioned earlier, was the only one of the sixteen guards to be executed.[49] Kim Wangun (Kanekado Kankon) was one of thirteen defendants in a British trial for brutality against and neglect of British and Dutch prisoners at sea and in camps on Ambon and neighbouring islands, including Haruku, where Kim had been stationed. Eight of the defendants in the subsequent trial were Japanese and five were Korean. All defendants were convicted of one or more of the charges against them, and six were hanged – a lieutenant-colonel, three captains and two sergeants-major. Utsumi, who uses Kim's case as a main focus of her book, passes over the fact that none of the five Koreans was sentenced to death. Two were sentenced to life imprisonment, two to ten years, including Kim, and one to seven years.[50]

Of the 911 defendants in British trials for whom information is available (Table 3), 121, or 13%, were acquitted. Other sentencing outcomes again clearly show that the lowest-ranking personnel were not treated harshly.

A total of 278 death sentences was handed down in the British trials (of which 245 were confirmed and carried out). Nearly 82% of the original death sentences were handed down on personnel of NCO/WO rank and above; NCOs and WOs alone account for 42% of the total. Only 17% of the Korean Guards who were convicted, and 12% of the privates, received the death penalty. It was more risky to be tried as an interpreter than a Korean Guard: nearly 36% of interpreters (including some Koreans and Taiwanese) who were prosecuted received the death penalty in the first instance.

The original sentences passed by the war crimes courts were not always confirmed. Sentences were reviewed by a confirming officer, whose job was to assess the court's verdict and sentence and to make a recommendation to higher authorities on whether they should stand or not. In many cases, sentences were commuted or reduced as a result of this process. Thirty-three prisoners condemned to death by British courts were subsequently reprieved (Table 3), according to the card index of prisoners in the War Office file.[51] Koreans and other low-ranking personnel who were found guilty were highly likely to have their sentences reduced at the end of the court process. Korean Guard Yi Hak-Nae (Hiromura Kakurai), for example, was sentenced to death in an Australian trial for inhumane treatment of POWs at Hintok Camp on the Burma–Thailand Railway in 1943, but the confirming authority reduced his sentence to twenty years.[52] In British trials in Southeast Asia (Table 3), none of the death sentences which had been passed on the most senior officers was commuted, whereas five of the eleven death sentences passed on Korean Guards, and one of the four passed on privates, were commuted. Another twelve Korean Guards and two privates had their prison sentences reduced at the confirmation stage of sentencing. Overall, Korean Guards had their sentences reduced at the highest rate of any category in the British trials in Southeast Asia, and at twice the rate (26.6%) of any other group, apart from those simply classed as 'civilians' (21%). In the Australian trials of forty-two defendants in Hong Kong, four death sentences were confirmed, resulting in the executions of one senior officer and three junior officers, but no junior enlisted men or civilian auxiliaries.[53]

Convicted prisoners were generally executed or imprisoned at or near the locations of their trials. Between 1949 and 1953, however, in accordance with arrangements made between each prosecuting government and either the Americans, during the Occupation of Japan, or the Japanese, after peace was restored in 1952, convicted war criminals were transferred to serve out the remainder of their sentences in Sugamo Prison in Tokyo. But Article 11 of the peace treaty decreed that the original prosecuting governments retained power over war criminals' sentences. Only they could grant parole or any form of clemency.[54] The Japanese government could only 'recommend' clemency for convicted war criminals. Under this system, Allied governments eventually had to face up to the problem of whether and how to grant parole or other forms of clemency to Japanese war criminals, and here again, it became evident that the authorities were sensitive to rank.[55]

Article 11 was intended as a way of keeping war criminals in prison for the duration of their sentences. In the ensuing years, however, the priorities of Allied governments changed rapidly as the Cold War escalated and as normal economic relationships with Japan began to seem possible again. All the prosecuting governments accepted that the need to incorporate Japan into the non-Communist camp overrode the imperative to keep punishing war criminals, and some sought to restore trading relationships. The Japanese government wanted war criminals released, and foreign governments began actively to seek the means of doing so. From 1952 onwards, Nationalist China, France, the Philippines, the Netherlands and Australia either released war criminals in their custody outright or developed formulas that effectively released them en masse. Only the UK and the United States continued to insist on examining each case on its merits. The United States had convicted only three Koreans in total, so the UK became the most important power as far as clemency for Koreans in the final period was concerned.

By the mid-1950s, the situation of the guards, few though they were, was more pressing than that of other low-ranking personnel. Very few enlisted privates remained in British custody by the time peace was restored. None had originally received a life sentence, and the average length of sentences before confirmation had been 7.7 years for privates. Sentences were counted from the date of first arrest on suspicion as a war criminal, and, in practice, all war criminals in British custody were granted a remission of one-third of the sentence for good behaviour in prison. As a result, many private soldiers still incarcerated overseas had been released by mid-1951, when the British government transferred the war criminals then under its control to occupied Japan to serve out the remainder of their sentences in Sugamo Prison. In the months between arrival in Sugamo and the formal restoration of peace in April 1952, the remaining prisoners came under the control of the Supreme Commander for the Allied Powers, that is, the U.S. military, which operated its own parole system in Sugamo, under which war criminals were eligible for parole after serving one-third of their sentences.[56] By April 1952, the Americans had paroled half of the war criminals in Sugamo who had been convicted by Britain,[57] including Utsumi's main subject, the Korean Guard Kim Wangung.[58] Thus, few junior enlisted men, who tended to have short sentences in the first place, would have remained. On the other hand, ten Korean Guards were originally sentenced to life imprisonment, which was 'quantified' by the British at twenty-one years minus seven years for good behaviour, meaning that the sentence in practice was fourteen years, and another five had had death sentences commuted. These men remained in prison, so the UK continued to be responsible for the sentences of Korean Guards well into the 1950s.

When the peace treaty came into force, 1,244 prisoners were still incarcerated in Sugamo.[59] This total included twenty-nine Koreans and one Taiwanese; another forty-eight Taiwanese prisoners were incarcerated on Manus Island under Australian jurisdiction.[60] Thus, only 2.3% of war criminals still in custody were Korean. The twenty-nine Korean prisoners appear to have comprised thirteen convicted by the UK, six by Australia and ten by the Netherlands.[61] The sixteen Korean interpreters convicted by Nationalist China seem to have been released by this point, either on parole or at expiration of sentence. In any case, in August 1952, the Nationalist Chinese transferred all ninety-one of their remaining prisoners to Japanese authority, effectively authorising a mass release. In the first half of 1954, the maximum total number of Korean Guards in Sugamo was twenty-three. By the beginning of September 1955, six Koreans remained in Sugamo, all in British custody, out of a prison population of around 570.[62]

The fact that only six Korean Guards remained in prison in September 1955, however, masks the problem faced by the British government as it sought to resolve the issue of war criminals more broadly, by deciding the means of clemency. Of the eleven former Korean Guards under British legal control in Sugamo in February 1954, all had had sentences of fifteen years or more.[63] Like the Americans, the British authorities were committed to a case-by-case analysis of each application for clemency, rather than devising a formula which would allow mass release. As a Foreign Office official noted, 'In general these men were convicted of crimes of particular brutality', so it was not easy to find justification for their release.[64] By the mid-1950s, the insistence on considering every case on its merits meant that both British and American officials were left with a core group of prisoners who had committed terrible crimes. In the effort to find a way to release them without authorising a mass release, UK and U.S. officials had little choice but to begin actively reassessing the original trials of and verdicts against Japanese war criminals. For Britain, the cases of the Korean Guards were among the hardest to resolve because of the nature, severity and public sensitivity of their crimes. Review of these cases thus prompted serious reconsideration of the basic assumptions about what constituted a war crime and what circumstances mitigated that crime. In the process, British officials increasingly accepted that military necessity, the circumstances of the war, and the imperative for subordinates to obey superiors as in any army mitigated the severity of the offences that convicted war criminals had committed. By this time, they included as subordinates not only the few remaining Korean Guards but also Japanese military personnel of much higher rank, since the soldiers of lowest rank had already been released. Sergeants, sergeants-major, lieutenants, majors and even a lieutenant-colonel could now be described as 'subordinate' in rank.[65] The civil governor of the Andaman Islands, Jochi Ryonosuke, was also included under this rubric.[66] In using this line of argument, it became important to stress that the most senior officers, who had been responsible for decision-making at the highest operational level, had been severely dealt with, in order to avoid giving the impression that crimes had not been sufficiently punished. Thus, the crimes for which Jochi had been convicted were said to have been the responsibility of the Japanese naval authorities and of six officers who had been executed.[67]

In 1955, the British government reduced the maximum sentence to be served by war criminals to fifteen years, except in the 'very worst' cases. With remission for good behaviour, that meant that prisoners would be released ten years after the date of their first arrest as suspected war criminals. The last six of the Korean Guards benefited from this decision. They included Matsumoto Meizan, who had committed crimes on the Burma–Thailand Railway. His case was said to have had 'no redeeming features' in 1949, and he had also been refused clemency in 1953.[68] The 'notorious guard' Toyoyama Kisei, too, was still in prison. Both these men, and four other Korean Guards, were included in a petition for clemency for thirty war criminals that was submitted to the Queen in August 1955. The Queen was informed that 'They [the thirty war criminals] were guilty of serious crimes but they were mostly of subordinate rank and in many cases they were guilty of only lesser responsibility for war crimes….The senior officers on whose orders they acted have in most instances paid the death penalty.'[69] The Queen, as was constitutionally expected of her, accepted the recommendation, and the last of the convicted Korean Guards were released.

Koreans had suffered the colonial rule of their country by Japan from 1910, and there was no international legal reckoning with Japanese authorities for crimes against humanity committed against them during the colonial period. For a variety of reasons, however – including duress, social pressure, lack of other opportunities and a desire to better themselves – many Koreans took part in the Japanese imperial venture. After the war, they faced, like Japanese and Taiwanese military personnel, the prospect of investigation and prosecution where their actions were likely to have been criminal under international law. The records relating to Koreans indicate that this prosecution, and subsequent deliberations over sentencing and clemency, took strong account of the implications of having a subordinate place in the Japanese military. Far from being the group upon whom 'the heaviest retribution' was visited, Koreans were singled out only when their distinctive individual initiative as brutal guards drew attention to them.

Notes

1. This chapter draws on collaborative work funded by an Australian Research Council Discovery grant. See Sandra Wilson, Robert Cribb, Beatrice Trefalt and Dean Aszkielowicz, *Japanese War Criminals: The Politics of Justice After the Second World War* (New York: Columbia University Press, 2017). I am grateful to Robert Cribb for providing the material in Table 3 and for other trial statistics.
2. Utsumi Aiko, *Kimu wa naze sabakareta no ka: Chōsenjin BC-kyū senpan no kiseki* (Tōkyō: Asahi Shinbun Shuppan, 2008), 21, 96–97; Utsumi Aiko, 'Korean "Imperial Soldiers": Remembering Colonialism and Crimes against Allied POWs', in T. Fujitani, Geoffrey M. White and Lisa Yoneyama, eds, *Perilous Memories: The Asia-Pacific War(s)* (Durham, NC: Duke University Press, 2001), 202–203.
3. The National Archives (UK) (hereafter TNA), WO 203/4936, SACSEA to ALFSEA, 14 Jan. 1946.
4. See, for example, TNA, WO 203/4936, Telegram, Mountbatten to Chiefs of Staff, SACSEA [18 Sept. 1945]; TNA, WO 203/5596, ALFSEA to AFNEI [April 1946].
5. Hayashi Hirofumi, *BC-kyū senpan saiban* (Tōkyō: Iwanami, 2005), 152–153.

6. Clifford Kinvig, 'Allied POWs and the Burma-Thailand Railway', in Philip Towle, Margaret Kosuge and Yoichi Kibata, eds, *Japanese Prisoners of War* (London: Hambledon and London, 2000), 51.
7. TNA, WO 203/4936, SACSEA to ALFSEA, 14 Jan. 1946.
8. 'Japs Gentlemen Compared with Korean Guards, says Ex-P.O.W.', *Border Watch* (Mt Gambier, SA), 16 Sept. 1948, 5.
9. Gavan McCormack, 'Apportioning the Blame: Australian Trials for Railway Crimes', in Gavan McCormack and Hank Nelson, eds, *The Burma-Thailand Railway: Memory and History* (St Leonards, NSW: Allen & Unwin, 1993), 87.
10. Utsumi, 'Korean "Imperial Soldiers"', 212.
11. Utsumi Aiko, Introduction to Gil Heong-yun, 'Lee Hak Rae, the Korean Connection and "Japanese" War Crimes on the Burma-Thai Railway', *Japan Focus*, 26 Aug. 2007. Available at http://www.japanfocus.org/-Gil-Heong_yun/2505 (accessed 16 Feb. 2015).
12. Utsumi, *Kimu wa naze sabakareta no ka*, 20.
13. McCormack, 'Apportioning the Blame', 87. For a similar viewpoint, though with less explicit argument, see Takahashi Tetsuya, 'Les Militaires coréens de l'armée japonaise et les procès pour crimes de guerre', *Cipango: cahiers d'études japonaises*, No. 15 (2008), 79–100, available at http://cipango.revues.org/395; DOI: 10.4000/cipango.395 (accessed 16 Feb. 2015).
14. The strong sense of personal responsibility towards Koreans that underlies Utsumi's work is evident, for example, in Utsumi, 'Korean "Imperial Soldiers"', 199–201.
15. Some sources place lance corporals (as leading privates) with privates rather than non-commissioned officers. See, for instance, the U.S. Army's *Handbook on Japanese Military Forces* of Sept. 1944: *HyperWar: Handbook on Japanese Military Forces ([US] War Department Technical Manual, 15 September 1944, TM-E 30-480)*, 2. Available at http://www.ibiblio.org/hyperwar/Japan/IJA/HB/HB-1.html (accessed 16 Feb. 2015).
16. Philip Warner, *Japanese Army of World War II* (Oxford: Osprey Publishing, 1973), 4; Gordon L. Rottman, *US Marine vs Japanese Infantryman: Guadalcanal 1942–43* (Oxford: Osprey Publishing, 2014), back of title page.
17. Warner, *Japanese Army of World War II*, 4.
18. Utsumi, 'Korean "Imperial Soldiers"', 202; Utsumi, *Kimu wa naze sabakareta no ka*, 21.
19. Utsumi, *Kimu wa naze sabakareta no ka*, 20–21.
20. Hayashi, *BC-kyū senpan saiban*, 153–154. Taiwanese civilian employees of the Japanese military served mainly in Borneo, and also in the Philippines. In the war crimes trials, Australia convicted the greatest number.

21. Utsumi, *Kimu wa naze sabakareta no ka*, 21. On the general mobilisation of Korean civilian labour, see Brandon Palmer, *Fighting for the Enemy: Koreans in Japan's War, 1937–1945* (Seattle: University of Washington Press, 2013), 139–182.
22. Utsumi, *Kimu wa naze sabakareta no ka*, 59–66. On pay and conditions for Korean civilians employed by the Japanese military, see also Palmer, *Fighting for the Enemy*, 153.
23. Utsumi, *Kimu wa naze sabakareta no ka*, 65.
24. Aiko Utsumi, 'The Korean Guards on the Burma-Thailand Railway', in McCormack and Nelson, eds, *The Burma-Thailand Railway*, 135.
25. Palmer, *Fighting for the Enemy*, 146.
26. Utsumi, *Kimu wa naze sabakareta no ka*, 60–61. Japanese and Korean names are given in the usual East Asian order, with surname first, but in other respects I have retained the form of the name used in the relevant archival record (without macrons, in the case of Western-language records). Where possible, I have given the Korean as well as the Japanese names of Korean military personnel.
27. Palmer, *Fighting for the Enemy*, 153, 170–171, 187.
28. Ibid., 154–156.
29. Utsumi, *Kimu wa naze sabakareta no ka*, 62. I Gil (Kasayama Yoshikichi) makes a similar point in Kasayama Yoshikichi, 'Korean Guard', in Haruko Taya Cook and Theodore F. Cook, *Japan at War: An Oral History* (New York: New Press, 1992), 113–114.
30. Takahashi, 'Les Militaires coréens de l'armée japonaise'.
31. Palmer, *Fighting for the Enemy*, 153.
32. Ibid., 153, 174.
33. Utsumi, *Kimu wa naze sabakareta no ka*, 60–61.
34. Ibid., 62.
35. Yi Hak-Nae, 'The Man Between: A Korean Guard Looks Back', in McCormack and Nelson, eds, *The Burma-Thailand Railway*, 121, 124. The entry on Yi Hak-Nae in the book's list of contributors states inaccurately that he was 'conscripted into Japanese Army in 1942 as *gunzoku* (civilian auxiliary)' (xii).
36. Palmer, *Fighting for the Enemy*, 153.
37. Utsumi, *Kimu wa naze sabakareta no ka*, 21.
38. Kasayama, 'Korean Guard', 114.
39. Utsumi, *Kimu wa naze sabakareta no ka*, 104.
40. Ibid., 112; Kasayama, 'Korean Guard', 114–118.
41. TNA, WO 235/963, Trial of Lt Gen. Ishida Eiguma and Four Others, Singapore, Oct.–Dec. 1946, 290.
42. Utsumi, *Kimu wa naze sabakareta no ka*, 224.
43. Trial of Ishida Eiguma and Four Others.

44. Australian and French figures are drawn from the digital collection of the Forschungs- und Dokumentationszentrum für Kriegsverbrecherprozesse (ICWC) at the University of Marburg. Philippine figures (which are for trials run by the Philippine government, not the U.S. government) are taken from Sharon Chamberlain, 'Justice and Reconciliation: Postwar Philippine Trials of Japanese War Criminals in History and Memory' (PhD diss., George Washington University, 2010), 71 (with total number of defendants adjusted to include civilians).
45. Hayashi, *BC-kyū senpan saiban*, 152.
46. TNA, WO 235/910, Judge Advocate General to Commander, Singapore District, 'War Crimes Trials – Kaneoka Kiko', 6 Nov. 1946, Trial of Kaneoka Kiko, Singapore, Oct. 1946.
47. TNA, WO 235/952, JAG to Commander, Singapore District, 'War Crimes Courts', 23 Oct. 1946, Trial of Hashisuka Kunifusa and Twenty-Three Others, Singapore, July-Sept. 1946, 6.
48. See the following documents in TNA, WO 235/1034, Trial of Lt Col. Banno Hirateru and Six Others (or Abe Hiroshi and Six Others), Singapore, Sept.–Oct. 1946, File 4: Wild, War Crimes Liaison Officer, ALFSEA, to War Crimes Legal Section, ALFSEA, Singapore, '"F" Force Case – Korean Guard Toyoyama Kisei', 30 July 1946, 2 (= 918); Col. Kappe, 'Affidavit of Actions and Misdemeanors on the Part of Toyoyama Kisai [sic] – Korean – in Thailand During Period April–December 1943' (1000); 'Toyoyama Kise [sic] (Korean)' (affidavit of Major Roderic Henry Anderson, Cowra, NSW).
49. TNA, WO 235/952, Trial of Hashisuka Kunifusa and Twenty-Three Others, Singapore, July–Sept. 1946.
50. TNA, WO 235/886, Trial of Lt Col. Anami Sanso and Twelve Others, Singapore, July 1946; Utsumi, *Kimu wa naze sabakareta no ka*, 112–35, 163–92.
51. The figure of 25 reprieves is given in TNA, FO 371/115292, 'Sentences on Japanese War Criminals Convicted by British Military Courts', appended to draft of 'Clemency for Japanese War Criminals Convicted by British Military Courts', 2 May 1955.
52. See National Archives of Australia (hereafter NAA), A471/81640, Barcode 721743, Trial of Hiromura Kakurai, Singapore, March 1947. Hiromura was Camp Commandant at Hintok at one point. Utsumi discusses Hiromura's case in *Kimu wa naze sabakareta no ka*, 207–255.
53. Information on Australian trials in Hong Kong is drawn from the digital collection of the Forschungs- und Dokumentationszentrum für Kriegsverbrecherprozesse (ICWC) at the University of Marburg.
54. Treaty of Peace with Japan, in John M. Maki, ed, *Conflict and Tension in the Far East: Key Documents, 1894–1960* (Seattle: University of Washington Press, 1961), 136–137.

55. On clemency for Japanese war criminals, see Sandra Wilson, 'The Sentence is Only Half the Story: from Stern Justice to Clemency for Japanese War Criminals, 1945–1958', *Journal of International Criminal Justice*, 13 (2015), 745–761.
56. Diplomatic Archives, Tokyo (Gaikō shiryōkan), SCAP Circular No. 5, 'Clemency for war criminals', 7 March 1950, D' 1.3.0.1, vol. 3, 388.
57. TNA, FO 371/110508, 'Japanese War Criminals Tried by UK Military Courts' [c. Nov. 1954]. In this list, the total number of war criminals sentenced by the UK is given as 756. This figure does not tally with a count of the cases recorded in the trials file WO 357/3, where the total is 911, the figure that has been used for calculations in this paper. The actual figure, as noted above, should be 920.
58. Utsumi, *Kimu wa naze sabakareta no ka*, 27.
59. Diplomatic Archives, Tokyo, D' 1 3 0 3-1, 39. Diplomatic Archives, Tokyo, D' 1 3 0 3-1, Vol. 2 (p. 39), Ministry of Justice, Japan, 'Release of War Criminals and its Progress [sic]', Sept. 1954, 2.
60. Utsumi, *Kimu wa naze sabakareta no ka*, 282.
61. Archival records give the figure of nineteen for Britain, but the records also note confusion about which war criminals had been convicted by British courts and which by Australian. Such confusion was exacerbated by the fact that both Britain and Australia had convened trials in Singapore and Hong Kong. The total of twenty-nine Koreans in April 1952 is known to be correct, because their names appeared on an (unsuccessful) petition to the Supreme Court seeking the release of Korean and Taiwanese prisoners on legal grounds. See the following documents in TNA, FO 371/99516: Dening, British Embassy, Tokyo, to Eden, Secretary of State for Foreign Affairs, 11 Aug. 1952; British Legation, Pusan, to British Embassy, Tokyo, 5 Dec. 1952. See also TNA, FO 371/99516, 'Copy of Note Verbale from Ministry for Foreign Affairs, Tokyo Dated 22nd July, 1952'; NAA, MP 729/8, 66/431/27, Barcode 444972, R. J. Percival, 'War Criminals of Korean and Formosan Nationality', 25 July 1955, 1.
62. The total was four according to Aide Memoire, 30 Dec. 1955, and cancelled draft of W. D. Allen, Foreign Office, to Myo Mook Lee, Korean Legation, London, both in TNA, FO 371/115293. But see Annex A and Annex B to TNA, FO 371/115292, Petition to the Queen from Harold Macmillan, Secretary of State for Foreign Affairs, 23 August 1955, 163–168.
63. TNA, FO 371/99516, A.J. de la Mare, British Embassy, Tokyo, to J.A. Pilcher, Foreign Office, London, 28 April 1952; TNA, FO 371/110514, 'Disposition of Prisoners Named in Enclosure to Korean Minister's Aide-Mémoire of November 27, 1953', [c. Feb. 1954].
64. TNA, FO 371/110514, C. T. Crowe, Notes for an Answer to Parliamentary Question, 9 Feb. 1954.

65. Petition to the Queen from Macmillan, 23 August 1955, 160–168.
66. Ibid.
67. Ibid.
68. TNA, FO 371/105435, Folder, 'Japanese Minor War Criminal: NOPAR Commission Recommendation for Parole for: MATSUMOTO, Meizan', 1953, esp. 102, 103.
69. Petition to the Queen from Macmillan, 23 August 1955, 162.

Sandra Wilson is a Professor at the School of Arts and a Fellow of the Asia Research Centre at Murdoch University, Australia. She received her BA (Hons) in History and her Master's in Japanese Studies at the University of Western Australia, and her D.Phil. in Modern Japanese History at Oxford University. Her research interests include the history of Japanese nationalism, post-1945 Chinese and Japanese films about the Second World War, and war crimes and war criminals in the Asian theatre after the Second World War. Her publications include *The Manchurian Crisis and Japanese Society, 1931–33*, London, Routledge, 2002, and, with Robert Cribb, Beatrice Trefalt and Dean Aszkielowicz, *Japanese War Criminals: the Politics of Justice After the Second World War*, New York, Columbia University Press, 2017.

Defining Colonial "War Crimes": Korean Debates on Collaboration, War Reparations, and the International Military Tribunal for the Far East

Deokhyo Choi

The event of prosecuting wartime Japanese militarist and political leaders at the International Military Tribunal for the Far East (known as the Tokyo War Crimes Trial or Tokyo Trial) left highly polarized views of its historical significance. While the Allied Powers celebrated the event as the "judgment of civilization," Japanese nationalists questioned the legitimacy of the Tokyo Trial as retaliatory "victors' justice." This kind of binary approach dominated debates on the Tokyo Trial for a long time. However, in the 1970s, some Japanese historians opened up new debates beyond such a binary methodology and offered a more nuanced and balanced understanding regarding the significance and limits of the Tokyo Trial. Since then, historians have examined how certain crucial issues were silenced and excluded from war crimes trials under the realpolitik of victorious nations. For those historians, as Japanese historian Yuma Totani succinctly explains, the Tokyo Trial

D. Choi (✉)
Research Institute of Korean Studies, Korea University, Seoul, South Korea
e-mail: dc353@cornell.edu

K. von Lingen (ed.), *Debating Collaboration and Complicity in War Crimes Trials in Asia, 1945–1956*, World Histories of Crime, Culture and Violence, DOI 10.1007/978-3-319-53141-0_3

was "problematic because *it did not do enough* to disclose Japanese war crimes or to punish responsible individuals."[1] Among the critical agendas that the Allied Powers never fully addressed in the Tokyo Trial were Japanese colonialism and crimes committed against Korean and Taiwanese colonial subjects. Many historians now agree that the absence of both the colonial question and voices of former colonial subjects exemplifies the serious limits of the Tokyo Trial.

This chapter aims to illuminate those Korean voices that were unrepresented at the time of the Tokyo War Crimes Trials. Although Koreans were given no significant role in the Tokyo Trial, Korean political leaders and intellectuals in both Korea and Japan created their own movements and debates on how to define Japanese and Korean "war crimes" committed within a colonial context. In this chapter, I examine how war crimes were discussed and framed among Koreans in the aftermath of liberation from Japanese colonial rule. I focus particularly on how Korean political leaders and intellectuals approached the problems of colonial collaboration and war reparations while appropriating ideas and principles – such as "crimes against humanity" and liberation from the "enslavement of the people of Korea" – that the Allied Powers had pushed forward through the Tokyo Trial and the Cairo Declaration of 1943. Through an examination of the Korean debates on war crimes and their critiques of trials, this chapter also shows how Koreans understood the limits of the Tokyo Trial beyond the binary of "victors' justice" and "the judgment of civilization." I argue that their unheard voices and critiques in fact heralded a different interpretation and historical assessment of the Tokyo Trial in the history of postwar Japan.[2]

***

To examine how the question of war crimes emerged as a critical agenda among Korean leaders and intellectuals, one needs to understand the historical background of the political debates on colonial collaboration in postliberation Korea. In August 1945, Korea was liberated from Japanese colonial rule as a result of Japan's defeat in World War II. Japan's sudden surrender brought U.S. and Soviet occupation troops into Korea and, as American historian Bruce Cumings argues, "a quintessential Cold War relationship marked Soviet–American interactions from day one in Korea."[3] The 38th parallel, which the United States and the Soviet Union had initially agreed upon as a temporary demarcation to disarm Japanese imperial soldiers, turned into the frontline of the U.S.–Soviet global Cold War confrontation by 1948. Under the U.S. and Soviet occupations, Korean political movements also divided into rightists and leftists, the North and the South, and proponents and opponents of the establishment of a separate regime. Korea's indigenous political struggles over the vision of a decolonized nation became a flashpoint of the nascent Cold War, developing into the internationalized civil war of 1950, the Cold War's first so-called hot war.

The Korean peninsula in 1945 was, in the words of Cumings, "ripe for revolution," swept by roaring "demands for thoroughgoing political, economic, and social change."[4] The Soviet Occupation encouraged indigenous revolutionaries and even radicalized and hastened Korean efforts for the revolutionary transformation of their decolonizing society.[5] For instance, the radical land reform enforced in the Soviet-occupied North was an especially good example of Soviet intervention and collaboration with the North Korean leadership. Historian Charles K. Armstrong argues:

> Land reform in North Korea is perhaps the most important example of rapid and radical change in the years after liberation that combined initiatives from above with input from below, decisions made in Moscow with decisions made on the ground in Pyongyang by the Soviet occupation authorities and the North Korean leadership. Here we can see clearly where the context of the Soviet occupation allowed for the implementation of radical reforms with deep roots in the Manchurian guerrilla struggles of the 1930s and the social conditions of Korea of the 1940s, the "Koreanization" of Marxist-Leninist communism.[6]

At the same time, the Soviet-facilitated radical social revolution in the North created a flood of political refugees to the U.S.-occupied South, turning them into fierce antileftist, anti-North political forces of the South Korean regime.

In the U.S.-occupied South, on the other hand, the political landscape of liberated Korea took a significantly different form. During the first three months of occupation, as Cumings has demonstrated, Americans in Korea overturned the indigenous "regime of liberation" created by left-leaning political leaders and hundreds of self-governing local organizations. The U.S. occupation denied the legitimacy of the Korean People's Republic (*Chosŏn Inmin Konghwaguk*) and the people's committees that had replaced central and local colonial authorities before U.S. troops established full occupation in South Korea.[7] Instead, the occupation forged a new order by reviving the colonial legal-governmental apparatus. The occupation also retained Korean colonial bureaucrats and police officers, despite Washington's initial directive to purge "[c]riminal and ordinary police agencies" of those who had "collaborated with the Japanese."[8] This new American-made order soon proved to be a failure and a betrayal of what the majority of Koreans had envisioned for liberation. In the fall of 1946, popular discontent over the first year of the occupation burst into violent uprisings against the remnants of the colonial regime, triggered by an incident in Taegu City on 1 October in which a demonstrator was shot to death by the local Korean police. During the months from October to December, crowds (mostly peasants) armed with clubs, hoes, rice-cutting hooks, and bamboo spears began to assault local police stations and municipal offices across the southern provinces and killed more than two hundred Korean police officers.[9]

Against this historical background, it is important to understand what the indigenous politics of liberation looked like in Korea. At its heart was the question of how to deal with the legacies of Japanese colonial rule. The majority of Korean political leaders understood and agreed that a new Korea had to be born out of the nation's collective efforts to dismantle the deeply entrenched structural edifice of the colonial regime. After the end of Japanese colonial rule, Korean political leaders immediately started to call for the elimination of colonial remnants (*Ilche chanjae*) and the removal of the so-called pro-Japanese elements (*ch'inilp'a*) and national traitors (*minjok panyŏkcha*) from the new nation-building efforts. As historian Koen de Ceuster succinctly explains, "collaboration was an issue on the minds of most politically active Koreans, from both the left and the right."[10]

On 28 August, 1945, within two weeks of Korea's liberation, a newly formed political organization called the Committee for the Preparation of Korean Independence (CPKI, *Chosŏn kŏn'guk chunbi wiwŏnhoe*) declared that the CPKI would promise to "confiscate properties owned by Japanese and Korean pro-Japanese elements and also nationalize public facilities, mines, large industries, and factories."[11] On 3 September, the Korean Provisional Government (KPG), the Korean government-in-exile in Chongqing, announced its future agenda for establishing national independence. Among fourteen concrete agenda items were specific policies toward Korean traitors and Japanese settlers in Korea. The KPG promised to "confiscate enemy properties and punish the enemy in consultation with Allied Powers" and also to "punish strictly and openly national traitors and those who sabotaged independence movements."[12] Major leftist and rightist political parties in both the U.S.-occupied South and the Soviet-occupied North also advocated with one voice for the swift elimination of colonial political and social structures and national traitors.[13] In the North, the Korean Communist Party in South P'yŏngan Province adopted in September a political manifesto that claimed to confiscate and nationalize the factories, mines, and transportation facilities owned by Japanese imperialists and Korean pro-Japanese elements.[14] Moreover, on 14 September, the Korean People's Republic (KPR) issued a policy statement emphasizing the question of colonial remnants. In its policy statement, the KPR promised:

1. to immediately eliminate the legal system implemented by Japanese imperialism;
2. to confiscate the land owned by Japanese imperialists and national traitors and to redistribute it to peasants for free [...];
3. to confiscate and nationalize mines, factories, railways, ports, ships, communication facilities, financial institutions, and all other facilities owned by Japanese imperialists and national traitors.[15]

Although many Korean political parties and organizations began to call for the elimination and punishment of colonial collaborators in the wake of liberation, the definition of "pro-Japanese elements" and "national traitors" was not self-evident. On 28 January 1946, KPR leaders made a clarification of the two categories as follows:

> The term "pro-Japanese elements" includes anyone who purposefully collaborated with Japanese imperialism. The term "national traitors" signifies extremely evil cases among pro-Japanese elements.[16]

The KPR leaders also specified categories of pro-Japanese elements and national traitors. These were, for instance, "traitors [*maegungno*] who sold out Korea to Japanese imperialism and also those who were related to them; nobles who were entitled by the Japanese emperor; Governor-General Advisory Council [*chungch'uwŏn*] members; high-ranking officials under Japanese imperialist rule (chiefs of the Governor-General bureaus and local governors); high-ranking officials in the police and the military police (deputy inspector level)." Other categories included police officers and colonial government officials who had become the "target of popular resentment," entrepreneurs who had owned war industries, leaders of wartime "fascist" organizations, and intellectual and political leaders who had actively collaborated with and participated in colonial policies such as assimilation movements and wartime labor mobilization.[17]

Moreover, the KPR leaders also expanded the scope of "national traitors" into the context of postcolonial Korea. They even included as national traitors those who "had not taken pro-Japanese attitudes" during the colonial period but later, after liberation, engaged in "reactionary terrorist" activities against "democratic groups and leaders." Obviously, the KPR leaders – who were mostly affiliated with the Korean Communist Party and other leftist political parties – targeted rightist political groups, particularly the Korean Democratic Party that mainly consisted of colonial landlords, entrepreneurs, and collaborators, and those who had forged close political ties with the U.S. occupation. In other words, bringing colonial collaborators to justice was an integral part of ongoing power struggles over the new nation-state building in Korea.

In Japan, a Korean leftist association called the Korean League in Japan (*Zainihon Chōsenjin Renmei*) took the initiative of ostracizing "pro-Japanese elements" and "national traitors" among *zainichi* Koreans (Koreans living in Japan). The Korean League in Japan was the predominant Korean organization that played a crucial role in managing *zainichi* Korean communities. After Japan's surrender, local Korean leaders immediately began to organize mutual assistance groups in order to protect Korean residents from possible Japanese reprisal and help those who wished to return to the liberated homeland. In some cases, Korean leaders took advantage of local Korean residential organs that had been formed through imperial wartime mobilization.[18] In mid-October 1945, various Korean mutual assistance groups that had mushroomed across Japan united into a single organization. By January 1946, the Korean League established local branches in almost all prefectures and had a total of forty-seven branches across Japan.[19]

In the Korean League's inaugural convention on 15 and 16 October 1945, *zainichi* Korean Communist leader Kim Ch'ŏnhae, who had just been released on 10 October from Fuchū Prison together with Japanese Communist leaders such as Tokuda Kyūichi and Shiga Yoshio, delivered a speech and called for the punishment of "pro-Japanese traitors." On 18 November, the central committee of the Korean League adopted a new resolution that included the "thorough investigation of pro-Japanese elements and national traitors" and listed thirty-six *zainichi* Korean traitors for a possible "people's trial."[20] Interestingly, those thirty-six *zainichi* Korean "pro-Japanese, national traitors" were apparently included in the "list of war criminals" (*sensō hanzainin meibo*) that the Japanese Communist Party (JCP) created and publicized at a political rally held on 8 December. At that rally, JCP leader Kuroki Shigenori read out the list of more than 1,500 names that the JCP had designated as war criminals, including Emperor Hirohito, and later submitted the list to the Japanese government and the U. S./Allied occupation.[21] A Korean newspaper reported that the names of thirty-six Koreans were included in the JCP-drafted list of war criminals.[22] In other words, leaders of the Korean League tried to expand the scope of war crimes trials in Japan by taking advantage of the JCP's efforts.

***

In fact, the idea of Korean "war criminals" (*chŏnbŏm*) also emerged in the political debate on anticollaborator legislation within the South Korean Interim Legislative Assembly (SKILA, *Nam Chosŏn Kwado Ippŏp Ŭiwŏn*). The SKILA was established in December 1946 by the U.S. occupation with the aim of creating a centrist coalition that would isolate both right- and left-wing extremists.[23] It consisted of forty-five elected members and another forty-five members appointed by the U.S. occupation authorities. Among the elected members, rightist leaders composed the great majority. Moreover, the elected members included a significant number of so-called pro-Japanese elements. General John R. Hodge, commander of the U.S. Army Forces in Korea, characterized them as follows:

> The elected members [of the SKILA] were a disappointment, not because they are Rightists which I generally expected, but because they are all, except two, of one block representing the pro-Japs, wealthy land owners, and conniving politicians [...].[24]

The remaining forty-five members of the SKILA were appointed from among moderate rightist and leftist politicians. Importantly, it was many of those appointed members who emerged as active proponents of anticollaborator legislation within the SKILA.

As the SKILA opened on 12 December, the members soon started discussing legislation on former colonial collaborators. On 21 December, assembly chairperson Kim Kyusik, from a moderate rightist group, announced in a press interview that the SKILA would carry out the drafting of a law for the prosecution of "pro-Japanese elements, national traitors, and evil profiteers [*akchil moribae*]" and also work on the establishment of a "special court" for them.[25] On 9 January 1947, the SKILA set up a committee for drafting an anticollaborator law, namely, the Committee for Special Legislation on Collaborators [*puil hyŏmnyŏkcha*], National Traitors, War Criminals and Profiteering Scoundrels [*kansangbae*].[26] The Committee was made up of nine SKILA members – all from rightist groups and mostly from among the appointed members – and many had political backgrounds that were related to the Korean independence movements of the colonial period. For instance, the committee was formed under the leadership of appointed member Chŏng Ihyŏng, who was a former anticolonial guerrilla fighter and had survived a nineteen-year imprisonment under the Japanese colonial regime.

The committee's efforts on anticollaborator legislation faced fierce opposition from the beginning, from inside and outside the SKILA. On 10 March, even before the committee officially submitted the first draft of the bill on 13 March, daily newspaper *Chayu Sinmun* published on its front page a protest letter from a man named Yi Haegin, the head of the Investigation Department of the National Police.[27] The letter was titled "An Open Letter to Leading Public Servants" (*cheilsŏn pongjikcha chehyŏng ege p'iryŏkham*). In his protest letter, Yi defended those who had collaborated with Japanese colonial rule by stating that they had done so against their will. Moreover, Yi characterized political advocates of the anticollaborator legislation as "parasitelike intellectuals" who were disrupting the unity of the nation for their own self-interest. Yi even went so far as to call for their exclusion from the current nation-building effort. This "open letter" from a high-ranking National Police official shocked and enraged supporters of the anticollaborator legislation within the SKILA. Assembly member Kim Pungjun called it the "National Police's declaration of war against the Assembly."[28] At the same time, strong opposition to the anticollaborator legislation also came from within the SKILA itself. As soon as the draft bill emerged on the discussion agenda in the 17 March session, one assembly member, Pak Yongŭi, immediately proposed removing it from the agenda. Pak claimed that the definition of collaboration was too broad and, thus, too problematic: "No one will be exempt [from the charges of collaboration] if this draft bill becomes law."[29] Another assembly member, Sŏ Sangil from the Korean Democratic Party, raised what he portrayed as "fundamental questions."

He asked: "Why do we have to define who the pro-Japanese are and who the national traitors are?"[30]

In fact, apropos assembly member Pak Yongŭi's question about the scope of collaboration, the anticollaborator bill targeted a broad range of cases as acts of collaboration. While the committee provided a relatively narrow definition of "national traitors" in the draft bill, the category of "collaborators" was very loosely defined.[31] According to the draft bill, "collaborators" signified "those who committed pernicious acts for Japan or for their own interest under Japanese rule during the period from Japan's annexation of Korea to [Korea's] liberation and thereby harmed Korean brethren."[32] The category of "collaborators" included, for instance, those who had served for the colonial government and municipal offices, entrepreneurs and employers who had committed the "exploitation" of Koreans in colonial industries, and intellectuals who had become an obstacle to revolutionary movements by praising Japanese rule and leading colonial assimilation (Japanization) movements. The committee even included as "collaborators" those who had "married a Japanese" or had "accustomed themselves to Japanese language in everyday life."

However, the punishment against collaborators was remarkably lenient compared to the other categories. While national traitors and war criminals could face the death penalty or indefinite banishment, the punishment against collaborators was limited to disenfranchisement for a maximum of ten years. The committee explained that the anticollaborator legislation was not intended to bring harsh punishment to collaborators, so long as they were not "national traitors" or "war criminals." Rather, as one of the committee members described it, the goal of the legislation was the "establishment of the nation's correct spirit,"[33] and hence the anticollaborator legislation was aimed at removing as many former collaborators as possible from the new nation-building process. Indeed, the committee estimated that the number of collaborators punishable under this legislation would be roughly 100,000 to 200,000.[34]

What is also important about this draft bill is that the committee created a separate category of Korean war criminals, in addition to the categories of collaborators, national traitors, and profiteering scoundrels. In the bill, the committee defined war criminals as follows:

> Those who have committed pernicious acts for their own interest during the time between the Mukden Incident (18 September 1931) and the liberation

of Korea (15 August 1945) and thereby caused harmful consequences to Korean brethren are considered to be war criminals.

- A person who abused Allied POWs;
- A person who ran a major war industry for the purpose of enhancing [Japan's] military strength;
- A person who voluntarily donated more than 10,000 yen or munitions to the Japanese military;
- A person who voluntarily joined the Japanese military;
- A person who advocated [Japan's] war through speech, writing, etc.;
- A person who joined the Japanese military and mistreated Korean brethren and Allied nationals.[35]

It is not clear how the concept of "war criminals" suddenly became incorporated into (South) Korean political discourse on colonial collaborators. As discussed earlier, colonial collaborators were mostly understood and framed as pro-Japanese elements and national traitors in post-liberation Korean society. Moreover, the definition of war criminals that the committee had proposed was obviously beyond what was generally understood as belonging to the definition of conventional war crimes as well as crimes against peace and crimes against humanity at the time of the Nuremberg trials and the Tokyo Trial. However, the incorporation of the concept of war criminals into the anticollaborator law can be seen as part of the Korean leaders' political efforts to appropriate the politics of the U.S./Allied democratization of Japan. For instance, the Tokyo Trial and the U.S./Allied purge of Japanese militarists became a reference point for Korean political leaders in criticizing U.S. occupation policy in Korea. On 8 January 1947, when the SKILA was forming the committee for anticollaborator legislation, the leftist Democratic National Front (*Minjujuŭi Minjok Chŏnsŏn*) in the South issued a statement urging General Douglas MacArthur to "purge war criminals in Korea" as he was doing in Japan. In its statement, the Democratic National Front pointed out the stark contradiction between the fates of war criminals in U.S./Allied-occupied Japan and wartime collaborators in U.S.-occupied Korea.[36]

In a sense, one can see that these Korean political leaders were attempting to appropriate the U.S./Allied politics of the war crimes trials. Given the reality that the national political landscape in U.S.-occupied South

Korea was dominated by former Korean colonial collaborators and colonial police forces, the proponents of the anticollaborator legislation needed to turn to a different moral and legal principle for bringing colonial collaborators to justice. Thus, by applying the concept of war crimes and crimes against humanity to the context of wartime colonial Korea, it could become possible to internationalize the domestically circumscribed question of pro-Japanese elements and national traitors.

Yet, the definition of war criminals became the major target of criticism within the SKILA and soon disappeared in the draft bill. In the SKILA session on 21 March, assembly member Yi Ilu questioned whether it would be fair to punish those who had been forced to participate in Japan's war against the Allied Powers, such as Korean conscripts and student soldiers. Yi argued that no single Korean had "voluntarily" joined the Japanese military and "mistreated Allied nationals." However, committee chairperson Chŏng Ihyŏng contended that some Koreans had indeed voluntarily worked for Japan's war by "donating airplanes and tanks" or by "agitating" for Korean enlistment. Chŏng insisted: "If they are not war criminals, then what are they?"[37] Another criticism was raised by some who started to question whether the concept of "war criminals" itself was applicable to Korea. For instance, in the SKILA session on 24 April, one assembly member simply dismissed the category of "war criminals" in the bill, saying, "Korea was not a party to World War II." But, committee chairperson Chŏng Ihyŏng refuted this view as well. He argued that "when overseas independence fighters were participating in the war against Japan, some domestic Korean leaders were collaborating with Japan by donating money." Thus, "We will punish war criminals from the position of a victorious nation."[38]

In the end, the category of "war criminals" was deleted from the draft bill. This occurred most likely because of the problem of how to define "war criminals" within the context of colonial Korea, rather than the question of whether or not colonial Korea had been a party to World War II. Indeed, one assembly member raised doubts about the "criterion for distinguishing war criminals from collaborators and national traitors."[39] After multiple revisions, the final draft of the anticollaborator bill was passed on 2 July, almost four months after the first draft bill was submitted to the SKILA. However, the U.S. occupation in Korea refused to enact the bill.[40] Later, after the South Korean government was established on 15 August 1948, the Constitutional

Assembly passed the new Anti-Traitor Law (*Panminjok haengwi ch'ŏbŏlpŏp*) on 7 September.

***

One can also find in Korean leaders' debates on war reparations their efforts to pursue judgments on colonialism and colonial crimes. In late 1947, Korean business leaders in the South drafted a report on possible war reparations from Japan.[41] In their report, these business leaders discussed the validity of claims for reparations by reframing the concept of war reparations. They argued that, although Korea "had not been a party to World War II from the standpoint of international law," it was a "liberated country." Thus, Korea's claim for reparations from Japan would be different from what victors usually claimed from the vanquished for compensation. In the case of Korea, reparations would be for "what Japan had exploited and plundered by force during the past decades of its colonial rule in Korea."[42] More importantly, the Korean business leaders referred to the Cairo Declaration of 1943 as the foundation of their claim for reparations from Japan.

The Cairo Declaration was one of the most significant international statements that challenged Japan's claim for the legitimacy of its modern imperial project. In the Cairo Declaration, the Allied Powers officially condemned Japanese colonial rule in Korea as the "enslavement of the people of Korea." The Allied Powers promised the liberation of Koreans from Japanese "enslavement" by declaring that "in due course Korea shall become free and independent." However, what the Allied Powers meant by "in due course," as the timeline for Korean independence, was not necessarily immediate independence in the aftermath of Japan's surrender. Although many Koreans understood the term "in due course" as the equivalent of "in a few days" or at least "very soon,"[43] the Allied Powers had in mind a different vision of Korean independence. As several scholars have already discussed, U.S. President Franklin Roosevelt was preparing a plan to administer post-colonial Korea under the trusteeship of the Allied Powers before establishing independence.[44] Moreover, the Cairo Declaration's promise of Korean liberation had a significant impact on U.S. occupation policy in Korea. After Japan's surrender, U.S. policymakers in Washington drafted a policy directive titled "Basic Initial Directive to the Commander in Chief, U.S. Army Forces, Pacific, for the Administration of Civil Affairs in Those Areas of Korea Occupied by U.S. Forces." This directive defined postwar Korea as a "liberated country." It stipulated that "[i]n conformity with the provisions of the Cairo Declaration your administration of civil affairs will be based upon the treatment of Korea as a liberated country to the maximum extent consistent with the security of your forces."[45]

Against this historical background, it is important to understand how Korean leaders formulated their claim for judgments on Japanese colonial rule. For instance, in his article titled "The Validity of the Claim for Reparations from Japan," Yi Sangdŏk argued as follows:

> As the Cairo and Potsdam Declarations characterized it as the "enslavement of the people of Korea," Japan's long-time domination of Korea was based not on basic principles of international justice such as morality, equity, and reciprocity, but on violence and exploitation.[46]

He continued, asserting that the "Japan-Korea annexation treaty" of 1910 had been enacted "by force" against the "Korean people's free will." Therefore, "reparations from Japan" would mean the "recovery of the loss caused by violence and greed."[47] Importantly, this formulation became the logical foundation for the South Korean government's approach to reparations issues. Later, when the South Korean government created a set of policy papers titled "Research for the Claim for Reparations from Japan" in September 1949, the government clarified its rationale for demanding reparations from Japan as follows:

> Japan's domination of Korea from 1910 to 15 August in 1945 was imposed by force and against the Korean people's free will. Because it was not based on the principle of justice, equity, and reciprocity and instead was domination through violence and greed, Korea and Koreans suffered the most among the victims of Japan.... [Through the Cairo Declaration,] this inhumanness and unlawfulness of Japan's domination of Korea was acknowledged in the world.[48]

The South Korean government also took its own initiative to pursue judgments on Japanese colonial rule in Korea. On 22 November 1948, South Korean Foreign Minister Chang T'aeksang announced that the South Korean government would work on bringing Class-A war criminals of the former governors-general in Korea – Koiso Kuniaki and Minami Jirō – into the South Korean courts to try them for crimes against humanity.[49] After the Tokyo War Crimes Trial issued a ruling on 12 November, Foreign Minister Chang held a press conference and expressed disappointment at the fact that Koreans had not been given any role in the Tokyo Trial."[50] On 29

November Foreign Minister Chang told the press that the South Korean government had requested that the Allied Powers transfer to the South Korean court both Koiso and Minami and also Itagaki Seishirō, former commander-in-chief of the Japanese army in Korea.[51] However, in a striking contradiction, the South Korean government simultaneously maintained a reluctant attitude toward its own colonial collaboration issues. As noted earlier, the South Korean Constitutional Assembly passed the new Anti-Traitor Law on 7 September 1948, and the Syngman Rhee administration reluctantly signed the law on 22 September. Unlike the assembly, the Rhee administration was unwilling to take action for the prosecution of former colonial collaborators. The Rhee administration made determined efforts to eviscerate the Anti-Traitor Law and to sabotage investigations launched by the Special Investigation Committee organized by the assembly.[52]

Simultaneously, Korean media's critiques of the Tokyo War Crimes Trial also brought to the fore the question of judgments on Japanese colonial rule and revealed the limits of the so-called judgment of civilization. The Korean news media, particularly *zainichi* Korean newspapers, published multiple articles and editorials on the Tokyo Trial when it was concluded.[53] For instance, the leftist *zainichi* Korean newspaper *Haebang Sinmun* published an editorial titled "Regarding the Ruling of the International Military Tribunal for the Far East" and criticized the Tokyo Trial for not prosecuting Emperor Hirohito. *Haebang Sinmun* also lamented the fact that the Allied Powers had not invited representatives of the Korean nation, which had been the "primary victim of Japan's invasion for the past four decades."[54] Another *zainichi* Korean newspaper, *Sinsegye Sinmun*, claimed that if the Tokyo Trial was supposed to be the trial held in the "name of civilization and humanity," then it was totally "contradictory and absurd" to exclude Koreans who were the "victims of [crimes against] humanity." *Sinsegye Sinmun* also complained about the fact that judgments on Japan's "invasion of Korea" had not been made by the Tokyo Trial.[55] *Chōren Chūō Jihō*, the bulletin of the Korean League in Japan, also criticized the Tokyo Trial for excluding Japan's war crimes that had occurred before 1928, particularly the Japan–Korea Protectorate Treaty of 1905 that was signed by force. *Chōren Chūō Jihō* argued that such exclusions manifested the "historical limits" of the Tokyo Trial.[56]

***

These *zainichi* Korean critiques raised crucial issues that Japanese historians would later bring to the fore in assessing the limits of the Tokyo Trial. As mentioned previously, in the 1970s some Japanese historians began to investigate serious flaws in war crimes trials in a manner unlike the existing "victors' justice" critiques that focused only on the retaliatory nature of the Tokyo Trial. One of the major criticisms that the Japanese historians presented was the absence of both the colonial question and voices of former colonial subjects in the Tokyo Trial. In this sense, it is important to note that the *zainichi* Korean critiques heralded a different interpretation and historical assessment of the Tokyo Trial in the history of postwar Japan.

Notes

1. Yuma Totani, *The Tokyo War Crimes Trial: The Pursuit of Justice in the Wake of World War II* (Cambridge, MA: Harvard University Press, 2008), 250.
2. Historian Chŏng Yŏnghwan has shed new light on those unheard voices in his recent works. See Chŏng Yŏnghwan, Kaihō chokugo no zainichi Chōsenjin undō to 'sensō sekinin'ron, 1945–1949," *Nihon shokuminchi kenkyū* 28 (June 2016); "Tōkyō Saiban o meguru zainichi Chōsenjin hakkō shinbun kikanshi no ronchō," *Nikkan sōgo ninshiki* 1 (2008).
3. Bruce Cumings, *The Origins of the Korean War: Liberation and the Emergence of Separate Regimes, 1945–1947* (Princeton: Princeton University Press, 1981), xxvii.
4. Cumings, *The Origins of the Korean War*, xx, xxvii.
5. Korean sociologist Kang Chŏnggu has discussed the consequences of the Soviet occupation of the North in terms of the "radicalization" of a Korean indigenous "historical course." See Kang Chŏnggu, *Chwajŏl toen sahoe hyŏngmyŏng: Mi chŏmnyŏngha ŭi Namhan, P'illip'in kwa Pukhan pigyo yŏn'gu* (Pusan: Yŏrumsa, 1989).
6. Charles K. Armstrong, *The North Korean Revolution, 1945–1950* (Ithaca: Cornell University Press, 2003), 75–6.
7. On 6 September 1945, the leaders of the Committee for the Preparation of Korean Independence declared the establishment of the Korean People's Republic. They hurried to form the Korean indigenous government in the face of the arrival of the U.S. occupation forces. On the significance of the formation of the Korean People's Republic, see Cumings, *The Origins of the Korean War*, Chapter 3; Kim Namsik, *Namnodang yŏn'gu* (Seoul: Tol Pegae, 1984), Chapter 2; Rim Ch'ŏl, "Chōsen Jinmin Kyōwakoku ni kansuru jakkan no mondai," *Chōsenshi kenkyūkai ronbunshū* 23 (1986); Ch'oe Sangnyong, *Mi kunjŏng kwa Han'guk minjokchuŭi* (Seoul: Nanam Ch'ulp'an, 1988), 77–119.
8. "Basic Initial Directive to the Commander in Chief, U.S. Army Forces, Pacific, for the Administration of Civil Affairs in Those Areas of Korea

Occupied by U.S. Forces" (SWNCC 176/8), in *Foreign Relations of the Unites States 1945*, vol. 6 (Washington: United States Government Printing Office, 1969), 1076. (Henceforth, *FRUS*.)

9. On the popular uprisings of 1946 in southern Korea, see Cumings, *The Origins of the Korean War*, 351–81; Chŏng Haegu, *10-wŏl inmin hangjaeng yŏn'gu* (Seoul: Yŏrŭmsa, 1988); Chŏng Yŏngjin, *P'okpung ŭi 10-wŏl* (Seoul: Han'gilsa, 1991); Sim Chiyŏn, Taegu *10-wŏl hangjaeng yŏn'gu* (Seoul: Ch'ŏnggye Yŏn'guso, 1991).
10. Koen de Ceuster, "The Nation Exorcised: The Historiography of Collaboration in South Korea," *Korean Studies*, 25, 2 (2001), 210.
11. Yi Kangsu, "Haebang chikhu Nam-Pukhan ŭi ch'inilp'a sukch'ŏng nonŭi yŏn'gu," *Chŏnnam sahak* 20 (2003), 27–8.
12. Kuksa P'yonch'an Wiwŏnhoe, *Charyo Taehan Min'guksa* 1 (Seoul: Kuksa P'yonch'an Wiwŏnhoe, 1968), 46–8.
13. Yi Kangsu, "Haebang chikhu Nam-Pukhan ŭi ch'inilp'a sukch'ŏng nonŭi yŏn'gu," 28–30.
14. Ibid., 39–40.
15. "Kŏnjun, ingong chungang inminwi kyŏlchŏng sŏnŏn chŏnggang sijŏng pangch'im palp'yo," *Maeil Sinbo*, 19 September 1945.
16. "Ch'inilp'a, minjok panyŏkcha ŭi kijun, chungang inmin wiwŏnhoe esŏ kyujŏng,"*Chayu Sinmun*, 31 January 1946.
17. Ibid.
18. See Ch'oe Yŏngho, *Chaeil Han'gugin kwa choguk kwangbok: haebang chikhu ŭi ponguk kwihwan kwa minjok tanch'e hwaltong* (Seoul: Kŭlmoin, 1995).
19. Pak Kyŏngsik, *Kaihō go zainichi Chōsenjin undōshi* (Tokyo: San'ichi Shobō, 1989), 61.
20. Pak, *Kaihōgo zainichi Chōsenjin undōshi*, 54–6, 60–1.
21. "Sensō hanzainin tsuikyū taikai," *Asahi Shimbun*, 9 December 1945; "Kyōsantō senpan meibo shukō," *Asahi Shimbun*, 12 December 1945; Shinobu Seizaburō, *Sengo Nihon seijishi I: senryō to minshushugi* (Tokyo: Keisō Shobō, 1965), 233.
22. "Chosŏnin chŏnbomja ilgong esŏ 36-myŏng chimyŏng,"*Chayu Sinmun*, 25 January 1946.
23. On the formation of the South Korean Interim Legislative Assembly and its role, see Kim Yŏngmi, "Mi kunjŏnggi Namjosŏn Kwado Ippŏp Ŭiwŏn ŭi sŏngnip kwa hwaltong," *Han'guk saron* 32 (1994). Also see Cumings, *The Origins of the Korean War*, Chapter 7.
24. Goodfellow Papers, Box 1, From Hodge to Goodfellow (28 January 1947), cited from Cumings, *The Origins of the Korean War*, 537.
25. "Ippŏp ŭiwŏn ŭijang Kim Kyusik, dong ŭiwŏn ŭi cheban munje e taehae kija hoegyŏn," *Seoul Sinmun* and *Tonga Ilbo*, 22 December 1946.

26. *Records of the South Korean Interim Legislative Assembly*, No. 12 (9 January 1947).
27. "Cheilsŏn pongjikcha chehyŏng ege p'iryŏkham," *Chayu Sinmun*, 10 March 1947. Also see *Records of the South Korean Interim Legislative Assembly*, No. 35 (14 March 1947).
28. *Records of the South Korean Interim Legislative Assembly*, No. 35 (14 March 1947).
29. *Records of the South Korean Interim Legislative Assembly*, No. 36 (17 March 1947).
30. Ibid.
31. "National traitors" were, for instance, those who "had signed the Korea-Japan Annexation Treaty"; those who "had defected from the national movement and collaborated with the Japanese"; and those who "had mistreated Korean brethren in collusion with foreign powers."
32. *Records of the South Korean Interim Legislative Assembly*, No. 36 (17 March 1947). The full text of the bill was also published on newspapers. For instance, see "Puil hyŏmnyŏkcha e taehan pŏmnyŏng (1)," *Chayu Sinmun*, 4 March 1947; "Minjok panyŏk, chŏnbŏm, kansangbae (2)," *Chayu Sinmun*, 5 March 1947.
33. *Records of the South Korean Interim Legislative Assembly*, No. 42 (26 March 1947).
34. *Records of the South Korean Interim Legislative Assembly*, No. 36 (17 March 1947).
35. Ibid.
36. "Minjujuŭi minjok chŏnsŏn, chŏnbŏmja ch'ubangnyŏng ŭi chejŏng kongp'o rŭl yoguhanŭn tamhwa palp'yo," *Chosŏn Ilbo*, 9 January 1947.
37. *Records of the South Korean Interim Legislative Assembly*, No. 39 (21 March 1947).
38. "Chŏnbom tŭng ch'ŏdanan, ibŭi ŭi nonjŏn paegyŏlhwa," *Chayu Sinmun*, 26 April 1946.
39. Ibid.
40. On the U.S. Occupation's stance on the anti-collaborator bill, see Hŏ Chong, "1947-nyŏn Nam Chosŏn Kwado Ippŏp Ŭiwŏn ŭi 'ch'inilp'a ch'ŏbŏlpŏp' chejŏng kwa kŭ sŏngkyŏk," *Han'gu Kŭnhyŏndaesa Yon'gu* 12 (Spring 2000), 174–8.
41. See Ōta Osamu, *Nikkan kōshō: seikyūken mondai no kenkyū* (Tokyo: Kurein, 2003), 39–46.
42. Ibid.
43. In mid-September 1945, a U.S. official in Korea reported on how Koreans had understood the Cairo Declaration and stated: "It was recently discovered that from the beginning the Korean translation of the term 'in due course' in the Cairo Declaration has been the equivalent of 'in a few days' or

'very soon,' and well-educated Koreans expressed surprise when the difference was pointed out to them." See "The Political Adviser in Korea (Benninghoff) to the Secretary of State" (15 September 1945), in *FRUS 1945*, vol. 6, 1049.

44. WM. Roger Louis, *Imperialism at Bay: The United States and the Decolonization of the British Empire, 1941–1945* (New York: Oxford University Press, 1978); Cumings, *The Origins of the Korean War.*
45. It is important to note that Washington did not mean by this that Korea would be treated as an independent country. The same directive further explained that U.S. occupation policy in Korea was to "contemplat[e] a progressive development from this initial interim period of civil affairs administration by the United States and the U.S.S.R., *to a period of trusteeship under the United States, the United Kingdom, China, and the U.S.S.R.*, and finally to the eventual independence of Korea with membership in the United Nations organization" (emphasis added). See "Basic Initial Directive to the Commander in Chief, U.S. Army Forces, Pacific, for the Administration of Civil Affairs in Those Areas of Korea Occupied by U.S. Forces" (SWNCC 176/8), in *FRUS 1945*, vol. 6, 1074.
46. Yi Sangdŏk, "Taeil paesang ŭi chŏngdangsŏng," *Sinch'ŏnji* (January 1948), 32, cited from Ōta, *Nikkan kōshō*, 44–5.
47. Ibid.
48. Ōta, *Nikkan kōshō*, 50.
49. "Kankoku, Minami to Koiso o yōkyū," *Asahi Shimbun*, 23 November 1948.
50. "Chang T'aeksang wemubu changgwan, Han'guk ŭn Chosŏn kwan'gye chŏnbŏm chaesimsa yogu kwŏlli rŭl poyu handago p'yomyŏng," *Minju Ilbo*, 20 November 1948; "Chang wemu changgwan ilmunje ŏngŭp," *Chayu Sinmin*, 20 November 1948.
51. "Koiso Minami tŭng chŏnbŏm Han'guk sŏ ŏmbol yogu," *Tonga Ilbo*, 30 November 1948; "Hanminjok ŭl ch'akch'wihan wŏnhyung Koiso Kuniaki wa Minami Jirō ŭl indo hara," *Chayu Sinbun*, 30 November 1948.
52. On the Rhee administration's attitudes toward the Anti-Traitor Law and its sabotage of Committee's activities, see Yi Kangsu, *Panmin T'ŭgwi Yon'gu* (Seoul: Nanam Ch'ulp'an, 2003), 155–218; de. Ceuster, "The Nation Exorcised," 212–4.
53. See Chŏng, "Tōkyō Saiban o meguru zainichi Chōsenjin hakkō shinbun kikanshi no ronchō."
54. "Kŭktong kunsa chaep'an p'angyol e taehaya" *Haebang Sinmun*, 9 November 1948.
55. "Han'guk ŭi chŏnbŏm chaep'an yogu," *Sinsegye Sinmun*, 26 November 1948. Chŏng, 54–5.
56. "Senpan wa mada iru genjū ni shobatsu seyo Kyokutō Kokusai Gunji Saiban ni nozomu," *Chōren Chūō Jihō*, 11 November 1948.

Deokhyo Choi is a research professor at the Research Institute of Korean Studies, Korea University. He received his Ph.D. in History from Cornell University in August 2013. His Ph.D. dissertation, "Crucible of the Post-Empire: Decolonization, Race, and Cold War Politics in U.S.-Japan-Korea Relations, 1945–1952," won the International Convention of Asia Scholars (ICAS) Best Dissertation Prize 2015 in the Humanities. He has published numerous articles in English, Japanese, and Korean. His recent articles include. "Writing the 'Empire' Back into the History of Postwar Japan" (*International Journal of Korean History*, February 2017) and "'Mindful of the Enslavement': The Cairo Declaration, Korean Independence, and the Ambiguity of the Liberation of Koreans in Defeated Japan" (*The Significance and Effects of the Cairo Declaration*, 2014).*The research leading to these results received funding from the European Research Council under the European Union's Seventh Framework Programme (FP7/2007–2013)/ERC grant agreement n°* 313382.

Oaths of Allegiance in the Singapore Trials

CHEAH Wui Ling

Introduction

The changing of national allegiance engages difficult questions about loyalty, choice and identity. In times of war or conflict, such change of national allegiance becomes even more complicated when it involves a switching of sides. Wartime changes of allegiance involving high-profile individuals or large numbers may have serious political and social consequences. It may demoralise fighting men on the front and civilians at home. Such changes of allegiance may undermine a country's narrative of cohesion and perseverance at a time when this narrative is particularly needed. It may give lie to a country's claims that the war is conducted in the name of its population and for the people's benefit.

How then should such changes in allegiance be treated by the law? More specifically, should such changes in allegiance deprive the individuals concerned from the protection of the law? Should such changes be treated differently by national law and international law? This chapter explores how these questions arose in war crimes proceedings conducted by the British military in Singapore after the Second World War (Singapore Trials). It should be noted that changes in allegiance should not be confused with the

The original version of this chapter was revised. An erratum to this chapter can be found at DOI 10.1007/978-3-319-53141-0_9

CHEAH W.L. (✉)
Faculty of Law, National University of Singapore, Bukit Timah, Singapore
e-mail: lawcwl@nus.edu.sg

K. von Lingen (ed.), *Debating Collaboration and Complicity in War Crimes Trials in Asia, 1945–1956*, World Histories of Crime, Culture and Violence, DOI 10.1007/978-3-319-53141-0_4

giving of parole. There were incidents where the Japanese military coerced Allied prisoners of war (POWs) to give parole or promise not to escape.[1] This is not considered an abandonment of allegiance. The defendants in the cases considered in this chapter argued that their acts should not be considered war crimes committed against POWs because the victims concerned had renounced their allegiance to Britain by taking oaths of allegiance to Japan. The victims were British Indian and were members of the British military before being taken captive by Japan. They had been ill-treated or summarily executed by the Japanese military. The accused were charged with POW ill-treatment and death.

This chapter examines how two cases dealt with this question of allegiance change in the Singapore Trials. It starts by setting out the legal and political context of British war crimes proceedings in Singapore. The questions raised about allegiance change during the war were particularly charged against this post-war socio-political landscape, as the returning British colonial authorities sought to reassert authority and re-establish order in Singapore and the region. The chapter then focuses on how the question of allegiance change was treated in two cases: *Ikegami Tomoyuki and others* and *Takashima Shotaro and another*.[2] Two different approaches may be identified in these cases: the impossible-to-renounce approach and the criminal law approach. The first approach focuses on whether changes of allegiance could be effected in times of war, the second on the mindset of the accused. This chapter critically examines the rationales and arguments underlying these two approaches. It concludes by highlighting fruitful lines for future research.

Legal Framework and Socio-Political Context of Singapore Trials

On 18 June 1945, the British executive passed a royal warrant that authorised the British military to establish military courts to try violations of the laws and usages of war.[3] British or Allied judges were to preside over these courts.[4] The courts established in Singapore did not issue comprehensive judgments with their findings. Legal issues were raised during trial proceedings and in the opening and closing statements of the prosecution and the defence, though the quantity and quality of legal discussion in these trials were generally lower than in contemporary war crimes trials. The guilty findings and sentences of these courts were subject to confirmation by a confirming officer.[5] Upon a trial's conclusion, those convicted had the right to submit petitions for the confirming officer's consideration.[6] During this post-trial confirmation stage, the Department of the Judge Advocate General based in Singapore would also prepare a review report (DJAG review report). This report would have a summary of the facts of the case and its legal issues.

These British military courts established pursuant to the 1945 royal warrant functioned alongside the Nuremberg and Tokyo Trials.[7] The latter trials targeted a select group of high-ranking political and military leaders, while the 1945 royal warrant trials prosecuted a broad range of individuals for diverse acts amounting to violations of the laws and customs of war. These 1945 royal warrant British military courts were established in various locations throughout Asia, including Singapore. Based on records in the UK National Archives, altogether 131 royal warrant trials were conducted in Singapore (the Singapore Trials).[8] In Singapore, these British military courts prosecuted crimes that had been committed in what is present-day Singapore, Malaysia, Brunei, Indonesia, Thailand, Vietnam, Cambodia, Palau, Papua New Guinea and the Andaman and Nicobar Islands. Among offences tried were those related to the building of the Burma–Siam Railway, the ill-treatment of POWs and civilians in detention camps, the massacre of civilians and the summary execution of suspected spies.

Some cases dealt with the ill-treatment or killing of Indian soldiers who had been part of the British army. These cases were of political significance to the British. When Singapore fell to the Japanese military on 15 February 1942, the 30,000 Japanese soldiers led by General Yamashita Tomoyuki had inflicted a loss on the British of 7,500 killed, 10,000 wounded and 120,000 captured, though exact numbers continue to be contested.[9] Altogether, the Japanese military took 55,000 Indians prisoner during their invasion of Malaya and Singapore.[10] These Indian prisoners were separated from other British troops and brought to Singapore's Farrer Park. There, they were urged to renounce their British allegiance and fight alongside Japan to liberate India from British rule, and immediately 20,000 Indian soldiers chose to take up arms against the British, with another 20,000 doing so from June to August 1942.[11] Thus was born the Indian National Army (INA). Those who did not join the INA were sent by the Japanese military to work on various construction projects as forced labourers.

When other surrendered British military personnel first heard about this change of allegiance by Indian soldiers, many reacted in shock and disappointment at what they saw as a betrayal.[12] There were in fact many reasons for the Indian soldiers' switching of allegiance. Some truly did believe Japan's promise to liberate Asia from the shackles of Western colonial rule.[13] Others were disillusioned and angry with the racial discrimination practised by the British military within its ranks.[14] There were those who remained suspicious of Japan's benevolent claims but who believed that Indian involvement was necessary to avoid the replacement of British rule with Japanese rule in India.[15] Others joined for private reasons of self-preservation.[16] Support of the INA was not limited to Indian military personnel. Many Indian civilians contributed money to the INA's cause.[17] In 1943, Bose's formation of the Provisional Government of Free India in Singapore inspired many more Indians to join the INA, which by then totalled 80,000 men.[18] By 1945, 18,000 Indian civilians had joined the INA.

Throughout the war, the loyalty of British colonies remained a sensitive issue for British leaders. Even before the war ended, the British government started discussing post-war colonial policies in Asia. Views ranged from a restoration of pre-war status to outright liberation, but there was eventually a general agreement that Britain would continue to administer her colonies in the Far East with a view to granting eventual self-governance. British leaders rationalised that they were best-placed to continue the administration of these colonies in the interest of the local populations as well as the wider international community. A joint memo by the Foreign Office and the Colonial Office recognised that continued British administration would ensure that Singapore's port continued to be the "life and trade of the Malayan archipelago, as well as the ocean trade of the East" and that the Malay peoples' well-being continued to be protected against "the more efficient and numerous Chinese and to a lesser extent the Indians".[19] The British established the Malayan Planning Unit under the War Office, which was charged with planning Britain's post-war reoccupation and civil administration of British Malaya.[20] The British thus expected their colonial rule of British Malaya to continue for a significant time, even if this was to lead eventually towards self-government.

When the British returned to Malaya and Singapore at the end of the war, some of them wrongly assumed that the colonial population would demonstrate a strong lingering loyalty to the British. Instead, they encountered a definite change in political and social attitudes. There were increased calls for political inclusion and independence. British civilians returning to Malaya had to be warned not to expect the same level of acceptance towards British colonial rule from locals.[21] In addition, the returning British faced numerous post-war reconstruction challenges in British Malaya. There were severe food shortages and a lack of water, electricity and other basic necessities.[22] An estimated 70,000 POWs in the region needed to be rescued and evacuated.[23] In the interregnum between Japan's unconditional surrender on 15 August 1945 and the return of the British to Malaya and Singapore in September 1945, anti-Japanese resistance groups had taken it upon themselves to punish Japanese collaborators throughout British Malaya.[24] There was a general breakdown in law and order in Malaya and Singapore.[25] Hospitals were in short supply of medicine and equipment.[26] The British military also had to deal with the demobilisation and containment of wartime guerrilla forces.[27]

Though the British military administration had to deal with many post-war challenges, British military leaders also believed that it was important to conduct war crimes prosecutions.[28] The British military was eager to begin the organisation of these trials. In October 1945, Admiral Lord Louis Mountbatten, Supreme Allied Commander South-East Asia, sent a message to the chiefs of staffs emphasising the need to start holding such trials: "I wish, however, again to stress my anxiety at the delays which are occurring in bringing to trial in particular those minor criminals identified as having committed acts of individual cruelty against British Nationals or our Allies whether they were prisoners of War, Internees or Civilians not interned."[29] British military officials believed that these trials would achieve a number of objectives in the region. The trials were to vindicate the demands of victims and the general public for justice. For example, it was decided that it would not be "useful" for General Tomoyuki Yamashita, who was to be tried by the Americans in the Philippines, to be retried by the British in Singapore for crimes committed during the Japanese Malayan campaign. However, information about his crimes was to be "released to the world" as it was believed that this would "satisfy to a large extent the strong local feeling against Yamashita".[30]

Many of the Singapore Trials dealt with war crimes involving Indian victims. In a number of these cases, the defence alleged that the Indian victims had sworn allegiance to Japan, renouncing their allegiance to the British, and should therefore be treated in accordance with Japanese military disciplinary rules. Here, I focus on two cases where the issue of allegiance was examined by the same court and where there were relatively extensive discussions of the allegiance question. Both of these cases concerned Indian victims who had been members of the British army but who had been subsequently captured by the Japanese. The defence argued that the victims had taken oaths of allegiance to Japan and were members of the Japanese Romu Tai or Special Labour Unit. These cases were decided by the same panel of judges. The post-trial DJAG review reports took a different approach and advised non-confirmation of the trials' findings. These trial findings were not confirmed.

The Impossible-to-Renounce Approach: The Trials of *Ikegami Tomoyuki and Others* and *Takashima Shotaro and Another*

Ikegami Tomoyuki and Others

The trial of *Ikegami Tomoyuki and others* involved six defendants.[31] All defendants belonged to the Ikegami Unit headed by the first accused, Ikegami Tomoyuki. Two charges were brought against the accused based on two separate incidents dated 27 June 1945 and 18 June 1945. The facts of the case were as follows. The first accused, Ikegami, was the commander of a unit which included the Romu Tai or Special Labour Unit. The defence argued that the Indian victims belonged to this force. The Ikegami Unit was operating in Lutong in the state of Sarawak, Malaysia. Four of the accused – Takahashi Yoichi, Takahashi Tatsuo, Miyoshi Ren, Hisano Jun – were technical officers working in the Lutong oilfield. The last accused, Takahashi Takeshi, was a quartermaster working in the Lutong oilfield. The unit came under Allied attack and started withdrawing from the area. On 18 June 1945, during the withdrawal, Ikegami received a report that five Indians from the Romu Tai had been arrested while attempting to escape. It was claimed that the Indians had with them a secret map that showed the locations of Japanese units. Upon investigating, Ikegami concluded that they were Romu Tai members who were conspiring to desert to the enemy with secret information. Ikegami then ordered the victims' execution. The victims were executed later that day.

On 26 June 1945, eleven more Romu Tai members escaped but were recaptured the same day. The second accused, Takahashi, reported this incident to Ikegami explaining, among other things, that secret documents had been lost and found. Ikegami then conducted investigations and found that the victims had similarly planned to desert and had stolen confidential documents. He decided the victims were to be executed. The next day, 27 June 1945, the second to sixth accused reported to Ikegami, who explained his execution order and its grounds to them. The said Romu Tai members were executed by the accused that morning. The first charge, relating to the killing on 27 June 1945, was brought against all accused. The second charge, relating to 18 June 1945, was brought only against Ikegami.

Three judges were assigned to the case: Lieutenant Colonel H.E.R. Smith, Major E.N. Hebden and Captain E.H. Dunsford.[32] The prosecutor was Major S.J. Smith, who was a solicitor.[33] The accused were defended by Japanese defence counsel Tatsuzaki Ei, who was a judge advocate from the Imperial Japanese Navy.[34] A British defending officer, Lieutenant Ward J.H., was assigned to assist the defence on rules of military procedure as required pursuant to the 1945 royal warrant framework governing the trials.[35] Altogether, the trial lasted seven days. One witness testified for the prosecution. The defence called nine individuals to testify, including five of the six accused. The first accused, Ikegami, who held the rank of major, was sentenced to death by hanging. The second, third, fourth and fifth accused were each sentenced to ten years' imprisonment. Both the second and third accused held the rank of first lieutenant, while the fourth and fifth accused held the rank of second lieutenant. The sixth accused, who held the rank of corporal, was sentenced to five years' imprisonment. The court's sentences were not confirmed for reasons explained in what follows.

The trial started on 19 November 1945 and ended on 2 December 1945. In his opening address, defence counsel point out that the Indian victims were all members of the Tokushu Romutai, who had "voluntarily sworn an oath of allegiance to the Japanese".[36] This point was referred to by the accused and defence witnesses in the trial and was specifically taken up by the court during its independent questioning of certain accused and defence witnesses. On 25 November 1945, when the court questioned the fourth accused, Miyoshi Ren, on the nature of the unit, the latter explained that he had been "ordered and instructed by my superior officer" that the unit comprised "Indians who had sworn loyalty to the Japanese".[37] Miyoshi went on to explain that he always saw the Indians "being treated the same way as Japanese soldiers".[38] Their commander was selected from among them, and there were Japanese officers employed in the unit for "liaison purposes" and to "lead" and "instruct" the Indians to prevent misunderstanding since they "did not know Japanese customs and manners".[39] The court also addressed the issue of allegiance during its questioning the third accused, Takahashi Tatsuo. Takahashi explained that part of the job undertaken by the Special Labour Unit was the "guarding of the oil fields".[40] The court asked Takahashi whether the Indian POWs had their own commanding officer and "a reasonable amount of freedom" within the area in which their camp was located. Takahashi answered in the affirmative to both questions.[41]

Facts about how the Special Labour Unit was organised, the relatively important job assigned to them and their unregulated movement alerted the court to potential jurisdictional concerns. The court then highlighted its jurisdictional concerns to the prosecutor, noting that there was "a certain amount of corroborated evidence" that the victims were not POWs but "persons of Indian birth formerly subjects of His Majesty the King" who "by oath of greater weight than a parole" to the Japanese authorities had renounced rights as British subjects.[42] The court asked the prosecutor to consider this issue and submit its advice to the court, adjourning till the next day.[43]

On 26 November 1945, when the court reassembled, it heard the prosecutor's arguments on the allegiance issue. In the course of his arguments, the prosecutor referred to a mixture of British law and international law. He argued that any divesting of nationality should be governed by the 1914 British Nationality and Status of Aliens Act and existing British case law, according to which a British national "can only throw off his allegiance to the Crown in favour of an enemy state while he is actually residing in that foreign state".[44] Furthermore, based on British case law, the prosecutor argued that as an individual cannot avoid "military obligations" that were due before the renouncement of nationality, he also cannot "avoid" the "privileges and benefits" of those with such military obligations.[45] More interesting are the prosecutor's arguments in relation to then existing treaties. The prosecution argued that there are "two classes of rights in law": those granted "for the protection of the Public at large" and those "solely for individual protection". The latter could not be renounced.[46] In other words, the latter interests were public rather than private in nature. Therefore, based on this argument, they could not be renounced by the individual.

Upon hearing the prosecution's arguments, the court asked defence counsel for his submissions, which were relatively weak, even in comparison with the prosecutor's.[47] Japanese defence counsel openly admitted that he did not know British law "very well".[48] He did emphasise that the prosecutor had not given evidence to rebut the fact that the victims had sworn allegiance to Japan and that the latter had treated the former as members of the Japanese military. Defence counsel argued that even though the victims could still be considered British subjects from the perspective of the British, they were also to be considered Japanese subjects from the perspective of the Japanese. This, defence counsel admitted, was "a very curious state of things".[49] The court adjourned for fifteen minutes to consider the submissions of the prosecution and the defence. Upon reconvening, the court explained its opinion that it was not "empowered" to decide on its jurisdiction over the accused and would adjourn to consult the convening authority. [50]

When the court met again on 28 November 1946, it announced that it had considered counsels' submission and the advice of the convening authority's legal advisors on the allegiance issue. Based on "International Law and the Constitutional Laws of the Empire", the court held that subjects were unable to renounce their allegiance during a state of war. Any attempt to get a subject to do so by a captor would be a war crime.[51] Thus, the trial continued. Ikegami was sentenced to death by hanging. The other accused who had held the ranks of first and second lieutenants were sentenced to ten years' imprisonment, while Takahashi Takeshi, who had been a corporal, was sentenced to five years' imprisonment.

Takashima Shotaro and Another

The same panel of judges addressed this same issue of allegiance in the later case of *Takashima Shotaro and another.*[52] The trial involved two accused, Sergeant Takashima Shotaro and Corporal Asako Koichi, who were charged with the ill-treatment of Indian POWs in a camp run by the two accused in Sankakuyama, New Britain. Takashima was in charge of the party of Indian POWs, and Asako was a medical orderly in the camp. The accused were charged with being involved in the ill-treatment of these Indian POWs. This alleged ill-treatment included forcing sick men to work and neglecting to provide proper medical attention in a camp where Takashima was the commanding officer and Asako was a medical orderly. The prosecutor in that case was Major S.B. Sahay.[53] The defence lawyer was Nakamura Takeshi, a barrister at the Tokyo civil court.[54] The defending officer was Captain D.F.H. Sinclair.[55] The trial took six days. Two witnesses testified for the prosecution, and three individuals testified for the defence, including the second accused, Asako. At the close of the prosecution's case, defence counsel argued that the prosecution had not provided enough evidence or made out a case against Takashima.[56] The court agreed with defence counsel and acquitted Takashima. The trial, however, continued against Asako, who was eventually sentenced to life imprisonment. The court's finding and sentence against Asako was, however, not confirmed.

The trial started on 25 January 1947 and ended on 30 January 1947. On the trial's fourth day, 29 January 1947, defence counsel made a submission to the court that the Indian victims had taken an oath of allegiance and were no longer considered POWs at the time of the crime. The crime was therefore not within the court's jurisdiction.[57] In response, the prosecution referred to Regulation 6 of the 1945 Royal Warrant Regulations, which prohibited jurisdictional challenges. Regulation 6 stated that an "accused shall not be entitled to object to the President or any member of the Court or the Judge Advocate or to offer any special plea to the jurisdiction of the Court". This meant that the accused could not argue that the court had no authority to try the case. The prosecutor stated that Regulation 6 provided a "complete answer" to the claims made by the defence.[58] He further argued that the British Manual on Military Law prohibited occupying forces from forcing inhabitants of occupied territories from swearing allegiance to the former. If this was so for the civilian population, the prosecutor argued that POWs "certainly cannot" change allegiance.[59] The prosecutor also argued that this question should only be referred to the convening authority if the court decided that the change in allegiance had taken place "voluntarily".[60] In response, defence counsel stated that he was "sure" he would be able to "produce ample evidence" if given time to do so.[61]

The court president then explained that the present court had been involved in an earlier trial where "an identical submission" had been made by the defence.[62] He was in all probability referring to *Ikegami Tomoyuki and others.* It explained that in the earlier case, the convening authority had advised that the court had jurisdiction over the case and that victims "were not able legally to forswear their oath of allegiance to the British crown".[63] The court president further noted that a "number of leading cases" had been discussed in that earlier case.[64] The court also later declined the prosecutor's suggestion to recall the prosecution's witness Naurang Khan, who had been a member of the British Indian Army and who had been detained in the same camp, to question him about the taking of this oath of allegiance.[65] In his closing address, the defence counsel repeated the argument that the victims were not "pure Ps.O.W", that they were "released from the status of Ps.O.W. by the Japanese Army" and that they were members of the Indian Labour Unit.[66] Asako was eventually found guilty by the court and sentenced to life imprisonment. This was not confirmed by the confirming officer based on the DJAG review report, which forms the basis of analysis in the next section.

Criminal Law Approach: DJAG Review Reports of *Ikegami Tomoyuki and Others* and *Takashima Shotaro and Another*

As explained earlier in this chapter, based on the 1945 royal warrant framework, the guilty findings and sentences of these British military courts were not final until confirmed by the confirming authority.[67] For the Singapore Trials, before confirmation, the Department of the Judge Advocate General based in Singapore reviewed the cases and prepared DJAG review reports that were considered by the confirming officer prior to deciding whether the trial's finding was to be confirmed. Neither *Ikegami Tomoyuki and others* nor *Takashima Shotaro and another* was confirmed. The review reports issued in these cases are particularly interesting for their legal consideration of the issue.[68] As explained in what follows, these reports took a criminal law approach to the question, which focused on the accused persons' state of mind.

In the DJAG review report for *Ikegami Tomoyuki and others* dated 13 February 1947, the Indian victims were described as being "originally Prisoners of War, but who had sworn allegiance to the Japanese".[69] The report recognised that defence counsel had argued that even if the victims were POWs, Ikegami, the highest-ranking defendant, had "acted in the bona fide belief" that the victims had "the status of Japanese soldiers" and were "subject to Japanese military law".[70] As for the other lower-ranking defendants, the DJAG review report noted how the defence had claimed they had been implementing an "apparently lawful" order and were therefore not culpable.[71] The DJAG report acknowledged that, though based on the "domestic law of England", it was not possible for a British subject to renounce his or her nationality while on enemy or enemy-occupied territory during a war.[72] Under this domestic law, an individual who did so would have committed an offence under the English law of treason.[73] However, under then-existing international law, when an individual who had "voluntarily" joined enemy forces, disciplinary action against the individual pursuant to the enemy's military law would not be considered a war crime.[74] The review report went on to note that "there was no evidence" that the Indians had been "suborned" or coerced.[75]

More interestingly, in line with the arguments raised by the defence, the DJAG review report explained that even when the victims had been coerced or "suborned" to join enemy forces, the disciplining officer should not be held culpable for that act of coercion. Specifically, the report noted that the accused may have been acting on "a bona fide mistake of fact" and may have truly believed that the victims were "persons properly subject to Japanese military law".[76] This observation is important given the prosecutor's closing address in *Ikegami Tomoyuki and others* in which the prosecutor argued that if Ikegami did not know of the correct status of these victims, he should have ascertained for himself the status of the victims, and that it is "a cardinal principle of our law" that "ignorance of law" is not a defence, though it may impact mitigation.[77] In contrast, the DJAG review report found that the mistake was one of fact and, if bona fide, would absolve the accused of criminal culpability.[78] Accordingly, the DJAG review report recommended that confirmation of the case be withheld.[79] The court's decision and sentences were eventually not confirmed.[80]

This approach was similarly taken by the DJAG review report on *Takashima Shotaro and another*. The DJAG review report dated 15 April 1947 observed that the defence had raised the point that the victims were originally POWs but had taken oaths of allegiance to Japan and had thus lost their POW status.[81] During the trial, the accused were questioned about the army order that had confirmed the non-POW status of these Indian victims. However, the prosecution's application to recall a witness to give evidence on this point had been "unfortunately rejected" by the trial court "as a matter of law".[82] The DJAG review report went on to explain that the accused could still "raise as a defence" that he "honestly believed that he was acting within his rights towards men whom it was his duty to treat as such".[83] In other words, the accused could raise the defence that he had honestly believed the fact that the victims had lost their POW status. The DJAG review report advised non-confirmation of the trial court's findings.

It should be noted that this issue was of sufficient concern for Department of the Judge Advocate General in South-East Asia Land

Forces to request advice from the JAG Office in London on the issue. In a message dated 10 January 1947, Brigadier Davis stated that he would be "grateful" for the "opinion" of JAG London on *Ikegami Tomoyuki and others* and another case tried at Jesselton, namely, *Kamikura and another.*[84] In a subsequent message dated 27 February 1947 to the JAG office in London, Davis explained the receipt of further information:

> Information has since been received to the effect that Indian prisoners of war who refused to join the Indian National Army were sent to various theatres as slave labourers and that the ROMU TAI, or Special Labour Corps, were formed of such men.[85]

This additional information showed that the oaths of allegiance concerned were most probably extracted from the victims under duress. However, it does not alter the position taken in the two DJAG review reports due to the criminal law approach taken. The accused, who had not been involved in getting the victims to take these oaths of allegiance, could have been under the mistaken belief that the victims had indeed switched their allegiance to Japan. This criminal law approach swung the spotlight from the oaths of allegiance to the culpability of defendants.

Conclusion

There are a number of possible reasons why the DJAG review reports in these two cases took a criminal law approach as opposed to an impossible-to-renounce approach. First, it should be noted that none of the judges at the trial court in this case had legal qualifications. However, the judges in *Ikegami Tomoyuki and others* had referred the question of the impact of oaths of allegiance to the convening authority, whose legal advisers advised that the changing of nationality was not effective. These British war crimes trials were widely reported by the media in Singapore. Perhaps owing to the public spotlight on these cases at the trial stage, British authority would have been further undermined if the nature of these oaths had been examined more closely at trial. It may have been easier to foreclose any such examination by holding that nationality could not be renounced. At the non-public confirmation stage, it would have been less contentious to acknowledge that international law recognised the possibility that the victims may have chosen to join enemy forces and that culpability in these cases should turn on the state of mind of the accused.

It is important to note that the state of international law was unclear and still evolving during the post-Second World War period. Other British war crimes trials involving oaths of allegiance emphasised different issues, and trial exchanges seldom covered all relevant legal points. To get a more comprehensive idea of how these oaths were treated by the British military in these royal warrant trials, it is necessary to consider a larger number of trials, including those conducted elsewhere in Asia. By highlighting the significance of oaths of allegiance in these trials and relevant legal issues, this chapter may serve as a springboard for further studies.

Notes

1. For the account of one infamous incident, the Selarang Barracks Incident, see *Syonan Years 1942–1945 Living Under the Rising Sun, Reflections and Memories of War, Volume* 2, 1st, ed. (Singapore: National Archives of Singapore, 2009), 378–85.
2. The original records of these trials and other British military records referred to in this chapter are housed at the National Archives of the UK (hereinafter "TNA"). The record group is "WO 235 – Judge Advocate General's Office: War Crimes Case Files, Second World War". The National University of Singapore also holds copies of trial transcripts. When relevant documents are available in the International Criminal Court's Legal Tools Database, reference links will be provided. The trials are cited in TNA as follows: "WO235/979 – Defendant Ikegami Tomuyuki, Place of Trial Singapore"; "WO235/974 – Defendant Takashima Shotaro, Place of Trial Singapore". Note that the name of the first accused in *Takashima Shotaro and another* is represented in the TNA citation as "Takashima Shoiaro", but the documents in the file represent his name as "Takashima Shotaro". The TNA staff have entered sequential pagination into the documents, many of which do not have original page numbers. This pagination appears on copies held by the National University of Singapore's Central Library. For reference accuracy and as done by other scholars working with these trial records, I use this pagination as reference by inserting a prefix "SP" before the number.
3. Royal Warrant 0160/2498, 18 June 1945, promulgated by the War Office, Army Order 81 of 1945, available at http://www.legal-tools.org/doc/386f77/ (last accessed 28 Nov. 2016). Hereinafter referred to as "1945 Royal Warrant and Regulations". In Asia, British war crimes trials were also governed by an army instruction issued by the British military operating in this area, namely Allied Land Forces, South-East Asia (ALFSEA). Note that ALFSEA was reorganised from 1 December 1946 into South-East Asia

Land Forces (SEALF). TNA, WO 203/6092, Allied Land Forces, South-East Asia, *War Crimes Instruction No. 1 (2nd Edition)*, 4 May 1946.

4. 1945 Royal Warrant and Regulations, regulation 5.
5. 1945 Royal Warrant and Regulations, regulation 11.
6. 1945 Royal Warrant and Regulations, regulation 10.
7. For the Tokyo Trial, see Yuma Totani, *The Tokyo War Crimes Trial: The Pursuit of Justice in the Wake of World War II* (Cambridge: Harvard, 2009).
8. The record group is "WO 235 – Judge Advocate General's Office: War Crimes Case Files, Second World War". The TNA maintains lists of these trials, which indicate where they were held, but caution must be exercised because, given the huge number of listed trials, there are a few minor errors on locations, and verification in the actual case files is necessary. There are 132 trials listed altogether, but it is indicated that the records of one of these trials was missing at transfer.
9. Peter Doyle, *World War II Numbers* (London: Quid Publishing, 2013), 58.
10. Alan Warren, "The Indian Army and the Fall of Singapore," in *A Great Betrayal? The Fall of Singapore Revisited,* Brian Farrell and Sandy Hunter, eds. (Singapore: Marshall Cavendish, 2010) 235.
11. *Ibid.*
12. *Ibid.*, 236.
13. *Ibid.*, 234.
14. *Ibid.*, 235.
15. *Ibid.*, 234.
16. *Ibid.*, 235.
17. Cheah Boon Kheng, *Red Star Over Malaya: Resistance and Social Conflict During and After the Japanese Occupation, 1941–1946* (Singapore: Singapore University Press, 2012), 49.
18. Warren, "The Indian Army", 236.
19. TNA, CO 825/35/4, Joint CO-FO memorandum, August 1942, paragraph 30.
20. Following British convention at the time, this chapter will use the term "British Malaya" to refer to Malaya and Singapore. Malaya and Singapore will be individually used when it refers to these two units individually. F. (Full Name) S.V. Donnison, *British Military Administration in the Far East 1943–46* (London: Her Majesty's Stationary Office, 1956), 139.
21. Tim Harper and Christopher Bayly, *Forgotten Wars: The End of Britain's Asian Empire* (London: Penguin, 2008) 274.
22. Of the situation in Singapore, Turnbull writes, "Food was short, shipping was disorganized and traditional rice-producing countries had no surplus to export. Prices of essential commodities soon soared to ten times the pre-war level, and regulations to control the price of rice, fish and vegetables broke down because they could not be enforced." C(Full Name)

M. Turnbull, *A History of Singapore 1819–1975* (Singapore: Oxford University Press, 1977), 224.

23. Romen Bose, *The End of the War: Singapore's Liberation and the Aftermath of the Second World War* (Singapore: Marshall Cavendish, 2005) 92.
24. Cheah, *Red Star Over Malaya*, 133.
25. Donnison, *British Military Administration*, 158, 161.
26. *Ibid.*, 159, 162.
27. *Ibid.*, 386.
28. It is important to bear in mind that responsibility for these trials was delegated to the British military, with decisions to be taken in a largely decentralised fashion away from London. For this reason, it is important to understand how the British military leaders viewed these trials.
29. TNA, WO 203/4926A, SACSEA to Cabinet Offices, 2 October 1945, paragraph 2.
30. TNA, WO 203/4571A, Chief Civil Affairs Officer to SACSEA Headquarters, 15 February 1946, paragraph 4.
31. TNA, WO235/979, *Ikegami Tomoyuki and others.* The names and ranks of the defendants are as follows: Major Ikegami Tomoyuki, Lieutenant Takahashi Yoichi, Lieutenant Takahashi Tatsuo, Second Lieutenant Miyoshi Ren, Second Lieutenant Hisano Jun, Corporal Takashi Takeshi.
32. TNA, WO235/979, Ikegami Tomoyuki and others, "Proceedings of a Military Court", SP 00019.
33. *Ibid.*
34. *Ibid.*
35. *Ibid.*
36. TNA, WO235/979, Ikegami Tomoyuki and others, "Opening Address by the Defence Counsel", 1, SP 00099.
37. Ikegami Tomoyuki and others, "Proceedings of a Military Court", Testimony of Miyoshi Ren, SP 00042.
38. *Ibid.*
39. *Ibid.*
40. Ikegami Tomoyuki and others, "Proceedings of a Military Court", Testimony of Takahashi Tatsuo, SP 00046.
41. *Ibid.*
42. Ikegami Tomoyuki and others, "Proceedings of a Military Court", Testimony of Takahashi Tatsuo, SP 00047.
43. *Ibid.*
44. Ikegami Tomoyuki and others, "Proceedings of a Military Court", Prosecution submission on oaths of allegiance, SP 00049.
45. *Ibid.*
46. *Ibid.*, SP 00050.

47. This was to be expected as defence counsel was Japanese and not to be expected to be familiar with British law, another problem in the Singapore Trials, which this author deals with in a more comprehensive manner elsewhere.
48. Trial of Ikegami Tomoyuki and others, "Proceedings of a Military Court", Defence reply to prosecution submission on oaths of allegiance, SP 00051.
49. *Ibid.*
50. *Ibid.*
51. Trial of Ikegami Tomoyuki and others, "Proceedings of a Military Court", SP 00052.
52. TNA, WO 235/974, Takashima Shotaro and another, "Proceedings of a Military Court", TNA, SP 00014.
53. *Ibid.*
54. *Ibid.*
55. *Ibid.*
56. *Ibid.*, SP 00036–00037.
57. *Ibid.*, SP 00054.
58. *Ibid.*, SP 00055.
59. *Ibid.*, SP 00054.
60. *Ibid.*, SP 00055.
61. *Ibid.*
62. *Ibid.*
63. *Ibid.*
64. *Ibid.*
65. *Ibid.*, SP 00067.
66. *Ibid.*, SP 00091.
67. 1945 Royal Warrant and Regulations, regulation 11.
68. TNA, WO 235/979, Department of Judge Advocate General, South East Asia Land Forces, 13 February 1947, "War Crimes Trial", prepared by Brigadier F.G.T. Davis. Hereinafter, TNA, WO235/979, DJAG review report on Ikegami Tomoyuki and others; Department of Judge Advocate General, South-East Asia Land Forces, 15 April 1947, "War Crimes Trial", prepared by Brigadier F.G.T. Davis. Hereinafter, DJAG review report on Takashima Shotaro and another.
69. TNA, WO235/979, Ikegami Tomoyuki and others, DJAG review report on Ikegami Tomoyuki and others, SP 00010.
70. *Ibid.*, SP 00012.
71. *Ibid.*, SP 00013.
72. *Ibid.*
73. *Ibid.*
74. *Ibid.*
75. *Ibid.*

76. *Ibid.* It is noteworthy that the report also found that the question of the victims' status "is one of fact, though dependent on considerations of law", thus categorising this as a mistake of fact.
77. TNA, WO235/979, Ikegami Tomoyuki and others, "Closing Address for the Prosecution", SP 00109.
78. TNA, WO235/979, Ikegami Tomoyuki and others, DJAG review report on Ikegami Tomoyuki and others, SP 00013.
79. *Ibid.*
80. TNA, WO235/979, Ikegami Tomoyuki and others, "Military Court for the Trial of War Criminals", summary of case, SP 00003.
81. TNA, WO235/974, Takashima Shotaro and another, DJAG review report on Takashima Shotaro and another, SP 0005.
82. *Ibid.*
83. *Ibid.*, SP 0006.
84. TNA, WO235/979, Ikegami Tomoyuki and others, F.G.T. Davis to JAG of the Forces, London, 10 January 1947, SP 0005. As this chapter focuses on trials conducted in Singapore and due to limitations of space, I will not consider the latter case.
85. TNA, WO235/979, Ikegami Tomoyuki and others, F.G.T. Davis to JAG of the Forces, London, 27 February 1947, SP 00004.

CHEAH Wui Ling has been Assistant Professor at the Faculty of Law of the National University of Singapore since 2007. She was educated at the National University of Singapore (LL.B., LL.M.), Harvard Law School (LL.M.), European University Institute and Oxford University (D.Phil). She is a qualified lawyer (called to the New York Bar) and holds a diploma in arbitration (Queen Mary University of London). Prior to entering academia, she served as a Legal Officer at INTERPOL's Office of Legal Affairs (Lyon, France). Her teaching experience includes periods at the Centre for Transnational Legal Studies (London, UK), Oxford University (UK), Université Jean Moulin Lyon 3 (France) and the Royal University of Law and Economics (Cambodia). Her work has been published in journals such as the *Harvard Human Rights Journal, Journal of International Criminal Justice* and *International Journal of Law in Context.* Currently, she is working on a book project on the Singapore war crimes trials. She is also co-founder of the Singapore War Crimes Trials Web Portal (http://www.singaporewarcrimestrials.com/).

Puppets, Profiteers and Traitors: Defining Wartime Collaboration in the Dutch East Indies, 1945–1949

Esther Zwinkels

For many years, the trials of Japanese criminals before the International Military Tribunal for the Far East (IMTFE) in Tokyo following the Second World War have aroused substantial controversy for being considered reflections of victor's justice.[1] Recent publications have nuanced this image of the prosecution of the twenty-eight so-called Class A war criminals. As state-of-the-art research shows, the Tokyo Trial was not primarily a showcase in which the victorious nations prevailed over the fate of the defeated. Although the trial had its flaws, the intention of eleven participatory countries, amongst them the Netherlands, was to have major war criminals convicted for crimes they had committed.[2]

Similar questions of victor's justice have been raised in relation to the Class B and Class C war crimes trials.[3] According to Philip R. Piccigallo, these local war crimes trials were "made to fit into the overall national and foreign policy objectives of each Allied country".[4] His admirable pioneering study was the first to provide an overview of the machinery created after the war. Yet recent research on the proceedings of the judiciary of the Allies in Asia allows us to build on his work and revise some of his

E. Zwinkels (✉)
Netherlands Institute of Military History (NIMH), The Hague, The Netherlands
e-mail: epm.zwinkels@mindef.nl

K. von Lingen (ed.), *Debating Collaboration and Complicity in War Crimes Trials in Asia, 1945–1956*, World Histories of Crime, Culture and Violence, DOI 10.1007/978-3-319-53141-0_5

findings.[5] Studies on the Australian trials show that political interests did play a role in decisions on procedures of war crimes trials but that the intention of investigators and the members of the judiciary was to conduct fair trials.[6] However, one must be aware of the differences among the political interests of the Allied powers in Asia. Australia, for instance, had a geo-political interest in a stable political situation in Asia, and particularly in its neighbouring countries. Although Australia was an important Allied power, the country was no colonial power; it had not been occupied by the Japanese army, and it therefore only had to take care of the relief and recovery of its own people who had suffered during the armed confrontation or in Japanese captivity. There seems to have been little incentive to use the trials for other purposes than to bring perpetrators to justice.[7]

The political situation was different in the colonial territories of the Allies in South-East Asia. The French, British, Dutch and, to a lesser extent, American colonial empires in this area were put under severe pressure and faced a new political reality with the outbreak of revolution, proclamation of independence and forms of social unrest caused by communist influences.[8] Western powers tried to curb these undesirable political developments and to reassert power over their (former) subjects.

One of the tools of the colonial powers to achieve this was the use of legal measures to settle wartime accounts of injustice and at the same time to purge society from politically undesired elements.[9] Many of the Asian revolutionaries had submitted themselves to the Japanese authorities in order to achieve their ultimate goal: free themselves from the colonial yoke. Those who had supported the enemy, the Japanese, could therefore be considered opponents of the colonial regime. The prosecution of the Class B and C war crimes and collaboration was left to the national courts and fell under local jurisdiction, albeit in the light of the newly formulated international laws.

The study of collaboration trials in Asia can reveal the dynamics of the power struggle, and especially the strategies applied to face changes in society which were strengthened during the period of Japanese rule over Asia. Not all colonial powers actively prosecuted collaborators with the enemy regime, but discussions about the policies and practices are just as insightful as the trials themselves.[10] If the war crimes trials in Asia were established to serve Allied or national interests, as Piccigallo argues, then this should also, if not even more so, be evident in the collaborator trials or the treatment of collaboration at large. Yet, the existing literature on decolonization hardly pays attention to the mutual influence of the trials and decolonization processes in Asia.[11] Fortunately, following the increasing amount of publications on collaboration in Europe, there has been growing scholarly attention on wartime collaboration in Asia, as this volume also shows.[12]

So far, a systematic study on collaboration in the Dutch East Indies has been lacking.[13] Extensive research shows that at least 312 cases of collaboration related to the Japanese occupation appeared before Temporary Courts-Martial in the Dutch East Indies between 1945 and 1949.[14] After May 1947 the number of collaboration trials declined, but sentences continued to be handed down, including death sentences, until days before the sovereignty transfer on 27 December 1949.[15] A number of case studies on collaboration in Indonesia have appeared, but, like publications on collaboration in Asia, they mainly cover a specific region, population group or type of crime and do not discuss the ideas behind the policies and prosecutions in detail.[16]

Therefore, this chapter is will be a first exploration into the ideas behind prosecution policies to determine to what extent these collaboration policies and trials were affected by the war of decolonization. To do so, the chapter is structured as follows. First, the initial pre-war ideas of the colonial government regarding the treatment of collaboration are described. Second, the legal definitions in the penal code and the legal provisions are introduced, followed by an overview of the different types of collaboration that were distinguished. Finally, attention is paid to factors which contributed to a change in policy with respect to collaboration and the extent to which this change can be attributed to the war of decolonization.

Collaboration in a Colonial Setting

Collaboration is in itself a difficult and far from neutral term.[17] As Timothy Brook states, collaboration "superimposes a moral map over the political landscape it ventures to describe".[18] In the colonial context, the term even brings in an extra dimension. In the Netherlands there was a clear division, because there were two parties: put simply, Dutchmen either cooperated with the German occupier, albeit in different degrees, or they did not.[19] By contrast, in the colony there were three parties involved. Not only did the Indonesian people experience the occupation by Japan between 1942 and 1945, but also the Dutch colonial presence in the past 350 years was in itself an occupation, being considered either lawful or unlawful.[20]

As a result, the occupying regimes in the Indies bring about different perceptions of collaborators. First, the occupation by the Dutch had, in the eyes of anti-Dutch Indonesians, produced collaborators consisting of local Indonesian elites and Chinese who had cooperated with the colonial administration during the period of trade activities and colonial rule to secure and enhance their own position.[21] For centuries, cooperation of traditional elites with the colonial administration had been essential for asserting control over colonial territory, and this way had been part of the colonial system to secure its existence.[22]

Second, during the Japanese occupation, some people cooperated with the Japanese authorities for various reasons. The Japanese authorities relied heavily on the traditional elite, the *pangreh praja* ('ruler of the realm'), to retain order and to mobilize the local people to meet targets for the war effort. According to the colonial government all persons who had cooperated with the Japanese authorities were collaborators for they had sided with the enemy and therefore betrayed the colonial government. They were held accountable for their actions – at least initially – as will be described in what follows.

In the eyes of the common Indonesian people, different ideas existed on collaboration with the Japanese. Although some local administrators and village heads had profited from exploiting villagers for the Japanese war effort for their personal gain, for the majority of the local rulers their shift of allegiance was predominantly for reasons of self-preservation and safeguarding their dynasty.[23] Discord had arisen on what stand to take regarding the traditional elites. In certain areas, the call for retributive actions was loud; in other areas, what happened during the war was left behind. Unlike the elites, the nationalist leaders who had overtly cooperated with the Japanese to achieve independence were generally considered true patriots by the Indonesian people.[24]

After but also during the Japanese occupation, retributive actions were taken by different groups of people to settle accounts for the wrongs that people had suffered in the past. They turned against the local elites, who were closely associated with the colonial system and against Indonesians and Chinese who had too eagerly submitted themselves to the Japanese orders. The actions were taken not only in revenge for the hardships they had endured during the war but also to prevent the traditional elite from restoring the old order. These social revolutions took place in several areas of the archipelago but took a most dramatic turn in North Sumatra and Central Java, where the majority of the traditional elite were murdered.[25]

At the same time, Europeans, Eurasians and Chinese, particularly on Java, fell victim to bands of revolutionary youth, the *pemudas*.[26] These young people had been members of the Japanese youth associations and believed more than the older generation of nationalists in the use of force as a means to achieve their goals, which were to realize an independent Indonesian republic and secure a prominent role for themselves within its administration.

The internal struggles between different population groups, nationalists and pemudas on one side and the Dutch East Indies government, reluctantly backed up by British military power, on the other formed the prelude to the war of decolonization during which the Dutch East Indies authorities tried to re-occupy the colony and restore its authority.[27] The colonial government had to formulate its policies to deal with the different stances towards "the enemy" and to regain its authority over the people. According to Thomas, Moore and Butler, the process of decolonization could be interpreted as "the attempt to renegotiate collaborative arrangements when the original framework had proved unable to meet the challenge of modernization, war and rapid social change in the colonies".[28] The prosecution of wartime collaborators could possibly contribute to such renegotiations.

Ideas and Expectations

The prosecution of wartime collaboration was in the hands of national criminal courts. The United Nations War Crimes Commission (UNWCC), the Allied committee established to formulate post-war policies in Europe and Asia, had recommended that it be the responsibility of the national governments to try their own nationals. The committee did not want to meddle in individual cases, in which the circumstances and the common national jurisdiction would be too different. Yet, since it was desired that "justice would be meted out to all war crimes", even if they technically could not be committed by one's own nationals, it was recommended that distinctions be made between so-called political quislings and people who had rendered assistance to the enemy.[29]

The local governments thus had to determine who was to be considered a collaborator and who was not. According to Brook, collaboration is determined by the moral prescriptions of a nation on how to act properly.[30] This implies that it is not only a variable definition which can differ between nations and states but that it is also prone to revision owing to changing sentiments among the people. The Dutch government had formulated such a moral prescription in a pre-war government document of instruction for civil servants on how to act in case of foreign occupation. This thirteen-page document was written in 1937 by the State Mobilisation Council (*Staatsmobilisatieraad*). The Dutch East Indies government had adjusted the instructions to the situation in the Indies before it was circulated in 1942. Although there was uncertainty among government officials regarding the scale of distribution of the instructions to its civil servants and private parties, at least around ten thousand copies had been printed.[31]

The instructions were well intended but were open to multiple interpretations and proved to be too removed from the reality faced by people during the Japanese occupation. The instructions assumed that the Indies government would remain in a lawful position and would be able to communicate with its people. Aside from members of the armed forces, it was forbidden to use violence or resistance against the enemy, since this would expose the people, as well as friends, family and fellow civilians, to severe acts of reprisal. Also, an instruction such as to "lodge a firm protest with the responsible institutions, or subordinate bodies or persons, in case events are taking place which are in breach of humanitarian laws" sounds naïve in hindsight given the character of the Japanese occupation.[32] Therefore, not only can one wonder how many people were aware of the existence of the instructions, but it also seems unlikely that the behaviour of those who cooperated with the Japanese stemmed from knowledge of the instructions. Yet several defendants in collaborator trials justified their behaviour of continuing their job under Japanese authorities by appealing to the government instructions, which required that they remain in their position as long as possible.[33]

Nevertheless, this document represented a point of departure for policies dealing with collaborators. During the Japanese occupation, the Dutch East Indies government-in-exile in Australia prepared for a return to power in its colony. The first measures for the restoration of Dutch civil administration in liberated Dutch East Indies territories were laid down in the Civil Affairs Agreement between the Dutch and the South-West Pacific Area, under the command of the American army. The principles included instructions for the administration of justice and investigating and prosecuting collaboration.[34] Lieutenant-Governor General H.J. van Mook declared in a radio speech on 15 August 1945, immediately after the Japanese capitulation, that "only for traitors, who have put their own interests before their fellow humans, this [the Japanese surrender] means the collapse of their own short and false glory".[35] Sukarno, one of the nationalist leaders who had supported the Japanese to recruit and mobilize Indonesians for the war effort, was denounced as a "quisling" and "puppet of the Japanese" who should be put on trial.[36]

Being far away from the Indies, in London or Brisbane, and with only limited sources of information at their disposal during the occupation, the administrators had become alienated from the developments on Java. They considered the proclamation of independence on 17 August an act of treason and did not believe that the ideas promoted by the independence movement would find wide support among the Indonesian people. The government refused to see that the political situation in the Indies had changed drastically and that the political stance of the people and their perception of collaboration were completely different than the Dutch government expected.[37]

On 25 August 1945, Van Mook gave an outline to the minister of Overseas Territories of the policies regarding the various types of conduct shown during the war against Japan by Dutch subjects, including Dutch, Chinese and Indonesians. According to Van Mook, a distinction should be made between the following groups of people:

"1. those who defended the interests of the people against the Japanese putting their lives at risk. They will be rewarded;
2. those who in the first place bore the interests of the people in mind during their cooperation with the Japanese. They need not fear punishment, even if they advocated a different policy than we did;
3. those who chose the enemy's side voluntarily and who actively took part in the war, which was positively rewarded by the enemy. They will be punished as well, although a distinction will be made between leaders and accomplices, and the possibility of intimidation should be taken into consideration;
4. those who committed crimes in exchange for goods, who must face punishment for that reason."[38]

In Van Mook's categories, it was in the first place not necessarily the actual act that distinguished one person's behaviour from another's but the intention behind the act. Those who had neglected the so-called interest of the people and solely and wilfully put their own interest first should be punished. Van Mook wished to communicate the tenor of the measures, which would have been supported by Lord Louis Mountbatten, to the people by newspaper or radio.[39]

Public arousal and insecurity compelled the government review its stance. In several areas, but predominantly Java and Sumatra, violent uprisings took place, in which especially the Eurasian and Chinese populations were victimized. After returning to Java in October 1945, Van Mook and his closest confidants were aware that they had to reconsider their point of view. Although they were not convinced that the majority of Indonesians would want to get rid of the Dutch colonial power, the administrators were aware that the number of people who might have supported the Japanese for ideological reasons was too large to be able to take legal action against them.[40] The plan to prosecute Sukarno was abandoned as well, even though Sukarno's role in the recruitment and mobilization of Indonesian work forces was condemned by several prominent Indonesians such as Sutan Syahrir.[41] However, Sukarno's prosecution would lead to the immediate termination of all negotiations with the Republicans. Also, it was feared, especially in The Hague and Washington, that taking action against Sukarno might harm public opinion in the United States and, hence, the Dutch diplomatic position.[42]

Jurisdiction

Ideas about punishment for collaboration were formalized in September 1945 by the addition of a number of articles to the existing criminal legislation of the Penal Code (*Wetboek van Strafrecht*).[43] The most prominent articles regarding collaboration were Articles 124 to 126 on rendering "assistance to the enemy" (*hulpverlening aan de vijand*). A broader definition of "supporting the enemy" of Article 124 was laid down in the new provision. It read as follows:

> "Anyone who wilfully in time of war provides support to the enemy or who disadvantages the state in relation to the enemy shall be sentenced to death or life imprisonment, or up to a maximum period of twenty years.
>
> By 'supporting the enemy' is understood:
>
> Reporting to the enemy or bringing to the power of the enemy, damaging or destroying defence lines, goods, weapons, money, fleet or army;
>
> Encouraging disorder, mutiny or desertion among armed forces;

> Providing the enemy with a map, plan, drawing or description of military installations or any intelligence about military movements or plans;
>
> Serving the enemy as a spy or takin in, hiding or helping an enemy spy; Encouraging the dissemination of enemy propaganda;
>
> Exposing another person to tracking, prosecution, deprivation or limitation of freedom, any form of punishment or any measure by or through the enemy and its supporters;
>
> Providing the enemy with any goods or money, committing acts to the advantage of the enemy, or hindering or obstructing or frustrating any act against the enemy."[44]

Another important change was that the sentences for several crimes became more severe. Providing support or any form of intelligence to the enemy could now be punished with sentences ranging from death, to life imprisonment or imprisonment for up to twenty years.[45] Conspiring to commit a certain crime which was already a crime according to Article 125 would now bring a sentence equal to that of persons who actually committed the crime.[46] Also, the criminal procedure in court was adjusted to the state of siege, and therefore the Revised Judicial Procedures of the Army (*Herziene Rechtspleging bij de Landmacht*) came into force.[47] This change in the criminal procedure had consequences, for instance, for the procedure of appeal and the carrying out of death sentences.

In a few essential points the Dutch collaboration trials differed from those held by other Allied countries. First, collaborators tried in the Dutch East Indies courts could not be enemy subjects, only Dutch subjects. War crimes, though, could only be committed by foreign subjects, because war crimes are committed by one nation upon another.[48] Second, as mentioned earlier, collaboration cases in the Dutch East Indies were handled by the same courts as war crimes cases, the Temporary Courts-Martial (TCMs) (*Temporaire Krijgsraden*).[49] Nineteen TCMs in the archipelago dealt with collaboration cases.[50] For serious crimes, civilians were tried by a military court because the state of siege was in force, which means that military authority prevailed over civil affairs.[51]

The Dutch East Indies was the only Allied country in which both war crimes and collaboration cases were tried before the same type of court and, partly, often with the same members of the court. The members of the TCMs were preferably civil law attorneys given a military rank to serve in court. The Japanese occupation had taken a toll on members of the judiciary, so there was a shortage of qualified staff. Still, many members of the court were former Indies judicial officers – civil law attorneys given a military rank – complemented by (reserve) officers stationed nearby.[52]

Remarkably, in the description it is mentioned explicitly that the decree applied to crimes committed "during the war, the period of occupation and thereafter, generally 'in times of war'", which includes the revolutionary period.[53]

But, although the period after 15 August 1945 was included in the provisions, the government did not intend to try all crimes that had been committed. In November 1945, a government statement was published which stressed that political collaboration would not be punished, provided the people had not severely harmed their fellow-subjects.[54] These messages were intended to ease the conscience of those Indonesians, like Sukarno and his supporters, who feared public condemnation. The agenda of the colonial government, which was not yet fully in power, was to convince the Indonesian people of the need for colonial administration. The government had to gain the support of Indonesians if they wished to re-establish their authority. Those who had been loyal to the Dutch during the war, primarily Chinese Indonesians, should be rewarded, not only materially with food and essential goods but also with respect, and enhanced social status and positions in the new civil apparatus.

With these two measures important steps were taken: the largest group of so-called political collaborators was drastically reduced to include only those who had committed serious political crimes, and measures were taken to prevent loyal members of the population from estrangement from the colonial authorities. Further categorization of crimes was desired, but different opinions existed on this matter. The Director of Internal Administration (BB) C.O. van der Plas and his advisor Abdulkadir Widjojoatmodjo wanted to deal with the crimes of past years, including crimes committed by revolutionaries. Therefore, they proposed an amnesty for most criminals, including those who committed crimes during the revolution, to prevent them from committing more serious crimes to keep them out of the hands of the authorities because of the likely sentences they would face for crimes committed under the Japanese.[55]

In February 1946, Van der Plas sent the proposal on granting amnesty to notable members of the Indies administration and army. Director of the Department of Justice N.S. Blom had analysed the proposal and approved the plans in broad terms. The main question remained, though, of whether Indonesian society would be restored when amnesty was granted for *all* crimes committed, including those committed after 15 August 1945, when independence was proclaimed, or whether exceptions should be made. Practical considerations played a part in this decision, for it would be difficult to determine which acts were committed for political reasons and which for other reasons. At the same time the authorities were of the opinion that the new society would not be well served if no past crimes were prosecuted.[56]

Eventually the administrators concluded that a general amnesty would stretch too far. Common criminal acts and acts committed to undermine colonial authority after August 1945 should be prosecuted as usual, but crimes that were done out of nationalistic sentiments would go unpunished. It was decided that acts of collaboration would be treated more leniently. In March 1946, an official government statement was published in the newspaper; it read, in part:

> "In this country, as well as in other countries, no one will be prosecuted for the sole act of collaboration, even politically, with the Japanese, because we have to close the past and start working on reconstruction. [...]
>
> Wherever peace shall be restored the need for a distinction between political offence and common crimes will arise. The future of Indonesia demands that such pacification shall not be accompanied by political prosecution or revenge, as it demands the reaffirmation of justice to safeguard the lives, the property and the morality of all good citizens. [...] Nevertheless, it is clear that certain people have committed heinous crimes which, according to the sense of justice of the people of Indonesia, of all classes and races, deserve to be punished. [...]
>
> After the current conflict, the government will also draw up lines of conduct regarding the period of upheaval following the Japanese occupation and acts which were done out of 'nationalist passion' and political confusion.
>
> The government is absolutely convinced of the need to distinguish between patriotic and criminal intentions [...] and between political offences and criminal acts."[57]

On the one hand, with this text the government tried to reassure the people that they would not be prosecuted for minor offences by appealing to the "future of Indonesia" and involving the people in the process by stating that people "of all races and classes" and their sense of justice would be heard and that the intentions behind acts of collaboration would be examined. On the other hand, the government statement shows that a clear line would be drawn between the period before 15 August and thereafter. Violence and crimes during the revolutionary period would not go unpunished.

Puppets, Profiteers and Traitors

The legal framework had thus been laid out briefly after the war, but so far it was not yet clear what kind of wartime behaviour was considered punishable. Attorney General Felderhof, who played a significant role in the formulation of the policies, identified three types of collaboration: political "assistance", economic collaboration and supporting the enemy.[58] Political assistance consisted of collaborating with the enemy for purely political goals, for the purpose of obtaining political advantages for one's population group and for fulfilling wishes under the assumption that Japan would win the war. Felderhof made clear that this type of collaboration in principle would not be prosecuted, unless it turned out that the local people felt otherwise or that there was evidence that the alleged collaborator had acted only for personal gain. Spreading enemy propaganda was considered a political act as well – at least for Indonesians. Indonesians who had worked, for instance, for the Japanese broadcasting station were generally left alone, whereas Dutch journalists who contributed to Japanese radio broadcasts were considered serious collaborators, or even traitors.[59]

Under economic collaboration Felderhof understood providing services and producing materials in favour or in support of the enemy. People with specialist knowledge, often Europeans and Chinese, were ordered to continue their work in their pre-war position, but now in Japanese service, for many offices, companies and factories had been taken over by the Japanese authorities. The attorney general considered it important to punish those who had seriously enriched themselves at the expense of others, but he was also aware that many people had seized opportunities to maintain themselves and their families.

The third category, "supporting the enemy", consisted mainly of treason, reporting individuals to the enemy, enlisting in the Kempeitai or other police organizations of the enemy and conducting espionage activities. According to the attorney general, it was self-evident that these latter acts would be condemned by everyone and all population groups, and therefore it was not necessary to consult population groups after their opinion or so-called sense of justice.[60] Treason was indeed considered a serious crime. At least in military circles, treason is considered the highest of all crimes, for it is considered betrayal of the state. If one looks at it in a wider sense, it can be considered a "crime against the nation, or "national betrayal", for you literally betray your fellow-subjects.[61]

During the period between the Japanese surrender and the sovereignty transfer to the Republic of Indonesia, the Dutch East Indies government continually revised its policies regarding collaboration, or rather the application of its policies. In this chapter only a small number of changes can briefly be addressed, but a few examples will be given to illustrate the difficulties of categorizing crimes and the dilemmas the government faced.

An interesting case study of political, or rather military, collaboration include the *heiho*, the Indonesian auxiliary troops recruited by the Japanese. Among the heiho were also Indonesians who had served in the colonial army, the Royal Netherlands East Indies Army (*Koninklijk Nederlands-Indisch Leger*, KNIL). Initially, the Indonesians were considered voluntary collaborators with the Japanese who needed to be prosecuted, or at least kept in detention. Soon the judiciary became more aware of the Japanese methods of recruitment. By far not all Indonesian troops had joined the auxiliary troops voluntarily.[62] Therefore, the attorney general decided not to prosecute this large group of (former) soldiers. Instead, the Dutch East Indies administrators hoped that the former heiho from the Moluccas, who were often former KNIL soldiers, could be recruited for the colonial army again and be mobilized in the armed conflict with the Republicans.[63]

A form of collaboration which is a combination of both political and economic collaboration, and even treachery to some extent, was the shifting loyalty of local village heads. As mentioned earlier, the traditional elite had an opportunistic attitude toward the ruling power in order to preserve their own position. Local administrators who not only had served under the Japanese but had also enriched themselves at the expense of the local people were strongly condemned by the Dutch East Indies government. In certain regions this was also expressed by the local people to the Dutch authorities. However, if the local village head was capable of retaining order in his administrative realm and was willing to swear allegiance to the Dutch again, no action would be undertaken to prosecute him.[64] As part of the discretionary powers the office of the prosecutor could decide not to prosecute if that served 'the general interest'. The political interests of preserving order and maintaining loyal local leaders in prominent positions would prevail.

Although economic collaboration was initially considered a cowardly act because it entailed profiting during wartime at the expense of others, it was relatively speaking considered the least harmful act of collaboration. As time progressed, investigators tended to place little importance on this type of crime.[65] Also, it became increasingly clear that not everyone involved in economic collaboration had committed himself voluntarily to Japanese activities.[66] Many, predominantly Chinese, tradesmen and industrialists were allowed, under force, to continue to run their businesses provided they delivered goods to the Japanese authorities or paid fair sums of money. The Chinese tended to preserve their family businesses and submitted to the Japanese. Politics should not interfere with economic interests, some Chinese would say.[67] After the war, the networks and capital of the business elites were more than welcome to engage in economic activities to revive the economy. As a result, only a small number of economic collaboration cases were brought to trial.[68]

What emerges from these examples are deviations between policies and practices, as well as their interactions. Judges and prosecutors sometimes took liberties with the demands from the office of the attorney general. The observations and opinions of the local prosecutors were taken into account by the attorney general and led to further adjustments in prosecution policies.

Amnesty Decree

Developments in the conflicts with the Republicans also affected the investigations and trials. Aside from the violent period of the *Bersiap*, armed confrontations with revolutionary bands hindered the Dutch East Indies authorities in their efforts to conduct investigations or establish courts in regions claimed by the Republicans. Investigators put their lives at risk in conflict areas to gather evidence of crimes outside the Dutch–British occupied territories, but even in certain occupied areas they were not always safe.[69] Several incidents took place in which Dutch or Allied investigators were nearly or actually killed.[70] Military and political tensions further increased as a result of difficult negotiations with the Republicans about the details of the Linggadjati Agreement, which was signed on 15 November 1946 but was not yet ratified because of disagreements over the interpretation of the treaty.

Another factor that affected policies was public opinion. Members of the judiciary emphasized repeatedly that they would take into account "the sense of justice" of the people when considering prosecution in certain cases.[71] In the various regions of the archipelago, the local dynamics between the different population groups and their attitude towards the Dutch differed, as did, therefore, their call for juridical measures against alleged perpetrators. As time went by, the government claimed to notice a diminishing interest in war crimes and collaboration trials among the people, although some administrators argued that among Eurasians and Chinese calls for retribution remained strong.[72]

Above all, the practical difficulties associated with investigating and prosecuting large numbers of suspects became an even greater challenge. There was a shortage of qualified judiciary personnel and facilities to investigate and try cases. As time went by, it became more difficult to collect evidence and depose witnesses, especially because of repatriation and the large number of displaced persons. It was also considered a weakness that no appeal was possible.[73]

These circumstances shifted the attention of the government and strengthened the political support to reduce the number of trials. On 7 May 1947, the Indies government agreed to an Amnesty Decree. According to the decree, so-called minor cases, including economic and political collaboration, propaganda and expressions of sympathy for the enemy, would not be prosecuted, and sentences for such crimes would be remitted.[74] The most severe crimes would be prosecuted. Among these were acts which directly contributed to the war effort of the enemy, acts by which someone else's body, honour or personal freedom was assaulted and acts which resulted in ill-treatment of a person who was in the hands of the enemy. In practice, treason was thus considered the most severe form of collaboration. Especially in cases in which the defendant was said to have joined voluntarily, had enjoyed his work or had participated in serious abuse, the court seemed to hand down severe sentences.[75]

Yet the lieutenant-governor general was wary of the reactions "the magical force of the word amnesty" could cause among the people in the Netherlands as well as the Indies.[76] It was suggested that the decree be published concurrently with the announcement of the birth of the new prince or princess of the royal family. This was rejected on practical and principle grounds, but it was acknowledged that the most pressing reason for the amnesty was the lack of capacity of the judiciary and that this should not be made public.[77]

Although the prosecution policies became more lenient over time, this did not mean that the trials related to the Japanese occupation were halted or that collaboration was no longer an issue. As mentioned earlier, the trials continued until the last days of 1949. In the meantime, the Indies authorities continued to make slight adjustments to the measures before the sovereignty transfer. Moreover, discussions on criminal and condemnable behaviour continued, or started anew, in purge committees to decide whether it was desirable to reinstate in their pre-war positions those who had been suspected or convicted of criminal behaviour.

Conclusion

This chapter shows how the ideas and policies of the Dutch East Indies government regarding wartime collaboration developed between 1945 and 1949. Can these be attributed to the process of decolonization? On the one hand, several changes are noticeable that seem to have been direct or indirect consequences of political developments since the end of the war with Japan. The initial plans of the Dutch East Indies government focused on the restoration of authority in reoccupied territories. The hard line regarding collaborators had to be abandoned and was replaced by a more lenient policy with narrow definitions of collaboration owing to the new realities faced by the returning administrators.

The policies related to wartime collaboration with the Japanese authorities were also closely related to the measures taken against crimes committed after 15 August 1945. This is evident in the assignment to the Allied investigation teams and the local investigators and prosecutors, but also in the provisions which mentioned that the measures would apply to "the time of war and the period immediately following the war". The outbreak of the revolution increased the negative effects of the occupational period even more.

In a practical sense, the lack of facilities and qualified staff, the limited accessibility to Republican territories and the difficulties of deposing witnesses owing to repatriation and the numerous displaced persons had repercussions for the investigations. By adjusting the instructions to prosecutors about what type of cases to file, the attorney general could influence the number and types of crimes that would be pursued, thereby prioritizing certain types of crimes over others. These instructions were to some extent politically motivated. Local circumstances and political interests could prevail over the prosecution of serious crimes if it seemed to contribute to bringing a specific area under control again and winning the support of Indonesians for returning Dutch authorities. But the limited capabilities of the judiciary also served as an incentive for policy adjustment, and eventually resulted in the Amnesty Decree.

On the other hand, one must be careful when attributing all changes to the process of decolonization. Certain factors also could have been a consequence of the post-war situation and not necessarily the process of decolonization. The practical difficulties were largely a result of the war; for instance, economic collaboration became increasingly less important in other countries of Europe and Asia. Moreover, political interests always weighed heavily on the minds of the colonial administrators. But the process probably strengthened or hastened certain decisions.

Also, it must be stressed that this chapter focused on the ideas and policies behind the prosecution of collaboration and did not take into account the sentences or reasoning behind the sentences handed down in the collaboration trials. Nor were the measures and trials related to the post-war crimes included in this study. Although the prescriptions and policies of the government must have affected the trials, these conclusions do not imply that members of the judiciary were not impartial or that the trials and outcomes were unfair.

The politicians and the judiciary did not completely dismiss all cases against collaborators. Perpetrators of serious crimes were still held accountable, and cases continued until the very last days of 1949. Punishment for collaboration and the purging of society, along with winning over the loyalty of the Indonesians, played an important role in renegotiating the collaborative agreements between the colonial authorities and the local people, as Thomas argued, and therewith shaping the new political relations between the Indonesians and the Dutch.

Notes

1. Strong criticism, as expressed, for instance, by Minear, was for long the dominant perception in Japan, as shown by Futamura: Richard H. Minear, *Victors' Justice: The Tokyo War Crimes Trial* (Princeton, NJ: Princeton University Press, 1971); Madoka Futamura, *War Crimes Tribunals and Transitional Justice: The Tokyo Trial and the Nuremburg Legacy* (London; New York: Routledge, 2008).
2. Yuma Totani, *The Tokyo War Crimes Trial: The Pursuit of Justice in the Wake of World War II* (Cambridge, MA: Harvard University Asia Center, 2008); Neil Boister, *The Tokyo International Military Tribunal: A Reappraisal* (Oxford: Oxford University Press, 2008). The countries represented in the IMTFE were the United Kingdom, the United States, France, the Netherlands, Australia, New Zealand, Canada, the Soviet Union, China, the Philippines and India.
3. See, for instance, Yuma Totani, *Justice in Asia and the Pacific Region, 1945–1952: Allied War Crimes Prosecutions* (New York: Cambridge University Press, 2015).

4. Philip R. Piccigallo, *The Japanese on Trial: Allied War Crimes Operations in the East, 1945–1951* (Austin: University of Texas Press, 1979), viii.
5. See on the British procedures R. John Pritchard, "The Parameters of Justice: The Evolution of British Civil and Military Perspectives on War Crimes Trials and Their Legal Context (1942–1956)," *International Humanitarian Law* 3 (2006): 277–326; Suzannah Linton, ed., *Hong Kong's War Crimes Trials* (Oxford: Oxford University Press, 2013) and in particular, Alexander Zahar, "Trial Procedure at the British Military Courts, Hong Kong, 1946–1948," 13–69.
6. An impressive in-depth study on the Australian trials and procedures is Georgina Fitzpatrick, Tim McCormack, and Narrelle Morris, eds., *Australia's War Crimes Trials 1945–51* (Leiden: Brill Nijhoff, 2016); Caroline Pappas, "Law and Politics: Australia's War Crimes Trials in the Pacific, 1943–1961" (unpublished PhD diss., University of New South Wales, Sydney, Australia, 1998).
7. Georgina Fitzpatrick, "War Crimes Trials, 'Victor's Justice' and the Australian Military Justice in the Aftermath of the Second World War," *The Hidden Histories of War Crimes Trials*, (Oxford: Oxford University Press, 2013), 327–47.
8. Martin Shipway, *Decolonization and Its Impact: A Comparative Approach to the End of the Colonial Empires* (Malden, MA: Blackwell, 2008).
9. An important volume on postwar policies on collaboration in Europe is István Deák, 'Introduction', in István Deák, Jan T. Gross, and Tony Judt, eds., *The Politics of Retribution in Europe: World War II and Its Aftermath* (Princeton, NJ: Princeton University Press, 2000).
10. According to Kratoska, Southeast Asian countries, except for the Philippines, were not inclined to try collaboration: Paul H. Kratoska and Ken'ichi Gotō, "Japanese Occupation of Southeast Asia, 1941–1945," in *The Cambridge History of the Second World War*, ed. Richard Bosworth (Cambridge: Cambridge University Press, 2015), 508–32. In the Philippines, 156 convictions in about 5,600 court cases: Konrad M. Lawson, "Wartime Atrocities and the Politics of Treason in the Ruins of the Japanese Empire, 1937–1953" (PhD thesis, Harvard University, 2012), 199; the British authorities decided that, except for military treason by members of the Indian National Army, it was not in the interest of the people to prosecute civilian collaborators in Asia. Civilians were tried in Malaya, though; see Denyse Tessensohn, "The British Military Administration's Treason Trial of Dr. Charles Joseph Pemberton Paglar, 1946" (MA thesis, NUS Singapore, 2006).
11. For example, C.A. Bayly and Tim Harper, *Forgotten Wars: Freedom and Revolution in Southeast Asia* (Cambridge, MA: The Belknap Press of Harvard University Press, 2007). Bayly and Harper do mention trials in

the different regions, but they do not go into the administration of justice. A valuable contribution to the field is therefore Kerstin von Lingen (ed), *War Crimes Trials in the Wake of Decolonization and Cold War in Asia, 1945–1956: Justice in Time of Turmoil* (Basingstoke: Palgrave Macmillan, 2016), which also reflects on the Dutch case: Lisette Schouten, "Netherlands East Indies' War Crime Trials in the Face of Decolonization", 195–220.

12. Recent studies on collaboration in Asia include Timothy Brook, *Collaboration: Japanese Agents and Local Elites in Wartime China* (Cambridge, MA: Harvard University Press, 2005); Koen de Ceuster, "The Nation Exorcised: The Historiography of Collaboration in South Korea," *Korean Studies* 25, no. 2 (2001): 207–42; David P. Barrett and Lawrence N. Shyu, *Chinese Collaboration with Japan, 1932–1945: The Limits of Accommodation* (Stanford, CA: Stanford University Press, 2001); Satoshi Ara, "Collaboration and Resistance: Catalino Hermosilla and the Japanese Occupation of Ormoc, Leyte (1942–1945)," *Philippine Studies: Historical and Ethnographic Viewpoints* 60, no. 1 (2012): 33–68; an important and innovative study in which different regions are compared is by Konrad M. Lawson, "Wartime Atrocities and the Politics of Treason in the Ruins of the Japanese Empire, 1937–1953" (PhD diss., Harvard University, 2012), in which Chinese, British and Philippine cases of collaboration by police and servicemen are described.
13. In my dissertation I attempt to fill this gap by providing an overview of the way in which the Dutch colonial government dealt with collaboration in the Dutch East Indies by studying how ideas, policies and the prosecution of collaboration and war crimes took shape and were put into practice.
14. This is not a definite figure. It is based on a wide range of primary sources, including trial records, clemency petitions, intelligence records, government documents and newspapers. In my thesis I will deal with figures and numbers more extensively. The number of cases was only a very small percentage of the total number of individuals under investigation, as is evident from the hundreds of intelligence and investigation records kept in the inventories of the intelligence services and judiciary in the National Archives in The Hague.
15. The first known collaboration trials related to the Japanese occupation were held at the TCM on Biak (Dutch New Guinea) in April 1945. One of the last judgments in a collaboration case was pronounced in public in Surabaya on 20 December 1949, only a few days before the sovereignty transfer. The defendant had worked as an interpreter for the Kempeitai in Malang and had assaulted several persons during interrogations. He was sentenced to a prison sentence of five years: National Archives, The Hague (NA),

2.09.19 Krijgsraden in Nederland en Nederlands-Indië 1923–1962 (KR), 80, Files TCM Surabaya 1947–1949.

16. Examples related to different population groups: Didi Kwartanada, "Competition, Patriotism and Collaboration: The Chinese Businessmen of Yogyakarta between the 1930s and 1945," *Journal of Southeast Asian Studies* 33, no. 2 (2002): 257–77; Twang Peck Yang, *The Chinese Business Élite in Indonesia and the Transition to Independence, 1940–1950* (Kuala Lumpur: Oxford University Press, 1998); Elly Touwen-Bouwsma, "Tussen Etnische Loyaliteit En Politieke Collaboratie: De Indo-Comités Op Java, 1943–1945," in *Het Einde van Indie: Indische Nederlanders Tijdens de Japanse Bezetting En de Dekolonisatie*, ed. Wim Willems and Jaap de Moor (Den Haag: Sdu Uitgeverij Koninginnegracht, 1995), 157–72, 286–88; Eveline Buchheim, "Victim, Accomplice or Culprit?: Marie-Therese Brandenburg van Oltsende's Relations with the Japanese Occupier," in *Under Fire: Women and World War II*, ed. Eveline Buchheim, vol. 34, Yearbook of Women's History/Jaarboek Voor Vrouwengeschiedenis (Amsterdam: Verloren Publishers, 2014), 127–40.
17. In the literature several definitions of collaboration are used. I will use the broad umbrella definition for collaboration encompassing all sorts of cooperation with the enemy in order to follow the terminology used by the Indies government.
18. Brook, *Collaboration*, 5.
19. Since the 1980s, the Dutch historiography has moved away from the dichotomy of "right" and "wrong" and paid more attention to the many "shades of grey": Chris van der Heijden, *Grijs verleden: Nederland en de Tweede Wereldoorlog* (Amsterdam: Contact, 2001).
20. C.J. Lammers, *Vreemde Overheersing: Bezetten En Bezetting in Sociologisch Perspectief* (Amsterdam: Bert Bakker, 2005), 244–59.
21. Heather Sutherland, *The Making of a Bureaucratic Elite: The Colonial Transformation of the Javanese Priyayi* (Singapore: Heinemann, 1979).
22. Ibid.; Ronald Robinson, "Non-European Foundations of European Imperialism: Sketch for a Theory of Collaboration," in *Imperialism – The Robinson and Gallagher Controversy*, ed. Roger Louis (New York: New Viewpoints, 1976), 128–51.
23. Shigeru Satō, *War, Nationalism and Peasants: Java under the Japanese Occupation 1942–1945* (Armonk, NY: Sharpe, 1994); Hendri F. Isnaeni and Apid, *Romusa: Sejarah Yang Terlupakan (1942–1945)*, ed. M. Yuanda Zara (Yogyakarta: Ombak, 2008); Sutherland, *The Making of a Bureaucratic Elite*, 153.
24. Hendrajit, Hawé Setiawan and Sudarto Murtaufiq, eds., *Japanese Militarism & Its War Crimes in Asia Pacific Region* (Jakarta: Global Future Institute, 2011). A few Indonesians openly condemned Sukarno for his role in the

recruitment of forced labourers and the maltreatment of fellow Indonesians: *Het Dagblad*, "Open brief aan H.M. de Koningin", 14 January 1946. This newspaper article was an open letter addressed to the Queen by Mas Slamet, who wrote several articles in which he appealed to the Indies government to punish the nationalist leaders for their misbehaviour during the occupation.

25. Anthony Reid, *The Blood of the People: Revolution and the End of Traditional Rule in Northern Sumatra* (Kuala Lumpur: Oxford University Press, 1979); A.J. Piekaar, *Atjeh En de Oorlog Met Japan* ('s-Gravenhage: Van Hoeve, 1949); Anton Lucas, *One Soul One Struggle: Region and Revolution in Indonesia* (Sydney: Asian Studies Association of Australia in association with Allen and Unwin, 1991).
26. William H. Frederick, "The Killing of Dutch and Eurasians in Indonesia's National Revolution (1945–49): A 'Brief Genocide' Reconsidered," *Journal of Genocide Research* 14, no. 3–4 (2012): 359–80; Mary Somers Heidhues, "Anti-Chinese Violence in Java during the Indonesian Revolution, 1945–49," *Journal of Genocide Research* 14, no. 3–4 (2012): 381–401.
27. The Dutch East Indies authorities used the word *re-occupy* in their correspondence with the British: e.g. Memo Lt-GG (Van Mook) to SACSEA (Mountbatten), 2 September 1945, in S.L. van der Wal, ed., *Officiële Bescheiden Betreffende de Nederlands-Indonesische Betrekkingen, 1945–1950*, [further: *NIB*] (The Hague: Nijhoff, 1971) Kleine Serie 36, vol. 1, 79–80. Until November 1946 the Dutch East Indies stood under British military command. Fabian Klose argues that it was not the intention of the European colonial powers to decolonize but rather to recolonize and to reinstate their hegemonic position: Fabian Klose, *Human Rights in the Shadow of Colonial Violence: The Wars of Independence in Kenya and Algeria*, trans. Dona Geyer (Philadelphia: University of Pennsylvania, 2013), 47–56.
28. Martin Thomas, Bob Moore, and L.J. Butler, "Introduction: Constructions of Decolonization," in *Crises of Empire: Decolonization and Europe's Imperial States, 1918–1975* (London: Hodder Education, 2008), 9.
29. The National Archives of the United Kingdom, Kew, Surrey (TNA), Treasury Solicitor and HM Procurator General (TS) 26/69 UNWCC, Report by Committee I on the treatment of Quislings, 28 October 1944. These recommendations were initially issued for the situation in Europe but were later also applied to the tasks in the Far East.
30. Brook, *Collaboration*, 4.
31. L. de Jong, *Het Koninkrijk der Nederlanden in de Tweede Wereldoorlog. Dl. 11a: Nederlands-Indië I: tweede helft.* (Leiden: Nijhoff, 1984), 670–74. Arsip Nasional Republik Indonesia, Jakarta (ANRI), Algemene Secretarie (AS) 283, "Aanwijzingen betreffende de houding, aan te nemen door de Bestuursorganen

van het land, de Zelfbesturende Landschappen, Provinciën, Regentschappen, (Stads)gemeenten, Waterschappen, Groepsgemeenschappen, Locale Ressorten en Inlandsche Gemeenten en door het daarbij in dienst zijnde personeel, alsmede de bevolking in geval van bezetting van Nederlandsch-Indisch gebied" [1941]; Idem, Letter Govt secretary to G. Beers, 14 Sept 1946. The *Staatsmobilisatieraad* consisted of commanders of the army and navy, the heads of the departments and the attorney general.

32. Original quote: "*bij de verantwoordelijke instanties krachtig protest aanteekenen wanneer deze instanties zelf, of wel daaraan ondergeschikte organen of personen, handelingen plegen, welke volkenrechtelijk niet geoorloofd zijn*" [Translation by author].
33. See, for instance, the case of a Manadonese man who worked as an interpreter for the Kempeitai: NA, 2.09.19, KR, 79 Files TCM Surabaya 1946–1948.
34. ANRI, AS 161, Principles concerning arrangements for civil administration and jurisdiction in Netherlands territory in the Southwest Pacific Area, 1944. In the agreement of 10 December 1944 it was laid down that Dutch or Indies officers of the Dutch East Indies Civil Administration (NICA) would handle civil affairs. See also "NICA-handboek", [s.l., ca. June 1945]. After 15 August 1945 command was handed over to the British of the South-East Asia Command.
35. Original quote: "*Slechts voor verraders, die eigen belang stelden boven dat van hun medemenschen, beteekent dit het ineenstorten van hun eigen korte en valsche glorie.*" [Translation by author]: Radio speech by H.J. van Mook on 15 August 1945, as published by Algemeen Nederlands Persbureau (ANP)-Aneta, in *NIB*, vol. 1, 42–43n.
36. Van Mook initially shared this opinion. Memo Lt-GG (Van Mook) to acting Director Internal Administration (BB) (Van der Plas), 26 August 1945, in *NIB*, vol. 1, 56–7; Memo Lt-GG (Van Mook) to SACSEA (Mountbatten), 3 September 1945, in *NIB*, vol. 1, 82–3; Tom van den Berge, *H.J. van Mook: 1894–1965: een vrij en gelukkig Indonesië: biografie* (Bussum: Uitgeverij Thoth, 2014), 198–201.
37. Van Mook spent a considerable amount of time during the war in London with the Dutch government-in-exile. Most other Indies government officials stayed in Melbourne and later at Camp Columbia near Brisbane.
38. Code telegram no. 25 Lt -GG (Van Mook) to min. Overseas Territories (OT) (Logemann), 25 August 1945, in *NIB*, vol. 1, 55–6.
39. Ibid., note 6.
40. In 1940 the population of the Dutch East Indies totalled about 70 million people, of which 50 million lived on Java. About 300,000 inhabitants were of European or Eurasian descent. If only a fraction of the Indonesians was considered collaborators, the colonial judicial system would not have been able to process them all.

41. Sutan Sjahrir, *Our Struggle*, ed. Benedict R.O'.G. Anderson (Ithaca, N.Y.: Cornell University, Department of Asian Studies, 1968). Also the Indonesian member of the Dutch Parliament, L.N. Palar, was of the opinion that Sukarno should resign because of his collaboration with the Japanese, although he did not consider him a traitor: *Het Vrije Volk*, 'Zeven getuigenissen over Indië', 8 October 1945.
42. ANRI, AS, 288, Letter of Dutch Ambassador to Washington (Loudon) to min FA (Van Kleffens), 10 December 1945.
43. Penal code for Dutch East Indies: Willem Engelbrecht, ed. Edwin Engelbrecht, *De Nederlandsch-Indische wetboeken benevens de Grondwet voor het Koninkrijk der Nederlanden, en de belangrijkste in Nederlandsch-Indie geldende algemeene verordeningen en besluiten, met verwijzing naar de op elk artikel betrekking hebbende Nederlandsch-Indische, Nederlandsche en sommige Fransche wetsbepalingen* (A.W. Sijthoff's Uitgeverij, Leiden, 1940).
44. Decree of 21 September 1945, "Definitie hulpverlening vijand en straffen", published in *Staatsblad voor Nederlandsch-Indië* 1945 no. 135 [translation by author].
45. Ibid.
46. Discussions and explanations on the changes and interpretation of the articles are found in ANRI, AS, 230.
47. Revised Judicial Procedures of the Army (*Herziene Rechtspleging bij de Landmacht*) *Staatsblad voor Nederlandsch-Indië* 1945 no. 112, 11 July 1945, revised by *Staatsblad voor Nederlandsch-Indië* 1945 no. 126, 29 August 1945 and *Staatsblad voor Nederlandsch-Indië* 1946 no. 57, 18 June 1946.
48. NIOD. Institute for War, Holocaust and Genocide Studies, Amsterdam (NIOD), 400 Indische Collectie (IC), 487 "Instructie inzake de nasporing naar oorlogsmisdaden".
49. Studies dealing with the TCMs in the Indies are mostly related to the Japanese war crimes trials and refer, if at all, only to a very limited extent to the collaborator trials: Peter Post et al., eds., *The Encyclopedia of Indonesia in the Pacific War*, in cooperation with Nederlands Instituut Voor Oorlogsdocumentatie (Leiden; Boston: Brill, 2010); L. van Poelgeest, *Japanse Besognes: Nederland En Japan 1945–1975* (Den Haag: Sdu, 1999); L.F. de Groot, *Berechting Japanse Oorlogsmisdadigers in Nederlands-Indië 1946–1949: Temporaire Krijgsraad Batavia*, 2 vols. (Den Bosch: Art & Research, 1990); Idem, "De Rechtspraak Inzake Oorlogsmisdrijven in Nederlands Indië (1947–1949)," *Militair-Rechtelijk Tijdschrift* 78 (1985): 81–90; 161–72; Idem, "De Rechtspraak van de Temporaire Krijgsraad Te Batavia (1947–1949)," *Militair-Rechtelijk Tijdschrift* 78 (1985): 248–57; 361–76; Fred L. Borch, "'In the Name of the Queen': Military Trials of Japanese War Criminals in the Netherlands

East Indies (1946–1949)," *The Journal of Military History* 79 (2015): 93–125; Lisette Schouten, "Colonial Justice in the Dutch East Indies War Crimes Trials," in *Trials for International Crimes in Asia*, ed. Kirsten Sellars (Cambridge, UK: Cambridge University Press, 2016), 75–99; L. de Jong, *Het Koninkrijk Der Nederlanden in de Tweede Wereldoorlog. Dl. 11b: Nederlands-Indië II: Eerste Helft* (Den Haag; Amsterdam: SDU Uitgeverij Koninginnegracht; Boom, 1995). In several paragraphs throughout the five volumes, De Jong points out specific cases of collaboration. He was criticised for condemning the collaboration by the Indonesian nationalists: Idem, *Het Koninkrijk der Nederlanden in de Tweede Wereldoorlog. Dl. 14: Reacties: tweede helft* ('s-Gravenhage: SDU-Uitgeverij, 1991), 820–25.

50. Confusion exists about the number of TCMs, because not all Dutch courts-martial were in the Dutch East Indies, not all courts dealt with the same types of cases (war crimes, collaboration, military cases) and not all were in operation during the whole period 1945–1949. The confusion existed at that time as well: ANRI, AS, Judge Advocate field court-martial (Bonn) to Govt Secr., 2 January 1948.

51. The state of siege was in force in the Dutch East Indies starting on 10 May 1940. Cases of instigation of insurgencies or revolutionary violence committed after the Japanese surrender could be tried by a TCM. Disciplinary cases in which Dutch or KNIL soldiers were involved would be brought before a field court-martial (*Krijgsraden te Velde*) KL or KNIL but were, for pragmatic reasons, occasionally brought before TCMs. Serious cases of collaboration with the enemy by KNIL servicemen were generally dealt with by a TCM. At a later stage of the decolonization war special courts-martial (*Bijzondere Krijgsgerechten*) were installed to deal with cases in the field: Rémy Limpach, *De Brandende Kampongs van Generaal Spoor* (Amsterdam: Boom, 2016), 468–530.

52. The pre-war judiciary consisted of about 300 persons. At least eighty-one members had died during the war, and a substantial number were considered unfit to return to their positions: NA, 2.10.14 AS, 4631, Report to Director of Justice regarding members of the judiciary, October 1945; "Lijst van overleden juristen (rechterlijke ambtenaren, advocaten en procureurs en ambtenaren van het departement van justitie)", *Tijdschrift voor het Recht* no. 1 (1947): 6–7.

53. The intelligence services and Netherlands War Crimes Investigation Teams were also instructed to collect information and intelligence about the period after August 1945: NIOD, IC, 442 Report Director Netherlands War Crimes Section (Benders), 8 March 1946. This implication was again stressed by Felderhof in NA, 2.10.17 Procureur-Generaal bij het Hooggerechtshof van Nederlands-Indië, 1945–1949 (PG), 52 Circular AG (Felderhof) to Judge Advocates, 8 April 1946.

54. Government statement, 6 November 1945, in *NIB*, vol. 1, 588–92; *Het Dagblad*, "Voorstel der Ned. Regering aan Indonesië", 7 November 1945.
55. NA, 2.10.62 Marine en Leger Inlichtingendienst, de Netherlands Forces Intelligence Service en de Centrale Militaire Inlichtingendienst in Nederlands-Indië (MLI), 2145, Memorandum Director BB (Van der Plas) to Blom, Van Bylandt, Spoor and Abdulkadir, 10 February 1946.
56. NA, 2.10.14 AS, 3313, Notes of the Department of Justice concerning amnesty, 25 February 1946.
57. *Het Dagblad*, "De collaborateurs. Uiteenzetting van de regeering", 1 March 1946.
58. NA, 2.10.17 PG, 52, Circular AG (Felderhof) to all CO AMACAB/CONICA, JAGs and substitutes, and prosecutors, 8 April 1946.
59. Leo Jansen, introd. Gerrit Knaap, *In deze halve gevangenis: dagboek van mr dr L.F. Jansen, Batavia/Djakarta 1942–1945* (Franeker: Van Wijnen, 1988); NA, 2.10.62 MLI, 2660 Ritman.
60. As described in article 124 2nd lid sub 6° and 7° W.v.S.
61. Lawson, "Wartime Atrocities", 22.
62. NA, 2.09.19 KR, 178 TCM in Hollandia, Plea by Aoki Naokichi in case of Matsumoto Kyoshi c.s., 16 March 1948; NA, 2.10.17 PG, 37, Letter Judge Advocate Tarakan to AG, 27 July 1945. See also Kaori Maekawa, "Heiho During the Japanese Occupation of Indonesia", in *Asian Labor in the Wartime Japanese Empire: Unknown Histories,* ed. Paul H. Kratoska (Armonk, NY: Sharpe, 2005), 179–96, 382–88.
63. Richard Chauvel, *Nationalists, Soldiers and Separatists: The Ambonese Islands from Colonialism to Revolt : 1880–1950* (Leiden: KITLV Press, 1990), 213–14; NA, 2.10.17 PG, 34 Heiho on Tarakan.
64. This was the case with the Sultan of Bima, who was considered "the only competent administrator" and his questionable role during the war was therefore forgiven: Leiden University Libraries, Leiden (UBL), 59 Collection B.J. Lambers, 28 Memorandum Lambers to AG (Felderhof), 29 May 1946.
65. NA, 2.10.17 PG, 44 Economic collaboration and execution.
66. Kwartanada, "Chinese Leadership and Organization in Yogyakarta during the Japanese Occupation," 69.
67. Peter Post, "The Oei Tiong Ham Concern and the Change of Regimes in Indonesia, 1931–1950," in *Chinese Indonesians and Regime Change*, ed. Marleen Dieleman, Juliette Koning, and Peter Post, (Leiden: Brill, 2011), 169–99.
68. NA, 2.10.17 PG, 44 Economic collaboration and execution. Judge advocates stated that only a limited number of cases was processed for prosecution.
69. For instance on Sumatra: NA, 2.10.17 PG, 44, Letter AG (on behalf, Van Maanen) to subst. Judge Advocate Palembang, 7 October 1946.

70. An Allied War Crimes Investigation Team was ambushed near Bogor on Java in April 1946. Three Australian investigators were killed. See, for instance, *Advocate*, "Australian officers ambushed by Indonesians. Shot from range of five yards", 22 April 1946. In Batavia Chief Assistant of the Attorney General B.J. Lambers was driven around by the driver of the Department of Justice with two armed soldiers. Private collection of B.J. Lambers, Letter Lambers to his wife, 29 August 1946.
71. NA, 2.10.17 PG, 20, Letter AG (Felderhof) to CONICA Banjarmasin (Ablij), 27 March 1946.
72. ANRI, AS, 37, Draft minutes meeting Council of Heads of Departments, 7 February 1947.
73. ANRI, AS, 277, Memos on the desirability of extraordinary clemency.
74. Decree Lt-GG 7 May 1947 no.14: Amnesty Decree, *Staatsblad voor Nederlandsch Indië* 1947 no. 79; NA, 2.05.117 Code-archief van het Ministerie van Buitenlandse Zaken, 1945–1954, 20903, Copy of telegram Lt-GG (Van Mook) to min OT (Jonkman), 11 February 1947.
75. See, for instance, the case of a Eurasian camp guard who had served in several internment camps where he would have maltreated and abused many internees. He was sentenced to fifteen years' imprisonment: NA, 2.10.62 MLI, 2567 Dinkelaar. A similar decree was issued in the Philippines in 1948: Konrad M. Lawson, "Universal Crime, Particular Punishment: Trying the Atrocities of the Japanese Occupation as Treason in the Philippines, 1947–1953," *Comparativ | Zeitschrift Für Globalgeschichte Und Vergleichende Gesellschaftsforschung* 23, no. 3 (2013): 57–77.
76. ANRI, AS, 37, Draft minutes meeting Council of Heads of Departments, 7 February 1947.
77. Ibid.

Esther Zwinkels is a researcher at the Netherlands Institute of Military History in The Hague. At Leiden University she is finishing her PhD thesis, which deals with investigations and trials of collaboration and war crimes cases after the Second World War in the Dutch East Indies. Her publications include "Containing 'potentially subversive' subjects: the internment of supporters of the National Socialist Movement in the Dutch East Indies, 1940–1946" in *Incarceration and Regime Change: European Prisons during and after the Second World War* ed. Christian G. De Vito, Ralf Futselaar, and Helen Grevers (New York: Berghahn, 2016) and *Het Overakker-complot. Indisch verzet tegen de Japanse bezetter op Sumatra 1942–1945* (Houten: Spectrum, 2011). This research is supported by the Netherlands Organisation for Scientific Research (NWO) as part of the research project "Recognition and Retribution. Transitional justice in the Dutch East Indies after the Second World War". The author would like to thank Petra Groen and the editors of this volume for comments on earlier drafts.

Between Postoccupation and Postcolonial: Framing the Recent Past in the Philippine Treason Amnesty Debate, 1948

Konrad M. Lawson

In the first two years following Philippine independence from the United States in 1946, the American embassy in Manila carefully collected reports on the debates over Filipino collaboration with the Japanese occupation of the archipelago from 1941–1945. How were the trials for their treason going? Would there be an amnesty? What did the broader population think about the wartime traitors? What were the political implications of this or that politician's prosecution or support for the prosecutions? Embassy reports were accompanied by attached summaries of conversations between Americans and Filipinos discussing the issue, along with bundles of newspaper clippings on the issue, a majority calling for an end to the treason trials, but with varying and sometimes contradictory lines of argument. The treason trials had not been going well. There was increasing frustration as, after months, almost none of the leading wartime leaders had appeared in a courtroom, let alone find themselves convicted. Among the clippings kept by the embassy can be found a *Manila Tribune* article published less than two weeks before a partial amnesty was proclaimed by Philippine president Manuel Roxas on 28 January 1948. The

K.M. Lawson (✉)
University of St Andrews, St. Andrews, UK
e-mail: kml8@st-andrews.ac.uk

K. von Lingen (ed.), *Debating Collaboration and Complicity in War Crimes Trials in Asia, 1945–1956*, World Histories of Crime, Culture and Violence, DOI 10.1007/978-3-319-53141-0_6

editorial worried that any amnesty for only the political collaborators would be unjust: Even if we believed in their sincere motives, it asked, was it then not possible that everyone else who collaborated did so "because they believed that the political collaborators were sincere? The truth is that political collaboration, whatever might have been its occult nature or purpose, influenced the intensity and scope of all other kinds of collaboration."[1]

In what follows we examine the remarkably extensive Philippine legislative debates in 1948 that constitute a key moment of contestation among political elites over the justifications for the wartime conduct but also a probing reflection on the fairness of issuing a partial amnesty that would exonerate almost all those who served in positions of greatest power but allow hundreds of treason cases of mostly lower class suspects to go forward. The two most detailed studies of the postwar treason trials in the form of Philippine People's Courts see the 1948 amnesty as the climax of a failed process. In his account of the progress of the People's Court up to the amnesty, David J. Steinberg traces the "growing sympathy" of the courts for claims of "justifying circumstances," until finally procedural issues came to dominate each case in the final lead-up to the 1948 amnesty in the form of Proclamation Number 51 by President Roxas, which resulted in the dismantling of the People's Court a few months later.[2] Steinberg and a more recent historian of the treason trials, Augusto V. De Viana, count 156 treason convictions, out of either 5,603 or 5,556 People's Court cases.[3] Steinberg ends his history of collaboration in the Philippines with the amnesty, and understandably so, given that he, like many historians of the occupation and aftermath, has been interested in explaining the almost complete co-optation of Filipino elites into the wartime administration by the Japanese military. Elsewhere, I have argued that there is much to learn from the continuation of trials for treason in regular criminal courts after the amnesty dismantled the special People's Court system.[4] Here, however, we will consider an example of how justice in the case of early postwar political retribution was determined as much by decisions in the legislature as in the courts of their creation.

If the 1940s brought to a climax the extremes of a century, it also gave birth to an *age of retribution*. At a global scale, and in uniquely interlocking ways, never has the world seen such a simultaneous combination of attempts to purge betrayal at the level of community, national or local, and punish brutality in the name of the universal. In her work analyzing this process of "political globalization" in the aftermath of World War II,

Margherita Zanasi has shown the ways in which the discourse on Chinese wartime collaboration with Japan closely paralleled and invoked the images and language of its French counterpart through what Rob Wilson and Wimal Dissanayake call "strategies of localization."[5] Zanasi outlines the way in which Chen Gongbo, one of the leading Chinese Nationalist Party figures to have joined and later led a wartime client state under Japanese occupation, embraces a "collaborationist nationalism" that mirrored similar arguments used by the former leading figures of Vichy France to justify their wartime conduct and argues that the invocation of the French example in postwar Suzhou treason trials situated the Chinese experience within a broader range of responses to the experience of occupation around the world.

The collaborationist nationalism embraced by those accused of national betrayal recast the traitor as a sacrificial martyr who, pretending to support the enemy, shielded the nation from the direct blows of the occupier and, in many cases, claimed to have secretly played a "double game" by covertly supporting the resistance. A form of this collaborationist nationalism can be found in the Philippines as it emerged from the destruction of almost half a decade of Japanese occupation from 1941 to 1945. There it was defended by the large number of political elites who accepted positions of authority throughout the Philippines during the Japanese occupation, both before and after the establishment of a nominally independent Philippine republic in October 1943, including José P. Laurel, Claro M. Recto, Jorge Vargas, Camilo Osias, and Quinten Paredes. Both the "shield" and "double game" arguments were extremely successful, aided in no small part by the rapid collapse of attempts to prosecute treason cases in a People's Court system established in the summer of 1945. Down to the present day it remains an important component of the dominant narrative of the wartime experience.

The richest harvest here does not come from weighing in on the moral questions being explored here, even if my sympathy for the critics of a partial amnesty may be inferred. Instead, the task in what follows is to connect, on the one hand, what was an intensely national discourse to a broader global one and, on the other, what was local in time – the 1948 debate – to the broader development of a postcolonial narrative of Philippine history since the Japanese occupation. These debates reveal the degree to which early postwar Philippine legislators portrayed the issue of retribution as part of a global process after the Second World War faced by many nations emerging from occupation, with wartime choices in the Philippines seen as comparable to those faced by others, especially under German occupations in Europe. These legislators, the first elected to a fully independent Philippine government, often described the issue in a language that would be entirely familiar to many a postoccupation state of the 1940s, going well beyond the transpacific commonalities in legal reasoning we would expect to find between the Philippines and the United States. Joining a trend in scholarship seeking to, as the historian Vicente Rafael calls it, "deprovincialize" the study of the Philippines, the moral arguments raised by legislators here thus contribute to a broader literature on political retribution and transitional justice.[6] However, this by no means reduces the Philippine experience to reflecting an undifferentiated universal pattern. As we shall see, the Philippine experience of colonial rule under Spanish, American, and, finally, Japanese rule, with the last of these explicitly proclaimed in anti-imperalist terms, adds a postcolonial dimension to the affair that offered an alternative interpretive framework for wartime conduct of those branded as traitors.

Other wartime allies of the Japanese, from the Indian nationalist Subhas Chandra Bose to Aung San in Burma and Sukarno in the Dutch East Indies, predominantly justified collaboration with Japan as a *proactive choice rather than a passive sacrifice* to minimize the evils of occupation, a strategic alliance with a new conqueror in the short term in order to achieve national liberation on their own terms. For a number of reasons, including the particular historical context of the Philippine path from colony to independent, if still largely U.S.-dependent status, in 1946, *this was not the way* most Philippine political debates in the early aftermath of Japanese defeat depicted their choices, even if later biographers, historians, and, with great hindsight, some of the participants themselves have highlighted the strategic use of a Japanese occupation to pursue nation-building initiatives.[7] Instead, seeing things from the perspective of participants of this highly public, and thus inevitably to some degree performative, series of exchanges in their own terms, the postcolonial translation or "strategy of localization" that can be identified in these postwar debates on treason in the Philippines is instead seen more often in disagreements over the transitive nature of loyalty: under what conditions does loyalty begin and end? Was it never owed, given there was no fully independent nation to be betrayed? Did the debt of loyalty expire at the moment the American colonial masters abandoned their colony to Japanese invaders in 1941? Or did all acts of betrayal vanish with a clean slate at independence in 1946? These issues, more or less delicately broached in these debates, represented a political mine field, as any answer would reflect a particular perspective on the nature of continuity of the state.

•

A more important difference with Europe was the reality that Japan's conquests in Southeast Asia, though often marked by significantly greater mass violence and atrocities, were nonetheless *occupations of already occupied* territory, the domination of one empire, Japan, replacing that of another, such as France, Britain, the Netherlands, or the United States. The defeat of Japan may have been welcome, and Japanese claims to be the vehicle of liberation for Asian peoples against their Western oppressors may have been thoroughly discredited thanks to a combination of the conduct of its own armed forces and its fate in war, but the reality was that an old master was on its way back. The decision of whether to collaborate with Japan or fight in alliance with the Western powers was, thus, for many based more on tactics than ideological affiliation, and for some, including Aung San's forces in Burma, it was a decision that could be reversed to great effect when the time was right.[8]

This key difference might lead us to expect the issue of wartime collaboration with the Japanese to take on a very different hue in early postwar Southeast Asia. Unlike the widespread trials that took place in countries across Europe and in China, and that were eventually attempted in Korea – where treason trials were held for collaborators with a colonial ruler embracing terms similar to other postoccupation states – the issue of collaboration with Japan in Southeast Asia might be expected to be a nonissue, as long as there was a new unity around the pressing nationalist cause against a returning European power. The Philippines differs substantially from its neighbors, however, in the extent to which Filipinos occupied positions of power throughout the American colonial period, no more so than in the period from the establishment of the 1935 Philippine Commonwealth, with its largely autonomous legislative and presidential administration representing a final transitional stage to independence. Though American promises of independence to the Philippines ought to have reduced the temptation to embrace Japan's wartime anticolonial message, the occupation was marked by an almost complete submission of elites to the occupation regime. Far from a reckoning with those who chose to wave the Japanese flag and take up leading government positions in one of Japan's most brutal occupations, leading figures in Japan's occupation regime, such as José P. Laurel, Claro

Recto, and Benigno Aquino, occupy positions as revered figures in the nationalist narrative, with the grandson of the last of these rising to the position of president of the Philippines in 2010.

Failed Trials and Amnesty in the Philippine Treason Trials

The leading political collaborators with Japan were quickly rehabilitated both politically and in memory. This was facilitated, above all, by the fact that none, save the very first to come to trial, were convicted of treason.[9] Some Filipinos who worked with the Japanese occupation, such as Benigno Ramos and Artemio Ricarte, did not survive the war. Others, such as Benigno Aquino, did not live to see the conclusion of their treason trial. The trials of some, including José P. Laurel, were delayed until an amnesty was passed. Many others were saved by a strict two-witness rule inherited from American treason law. As clarified in a key 1944 U.S. Supreme Court ruling, "every act, movement, deed and word of the defendant charged to constitute treason must be supported by the testimony of two witnesses."[10] Similarly binding in the Philippines, this would pose a severe obstacle for postwar trials in the Philippines. It was understandably difficult for Solicitor General Lorenzo M. Tañada to find the testimony of two witnesses to the signing of a treasonous document or the issuing of a treasonous order when such acts were often carried out in the relative privacy of an office. The overwhelming case load did not help move the process along, either. The special People's Courts established by Commonwealth Act No. 682 in September 1945 to handle all occupation-period violations of Article 114 of the Revised Penal Code, that is, the crime of treason, consisted of a mere five courts with three judges each.

Finally, even without the amnesty to come in 1948, many collaborators had little to fear from the People's Court after it ruled that the holding of government offices during the Japanese occupation neither constituted an overt act rendering "aid and comfort" to the enemy nor provided sufficient evidence of adherence to the enemy – the two required components of any treason conviction in the Philippines as it is in the United States.[11] This is a far cry from European examples, where membership in a party might be a sufficient condition for a treason conviction, such as the case of Norway, or propaganda efforts on behalf of the enemy might result in a death sentence.

At least at the level of laws and legal rulings, this was also a marked contrast with those targeted for collaboration with Japan in, for example, Nationalist- or Communist-controlled territories of China or even in the half-hearted attempt to punish collaboration in South Korea, for example, where high office holders were explicitly targeted by early postwar treason laws, even if mitigating clauses offered judges great flexibility. In the Philippines, the bar for adherence to the enemy was set so high that it required the prosecution to virtually step into the hearts of the accused and prove they were completely empty of patriotic feeling. Words spoken in praise of the Japanese Empire or calling for guerrillas to lay down their arms were but the moving of a helpless puppet's lips; war materials sold to the enemy were just the everyday business of an honest merchant. As long as a collaborator spoke other words in private against the occupier or contributed some percentage of their profits to the resistance, the possibility of "feigned cooperation" – the favorite term of the accused and judges alike – could not be ruled out.

The 1948 presidential amnesty in the Philippines did not eliminate the issue of collaboration; it transformed and contained it. The proclamation states that while the People's Court had been trying cases for more than two years, it had not reached a final judgment on any "treasonable collaboration with the enemy." Assuming that final judgment was taken to mean that the appeal of convictions had been ruled upon by the Supreme Court, this was simply untrue. Over two dozen treason convictions by the People's Court had received final rulings from the Supreme Court *before* the amnesty, and the original conviction was upheld in the majority of these cases.[12] The claim by Roxas only makes sense if, instead of all People's Court cases, it was limited to treason charges against those emphasized in the opening clause who "occupied positions in [the occupation] government, as well as against those who traded with the enemy."

The amnesty for those accused of treason arising from "the last war" justified itself on three basic grounds: a two-witness rule inherited from American treason law made prosecutions almost impossible, the issue divided the nation at a time unity was needed, and a "majority of the Filipino people" realized that the political collaborators were working under duress as a shield against Japanese brutality. However, the amnesty was limited in a way that would become controversial. It stated that "public sentiment [did] not extend" to military collaborators and those guilty of atrocities in the service of the enemy. Anyone who "voluntarily acted as spies or informers of the enemy, or committed murder, arson, coercion, robbery, physical injuries, or any other crime against person or property, for the purpose of aiding and abetting the enemy," would continue to face prosecution for treason.[13]

In effect, cases for the crime of treason would continue, though in regular criminal courts, for anyone guilty of having transformed their acts of betrayal into acts of violence or bore arms or supplied intelligence to the enemy.[14] This amnesty was an exercise of executive power rather than the product of legislation, but it required the concurrence of the Philippine Senate and House of Representatives before it could take effect. These debates revealed significant disagreement with the president, not only over whether such an amnesty was appropriate, but even more over the fairness of its limited scope.[15] It is in these debates that we find illuminating clues as to the way in which Philippine legislators viewed their own struggle to deal with the recent past within the broader context of a global process unfolding around the world.

Let us begin with how the story ends. Though many were absent for the vote, the resolutions supporting the amnesty passed on the evening of 13 February 1948 with overwhelming majorities of 50 to 8 in the House of Representatives and 14 to 2 in the Senate. Those who voted against the amnesty in the House included resistance veteran, future leader of the suppression campaign against the Huk rebellion, and eventual President Ramon Magsaysay. In the Senate, opposition included the same Lorenzo M. Tañada, who led the treason prosecution effort as solicitor general until he turned to a political career in the Senate. Despite the easy victory of the concurrence resolution that would end any serious attempt to hold elites accountable for some of the violence of the Japanese occupation or, at the very least, contrast their decision to take up leading positions with those who joined resistance forces that would be hunted and slaughtered by Japanese military and Philippine constabulary forces, the debates over the amnesty revealed a complex array of positions on collaboration and the violence of military collaborators. It generated over a hundred packed pages of transcripts in the Congressional Record, with a significant portion of this including speeches justifying the votes as they were taken.

Some members of the House of Representatives opposed the amnesty on principle. Hermenegildo Atienza, who represented Manila and was formerly the first postliberation mayor of the city, was disgusted with the fact that collaborators were not only going free but felt no shame at what they had done. "I cannot be merciful . . . I cannot vote now for an amnesty under an atmosphere that glorifies collaboration," he declared.[16] Atienza spoke movingly of his time as a prisoner of the Japanese in Fort Santiago where his friend, the guerrilla leader Guillermo Nakar, was offered an alternative to execution: if he accepted a position as the governor of Isabela, the eastern Luzon province where his guerrillas were once active, his life would be spared. He refused and was executed, and Atienza promised his friend that his memory would not be forgotten. "If I vote for amnesty I would have betrayed that trust: I would've been recreant to that word I pledged before a dying man."[17] Both Enrique Medina of Negros Oriental and Elisio M. Limsiaco of Negros Occidental, one of the few legislators to deliver his speech in Spanish, also appealed to the painful experience of guerrillas and cited many specific examples of the damning conduct of collaborationist leaders on the island of Negros in the Visayas. He felt that any mercy offered to the collaborators would "annihilate the patriotic fervor which was the base of the moral character of the people."[18]

"Different Conceptions of Serving One's Country" – Quintin Paredes and Charles de Gaulle

One of these collaborationist "heroes," who had served in a number of positions during the war, including justice minister and as one of the "Peace and Order Committee" members that oversaw the "pacification" of resistance "bandits," was among the representatives who participated in the debates: Quintin Paredes. Paredes had a long and distinguished career in the colonial period before the Japanese invasion, serving as Attorney General, Secretary of Justice, Speaker of the House, and the nonvoting Philippine Resident Commissioner in the U.S. House of Representatives in the opening years of the Commonwealth from 1935–1939. A short U.S. collaborator profile compiled about Paredes during the war, however, added an unusually acerbic comment to his profile: "Utterly selfish and probably cooperated with the Japanese because he believed they would win the war."[19] In the final vote, Paredes abstained because he was himself involved in "that drama which we might call a tragic comedy of 'collaboration'," but his long speech to the House offered an eloquent defense of his wartime conduct.[20]

Nowhere here does Paredes invoke the defense that would become somewhat more common in later narratives, which was that the Japanese were but one poor choice among two colonial masters, who could serve to eject the Americans and hasten freedom and release the Philippines from its cultural and economic bondage to the United States. There is anger directed at the United States, but, as in the case of many of the accused collaborators, as well as among resistance forces, it was anger at the United States for its abandonment of the Philippines in its hour of greatest need when it withdrew its forces in the face of the Japanese invasion. This abandonment was said to strip Filipinos of their legal responsibilities to defend and obey the Commonwealth of the Philippines or the United States government it served. In other words, at this crucial moment of transition it was a technical legal argument rather than than an explicitly anticolonial (against the United States) or pronationalist (for the independence of the Philippines) argument that was deployed. It was the centrality of the argument that collaboration protected the people, rather than helped accelerate their liberation, that separates Filipino wartime collaboration with the Japanese from all its counterparts in Southeast Asia and places it comfortably within a familiar global discourse over wartime conduct under occupation.

By far the longest legislative speech in these debates, the arguments put forward by Paredes shared both in structure and in specific claims many features of the speeches and testimonies of accused collaborators around the world of the time: that collaboration with a brutal occupier was one of the purest expressions of patriotic sacrifice. This was why, he argued, some of the other elite resistance leaders spoke up for him and his continued postwar service in government. Paredes quoted Charles de Gaulle's justification for including in his 1944 cabinet Jules Jeanneney, who was instrumental in the creation of the Vichy regime in 1940: "I did not go to Vichy then, but many who were there believed they were serving their country in their own way."[21] Whereas some took up arms against the Japanese, others chose the hard task of working with the occupier, it was claimed. De Gaulle is quoted as having put it in another way: "It was possible to have different conceptions of serving one's country. Today there is only one thing that counts: service to the country."[22] It was well known that de Gaulle favored a relatively lenient policy toward wartime collaborators in the Vichy government, but all the same, he made no effort to stand in the way of the execution of a political collaborator such as wartime prime minister Pierre Laval a few months earlier, denying an appeal for a retrial.[23]

In the Senate debates going on at the same time it was Camilo Osias, wartime education minister under the Japanese and a prominent voice of Japanese propaganda aims, who served as the voice for the political collaborators. He was case number 3,528 for treason in the People's Court and served as Resident Commissioner to the U.S. House of Representatives, and his reelection in 1947 was widely quoted as proof the Philippine people accepted his claim when he declared, "I yield to no man in patriotism, and when I served under the Japs I did so because I thought it was my duty to serve my people."[24] Of course, Osias and Paredes avoided dwelling on whether those lower in the chain of command who hunted down guerrillas or identified guerrilla suspects to the Japanese military might have shared the same desire to serve their country "in their own way." On the other hand, Paredes did not distinguish between himself and the more overtly anticolonial collaborationists more closely associated with the most violent strain of military collaboration at the end of the conflict, such as Benigno Ramos and Artemio Ricarte, who helped lead the most enthusiastic auxiliaries that fought with Japanese troops against the returning Americans and guerrillas, calling them both "real patriots."

As for the guerrillas, Paredes was somewhat sympathetic but justified his own wartime appeals for them to abandon their cause. Vicente Rafael has pointed out that during the occupation, elite collaborators "reversed the meaning of signs: 'collaboration' was really 'resistance' against the Japanese while 'resistance,' especially on the part of guerrillas in the countryside, was really 'collaboration' with the United States," but in the early postwar period Paredes recasts his own wartime "pacification" speeches by claiming his real message to the guerrillas at the time was that they should not act "until you have the *triunfo* cards in your hands..."[25] In other words, Paredes diverged somewhat from his French counterparts, who, he liked to point out, described a "sword and shield" relationship between the resistance and the Vichy regime. In France, the resistance was a sword against the Germans, while Vichy was to have served as a shield against German atrocities; the message Paredes had for his wartime opponents in the countryside was to put down the sword until victory was imminent.

"That Which is Reasonably Required by Civilized Justice"

Whatever the final vote, many more spoke out in favor, not just of a partial amnesty for economic and political collaborators, but a complete and universal one for all crimes of treason during the war. Again, their arguments stemmed from different basic principles. Damaso T. Samonte, representing Ilocos Norte on the northwestern tip of Luzon, saw the very idea of amnesty as "putting a bandage on a gangrenous wound," which could not "cleanse the nation's wounds of a highly potent and virulent virus."[26] Did heroes such as Jose Abad Santos, a judge on the Supreme Court of the Philippines who was executed by the Japanese for refusing to collaborate, he asked, die in vain? The Philippines was not alone in facing this problem after the war, but its other allies did not exhibit the "sickly sentimentality of Christian charity and a mistaken concept of unity" shown by President Roxas. He went on:

> Where are the Quislings now? Laval of France had long been carted away to the eternal sleep of infamy. Vidkun Quisling of Norway, Josef Tiso and Karl Hermann Frank of Czechoslovakia, Anton Mussert, the Fuehrer of the Netherlands, Leon Maria Joseph Ignace De Grelle of Belgium, and many others have long been liquidated without much of a ceremony except that which is reasonably required by civilized justice.[27]

However, if amnesty was inevitable, Samonte argued, then it should be for everyone: "I do not see any justice in exculpating the brain that schemes and convicting the hand that executes. The finger man is just as guilty as the trigger man." On the contrary, if anything, it was the political collaborators who deserved more punishment. "His racket is wholesale. He encompasses the entire mass of citizenry within the broad sweep of his perfidy."[28]

Lorenzo Sumulong, a representative from Rizal, east of Manila, who later became known worldwide for sparking the Krushchev shoe-banging incident when he was the Philippine representative at the United Nations in 1960, was also disturbed to learn that "the mercy to be extended will be given only to the brains and buy and sell tycoons of the occupation" and not the "ignorant simpleminded credulous Filipino," whose only crime was that he was "ready to believe the utterances of the prominent men of his time."[29] As was repeatedly pointed out in the debate, only a paltry 15% or so of treason cases were covered by the amnesty. According to a count by Representative Toribio Perez, there were some 472 cases involving political collaboration, 355 economic, and 100 related to cultural collaboration that were eligible for amnesty. However, those ineligible for the amnesty being debated were 2,677 cases involving espionage, enemy agents, spies, and informers, and another 2,925 cases involving military collaborators who were members of the Bureau of Constabulary, an infamous auxiliary organization known as the Makapili, as well as police and related organizations.[30]

Overt comparisons between the current issue of collaboration and similar moral challenges under the colonial rule of the United States or Spain were relatively rare in the speeches of the debate. One such reference came not from accused collaborators or their supporters but from Sumulong, who was deeply critical of a partial amnesty for elite collaboration. Was not Goebbels, he asked, "more monstrous and formidable" than the ordinary soldier, even he if never entered the field of battle? Sumulong was willing to accept the fact that the prominent men were "unwilling instruments," but were they not "bigger and deadlier enemies than the ordinary soldier who takes up arms in the fields?"[31] When Mateo M. Nonato questioned how one could call for a full amnesty for those "bastards that ought to be hanged" for serving as informers and spies who were directly responsible for the deaths of many Filipinos, Sumulong reminded the assembly that Filipinos had killed each other and acted as informers during the Philippine–American war, but the United States had been willing to forgive and forget in the aftermath. "Why should our government be more strict or rigorous with these countrymen of ours who are misled perhaps during the occupation?"[32] Sumulong was not referring to the Philippine–American war in order to laud the anticolonial efforts of that earlier age, including the efforts of the recently deceased Artemio Ricarte, who got to fight his cause one last time under Japanese sponsorship, but rather to propose the emulation of the supposed indiscriminate magnanimity of the United States in the aftermath of a bitter war in which the colonial power was itself guilty of torture and brutal counterinsurgency campaigns.

Another reference to the unusual challenges Filipinos faced under their dual occupation of the United States and Japan is found in Samonte's speech also calling for equal treatment of elites and lower-level collaborators. While he does not directly invoke the previous anticolonial war, he reminds Congress that the maze of loyalties was not easy to navigate:

> The Filipino soul, if we may be permitted to glean from this dismal state of affairs, is a sorely harassed soul. It is laboring in a labyrinth of perplexing contradictions. It is confused and bewildered. It is suffering from spasmodic contortions and distortions, as if undergoing the throes of penitential ablution.[33]

Overall, however, for Samonte, Sumulong, and several other representatives, such as Tapacio Nueno, the most troublesome aspect of the partial amnesty was that it was a clear case of social injustice that effectively discriminated on the basis of class. Esmeraldo Eco, representing Camarines Norte in the southeast Bicol region of Luzon, was outraged for the same reason: "The most lamentable fact is that those men who held important positions during the occupation, the ranking officers of the

Philippine Constabulary who issued orders to the buck privates…who were responsible, perhaps, for all the miseries and sufferings of our people, are the only persons who will be benefited by this grant of amnesty." He was not against either a general amnesty or even a partial one, but "if amnesty is ever to be given, I repeat, it must begin not from the very top, but from the rock bottom."[34] Alejo S. Santos, representing Bulacan to the north of Manila, protested, how could Eco suggest that those with blood on their hands go free first? It was, said Eco, a matter of command responsibility – a relatively new legal principle making its first major debut with the prosecution and execution of General Yamashita Tomoyuki in a Philippine-based American military court in December 1945. Santos disagreed, embracing a remarkable inverted version of the "just following orders" defense that Japanese soldiers prosecuted for war crimes in the Philippines would have little luck with in their own trials.[35] While the soldiers carrying out atrocities were culpable, Santos argued there could be no command responsibility for commanders who were themselves not free to act.

In the Senate, Lorenzo M. Tañada, speaking from his experiences prosecuting treason cases, also denounced the "discriminatory, unjust and vague" partial amnesty that left the "poor and ignorant" to languish in prison. In addition, he already foresaw one of the weaknesses in the exception provided by the amnesty. Was it not strange, Tañada argued, that someone accused of treason for acts of rape would go free, because it was not explicitly mentioned in the amnesty, while someone accused of treason for acts of robbery would not?[36]

These opponents of partial amnesty concentrated on the objective fact that it was overwhelmingly members of the lower classes who were accused of the crimes of torture, murder, and other acts of violence carried out on behalf of the enemy, or of enabling such atrocities in their capacity as informants. Calling for equal treatment of crimes likely to have been carried out by those higher (not directly violent but complicit) and lower (likely to be actually carrying out the acts of violence) in the wartime hierarchy, these arguments were often tinged with not a little patronizing language. It was implied that it was only their poverty, their ignorance, and their susceptibility to propaganda that led them to commit such acts. Just as many of those who favored amnesty for political collaborators took at face value their claims to have been motivated only by patriotic sacrifice, most of those who argued for a general amnesty studiously avoided confronting the possibility that the common man might also act out of personal revenge, greed, or a love of power. If political collaborators were innocent because, it was suggested, they could not prevent the brutality of the Japanese, the "smaller fries" or "los pequeños colaboradores," as they were referred to, were innocent because, in their ignorance, they could not be expected to refuse orders to carry it out.

As we saw earlier, Alejo S. Santos was not so sympathetic to military collaborators among the lower classes, and he was in a better position to speak against them. Santos was a wartime guerrilla leader, a future defense minister, and formerly one of the few delegates elected to the House of Representatives from the leftist Democratic Alliance, which included the Communist Party and representatives of the Hukbalahap guerrillas who would be formally declared an illegal organization only two months later.[37] Santos argued that it might be true that a partial amnesty would mostly favor the elites, but it was equally true that the help of some of these collaborating elites was of great assistance to the guerrillas. It was also undeniable which of the traitors were the most despised by the wartime resistance: the auxiliary organizations such as the Makapili, active only in the final months of the war, would meet a harsher form of justice beyond the courts of law if released.[38]

Santos did not buy the argument that the masses were docile creatures merely following the orders of the leading puppets. Directly countering the argument of the editorial that opened this piece, he said, "Makapilis could never say that they became Makapilis in response to the speeches of Mr. Vargas or Dr. Laurel or anybody else."[39] Yet even Santos preferred a general amnesty to a partial one so that the country could finally "give this collaboration question to oblivion," perhaps because he knew a different kind of justice awaited the military collaborators upon their release – that of liquidation at the hands of Huks, other guerrillas, or members of their own communities.[40] Though many representatives made calls for a general amnesty instead of a partial one, they acknowledged that they stood on weak constitutional grounds when they contemplated a refusal to concur with an executive proclamation and demand its modification. Some representatives, including Cosme P. Garcia, Marcial O. Rañola, and Simeon G. Toribio, did not think it was worth the effort to make a rousing speech in favor of a more general amnesty and merely declared their preference for it when announcing their vote.

"The Glorious Pages of Our Past"

We have seen that the debate over the crime of collaboration was carried out without much reference to the peculiar colonial predicament of the Philippines, that of having faced Spanish, American, and then Japanese occupiers. The debate made use of contemporary European examples to situate its treason debate in a global context. Those who supported the amnesty largely depicted the wartime conduct of elite collaborators as that of men who made a bold sacrifice to protect their people, a language that would be recognizable in many other early postwar debates in Europe, China, and Korea. The work of rebranding the Philippine wartime experience from a postcolonial perspective and one that accounted for the complexity of tangled loyalties would come, but it was not dominant in these debates two years after independence. In this early postwar period, the more narrow legal argument of cancelled loyalties in the face of an abrupt American withdrawal or the legal obligation of a people to occupation governments in war was more prominent; it was raised by Paredes in his speech but most well developed in the postwar writings of the wartime foreign minister, Claro Recto.[41]

One other significant reference to the colonial past would be found, not in the English-language speeches that comprise the vast majority of debate in the Congressional Record, but in the Spanish-language speech of Congressman Vicente Logarta from Cebu. Logarta, a former journalist, went on to serve in various positions for the Nacionalista Party. He was, thus, no radical but had witnessed Japanese atrocities first hand, early on in the Japanese invasion, rather than during the desperate and violent Japanese retreat in the face of the American reinvasion that shaped the most violent war memories of many Filipinos. According to the diary of former Philippine Governor-General Francis Burton Harrison, on a visit to Bulacan Province in 1942, Logarta had found that 110 of 176 teenage girls raped by the invading Japanese had died.[42] When the war ended, however, and he joined the debate on treason in Congress, Logarta did what none of the other legislators did in the same explicit manner: he immediately invoked "the glorious pages of our past" that had served as a rallying cry under Japanese and collaborator propaganda. He reminded the chamber of the 1896 execution of José Rizal at the hands of fellow Filipinos in Spanish service. After recounting the heroic career of Rizal and his fate, Logarta concludes:

> And there you have the strange paradox of a man who died, executed as a traitor, and yet, nevertheless, in the hearts of his people, his memory lives as the embodiment of the most sublime patriotic desire.[43]

This was not the 'patriotic' sacrifice argument of Quintin Paredes, who argued that his difficult choice was made out of necessity to save lives. It appealed to another kind of patriotism: the cause of Filipino independence, which had been invoked against Spain and the United States, which the Japanese occupiers attempted to co-opt. It was this last case, so recently on everyone's mind, that had, to some degree, contributed to its temporary discrediting, even if the Philippines was now two years from the end of formal colonial rule. While he would go on to echo some of the other oft-repeated defenses of elite collaborators, in the opening of his speech, Logarta cut through the so-called shield defense and bypassed the debates over wartime violence to consider what he thought was the heart of the matter:

> For us, in contrast with the theorists, those who, driven by a blind scholasticism, insist on framing the philosophy of the crime of treason with their jargon and a rigid and inflexible canon – those of us who live in a world of realities, we want to understand the crime of treason always in relation to the idea of the nation. We might even venture to say that this crime is almost always a patriotic act, found legitimate or base according to how and by who it is judged.[44]

It was all a matter of perspective. Building on a foundation of references to Rizal and the Philippine revolution of the late nineteenth century, Logarta would in rapid succession invoke examples ranging from the signatories to the U.S. Declaration of Independence to General Philippe Pétain and Gandhi, all as examples of how leaders might be variously seen as patriots to some and traitors to others. Gandhi was used as an example, not of a traitor to the British Empire and an anticolonial hero to supporters of Indian independence, but of someone who might be seen as a traitor to both the supporters of a "united India and a free Pakistan."[45] In the face of such tragic confusion, Logarta's speech culminated in a call to defend the charismatic leaders or "caudillos" of "our political, social, and economic life."

It seems unlikely that the "long view" of history invoked by Logarta necessarily had any connection to the language of its delivery, as we saw with other Spanish-speaking legislators such as Elisio M. Limsiaco, who used familiar terms in speaking out against the amnesty. Spanish, though a minority language in the debates considered here, mixed in smoothly with

English in both legislative debates and other legal contexts through the Spanish–Filipino elites who used it, including in supreme court rulings by judges such as Guillermo Pablo, and serves as a linguistic reminder of the historical and ethnic layers in Philippine society. Vicente Rafael has explored the "linguistic dimension" of wartime collaboration and suggested that the "emptiness" of collaborationist speeches stems from the foreignness of the English language to elites who spoke mostly Spanish to each other, allowing them more easily to "separate their intention from their words."[46] This may have been the case, but taking this too far would complicate the task of a historian examining the diversity within the English-language speeches that constitute the majority of these postwar debates. Did Quintin Paredes, who spoke in English, find it just as easy to separate his intentions from his words when he defended his wartime speeches in 1948? Are we to view the words of Timoteo P. Ricohermoso, who spoke both languages in the debates, with more suspicion when he spoke English than when he switched to Spanish? Identifying where language ends and race or class and race begin could also be a challenge. The Counter Intelligence Corps officers of the United States military, which compiled reports on suspected collaborators upon its return with MacArthur's forces, if anything was deeply suspicious of anyone from the Spanish and Spanish mestizo elite community of Philippine society, seeing them as particularly prone to Falange-inspired fascist conspirators, even if prewar sympathy for the Nationalists in Spain's civil war had in fact cooled considerably.[47]

Logarta's invocation of older national heroes was unusual, but his broader points match a strategy found more broadly: turning the focus away from particular acts or the moral dilemma faced by all Filipinos in wartime to an alternately more philosophical or at least legal question of who owes loyalty to who and when. We have seen this already in other examples, but variations of this can be found throughout early postwar debates. The entire speech of Cipriano S. Allas, a lawyer and representative from Pangasinan who was part of a presidential committee established to study the amnesty, might be given the title of one of questions he posed: "What is allegiance?" The highly technical answer he offered took him on a historical journey that included stops in 1600 England, the U.S. state of Maine in 1812, the American treason case of Eva Tagore, and pardons and amnesties following the American Civil War. His primary argument rested on a theory of "abrogated sovereignty," which meant that the political law of treason was abrogated in 1946 with the establishment of the new Republic of the Philippines.[48]

Skipping over the issue of wartime harms or collaborationist nationalist strategies entirely, his long discourse, steeped in the Anglo-American legal tradition, ironically leads him to make one of the statements with the most postcolonial ring of the entire debate: "why should we be harsh against our people if it is a crime against the United States?"[49]

•

The votes to concur with the amnesty brought to a close political debates on collaboration for half a decade, even though it affected a small minority of cases.[50] The People's Court itself was, despite its modest scope, an expensive burden on the state treasury and abolished by Republic Act 311. The 1946 budget set its cost at P650,000 (P = Philippine pesos), and during the 1948 debates its annual cost was quoted at P1,126,570. Putting this into perspective, the operating budget for the Department of Justice as a whole in 1947 was only P1,700,000, and the entire estimated government revenues for the 1947–1948 fiscal year was P130,000,000.[51] Those costs did not entirely disappear, however. As we have seen, the majority of treason cases were not covered by the amnesty and were thereafter returned to regular criminal courts. Though the budget provided was cut well out of proportion to the number of cases eliminated by the amnesty, Act 311 still allocated P375,000 to pay the costs of the remaining treason prosecutions and wages for fifteen special attorneys dedicated to those cases. The dismantling of the People's Court, an institution that represented the surgeon who operated upon the "gangrenous" wounds of the nation, together with the amnesty proclamation and resolutions of concurrence supported widely across party and factional lines, did much to take the issue out of the public eye.

The 1948 debate over the amnesty, whose outcome was never much in doubt, nonetheless provided an unparalleled moment to see a full range of possible interpretations of the dilemmas faced by the Philippine people under Japanese occupation. Though opponents of a partial, as opposed to a full, amnesty appealed to a sense of the class injustice of punishing only those most proximate to the violence, rather than those who held power above them, only a few of these legislators could claim strong personal familiarity with the lives of the poor. Sumulong could, at best, claim a grandfather who was originally a tenant farmer. Perhaps the most prominent exception was Ramon Magsaysay, whose humble origins as the son of a trade-school teacher would become one of his most beloved biographical facts in his future presidential campaign. Though no clear pattern emerges in terms of what position they took in the debate, many of the most active participants in the 1948 debate, including Samonte (b. 1901?), Sumulong (b. 1905), Magsaysay (b. 1907), Santos (b. 1911), and Eco (b. 1908), are all of a younger generation of politicians born in the first dozen years or so of American colonial rule, as compared to those whose wartime conduct gave rise to the debate, such as Quintin Paredes (b. 1884), Camilo Osias (b. 1889), Claro Recto (b. 1890), and José P. Laurel (b. 1891).

One of the most appealing aspects of these debates was a relative lack of uniformity or adherence to clearly identifiable factions. The positions put forward are marked by considerable internal diversity, and an impressive range of moral, legal, historical, and – as we have seen – globally connected lines of argument are advanced. In a now classic lecture from 1997, "Orientalism and the Study of Philippine Politics," Reynaldo Ileto critiques a series of historians of the Philippines, in some cases for their habit of "highlighting cultural differences" of Filipinos, invoking their "peculiarities," or producing explanations of them on the basis of basic traits that are seen as naturally guiding the political process in the Philippines.[52] There is, of course, no shortage of unique aspects to the postwar Philippine debates over wartime collaboration, the most important omission here being an exploration of the way in which important differences in local and regional experiences before and during the war shaped the positions of the legislators. To this we must certainly add the particular postcolonial nature of their context. However, whether through the deeply historical legal heritage appealed to by Allas within a specifically Anglo-American context or the European comparisons made by opposing legislators such as Samonte and Paredes, an overemphasis on what is singular denies a place to these rich debates in a broader global history of the politics of retribution, one that the participants clearly saw themselves as taking part in.

Notes

1. *Manila Tribune*, January 19, 1948 clipping included in RG59 896.00/1-2848. Philippines Republic: Internal and Foreign Affairs 1945–1949 Confidential U.S. State Department Central Files Film A 575.26 Reel 1 of 35.
2. David Steinberg, *Philippine Collaboration in World War II* (Ann Arbor: University of Michigan Press, 1967), 152–63.
3. *Ibid.*, 162. See also note 42, 207. He lists 229 "political prisoners" in custody by June 1948, excluding the Hukbalahap rebels. Augusto V. de Viana, *Kulaboretor!: The Issue of Political Collaboration during World War II*

(Manila: University of Santo Tomas Pub. House, 2003), 180. The source of de Viana's count is unclear.

4. Konrad Lawson, "Universal Crime, Particular Punishment: Trying the Atrocities of the Japanese Occupation as Treason in the Philippines, 1947–1953." *Comparativ*, vol. 23, no. 3, pp. 57–77.
5. Margherita Zanasi, "Globalizing Hanjian: The Suzhou Trials and the Post–World War II Discourse on Collaboration," The *American Historical Review*, vol. 113, no. 3 (June 1, 2008), p. 733. Rob Wilson and Wimal Dissanayake, *Global/Local: Cultural Production and the Transnational Imaginary* (Durham: Duke University Press, 1996), 2.
6. Vicente L. Rafael, "Reorientations Notes on the Study of the Philippines in the United States." *Philippine Studies,* vol. 56, no. 4 (2008), p. 485.
7. For example, David J. Steinberg, "Jose P. Laurel: A 'Collaborator' Misunderstood." *The Journal of Asian Studies,* vol. 24, no. 4 (1965), pp. 651–65. One of the most recent examples of this is Jeremy A. Yellen, "The Two Pacific Wars: Visions of Order and Independence in Japan, Burma, and the Philippines, 1940–1945." PhD diss., Harvard University, 2012.
8. This is not limited to non-Western colonial examples. We might note that similar choices faced Ukrainians in Europe, as well as many other irredentist and minority causes in the European context.
9. The exception was a wartime Minister of Justice and Minister of Home Affairs, Teofilo Sison, who was sentenced to life in July, 1946. Steinberg, *Philippine Collaboration in World War II*, 136.
10. In the majority opinion by Robert H. Jackson in the 5–4 US Supreme Court ruling of 1944, Cramer vs. U.S. Paul Finkelman, Melvin I. Urofsky, and United States. Supreme Court, *Landmark Decisions of the United States Supreme Court* (Washington, DC: CQ Press, 2003), 219.
11. Steinberg's *Philippine Collaboration* provides a good overview of the background of the People's Court.
12. See Appendix B of Konrad M. Lawson, "Wartime Atrocities and the Politics of Treason in the Ruins of the Japanese Empire, 1937–1953." PhD diss., Harvard University, 2012, 366–70 for a table very close to this number, which was eventually to receive Supreme Court rulings.
13. Proclamation no. 51, "A Proclamation Granting Amnesty." *Official Gazette* http://www.gov.ph/1948/01/28/proclamation-no-51-2/ (last accessed 28 November 2016).
14. I have explored these postamnesty trials in Konrad Lawson, "Universal Crime, Particular Punishment."
15. American Embassy, Manila to Secretary of State, Despatch No. 176, "Concurrence of the Philippine Congress with the President's Proclamation of Amnesty for Certain Wartime Collaborators" (18 February 1948) RG 59 896.00/2-1848.

16. Republic of Philippines *Congressional Record: House of Representatives* vol. 3, no. 15 (13 February 1948), 330.
17. *Ibid.*, 334.
18. *Ibid.*, 346.
19. In a collection of collaborator profile cards attached to State Department RG 59 896.00/2-747, comment dated July 1944.
20. One harsh critic of the political collaborators counts twenty out of ninety-eight members of the early postwar House of Representatives who had served in the wartime national assembly. Abaya, *Betrayal in the Philippines*, 70.
21. *Congressional Record: House of Representatives* vol. 3 no. 15 (13 February 1948), 377.
22. *Ibid.* A portion of this response by de Gaulle can also be found in "Home Problems of France," *The Times*, 28 December 1944, 3.
23. On de Gaulle's perspective on the trials, see Peter Novick, *The Resistance Versus Vichy: The Purge of Collaborators in Liberated France* (London: Chatto & Windus, 1968), 157. On his conduct in the final stage of the Laval trial, Geoffrey Warner, *Pierre Laval and the Eclipse of France* (New York; Macmillan, 1969), 415.
24. Armando J. Malay, "Osias Clashes with Pendatun On Amnesty," newspaper clipping attached to American Embassy, Manila to Secretary of State, Despatch No. 176 (18 February 1948) RG 59 896.00/2-1848.
25. Rafael, Vicente L., *White Love and Other Events in Filipino History* (Durham: Duke University Press, 2000), 110. *Congressional Record*, vol. 3, no. 15 (13 February 1948), 383.
26. *Congressional Record: House of Representatives*, vol. 3, no. 12 (10 February 1948), 211.
27. *Congressional Record: House of Representatives*, 215. Laval and Quisling were shot in October 1945. Karl Hermann Frank was publicly hanged and Mussert shot in May 1946. The wartime Slovakian leader Jozef Tiso was hanged in April 1947. However, Samonte was wrong about Leon Maria Joseph Ignace Degrelle, who escaped capture and fled to Spain.
28. *Ibid*, 212.
29. *Ibid.*, vol. 3 no. 13 (11 February 1948), 243.
30. *Ibid.*, vol. 3 no. 8 (4 February 1948), 86. These numbers are not mutually exclusive. It is not clear how many individuals the cases covered since most individuals were prosecuted on multiple counts of treason that could fall into more than one category.
31. *Ibid.*, vol. 3 no. 13 (11 February 1948), 242–43.
32. *Ibid.*, 249.
33. *Ibid.*, 212.
34. *Ibid.*, no. 14 (12 February 1948), 286.

35. For work in English on the prosecution of Japanese war criminals in Philippine courts, see Sharon Williams Chamberlain, "Justice and Reconciliation: Postwar Philippine Trials of Japanese War Criminals in History and Memory" (Ph.D. diss., George Washington University, 2010).
36. "Tañada Blasts Amnesty Move: 'Unjust, Vauge': Favors Top Men, Leaves Lowly to Suffer Penalties," newspaper clipping attached to American Embassy, Manila to Secretary of State, Despatch No. 176 (18 February 1948), RG 59 896.00/2-1848.
37. Santos would later join the Nacionalistas, serve as defense secretary, and run against Marcos for president in 1981. The Huks were declared illegal by Roxas on 6 March 1948. "The President's Month in Review: March 1948." *Official Gazette* http://www.gov.ph/1948/03/01/official-month-in-review-march-1948/ (last accessed 28 November 2016).
38. *Congressional Record: House of Representatives,* no. 14 (12 February 1948), 293–4.
39. *Ibid.*, 298.
40. *Ibid.*, 303.
41. See, for example, Recto's defense of the wartime collaborators in Claro Recto, *Three Years of Enemy Occupation: The Issue of Political Collaboration in the Philippines* (Manila: Cacho Hermanos, 1985).
42. Francis Harrison, *Diary of Francis Burton Harrison*, 13 June 1942 republished on the *Philippine Diary Project* http://philippinediaryproject.com/1942/06/13/june-13-1942-3/ (last accessed 28 November 2016).
43. *Congressional Record: House of Representatives* no. 13 (11 February 1948), 262.
44. *Ibid.*, 263.
45. *Ibid.*
46. Vicente Rafael, *White Love,* 111–12.
47. See Florentino Rodao, "Spanish Falange in the Philippines, 1936–1945," *Philippine Studies* 43, no. 1 (1 March 1995), 3–26.
48. *Congressional Record: House of Representatives* no. 14 (12 February 1948), 278–9, 284.
49. *Ibid.*, 278.
50. The debate would emerge again when Quirino pardoned several hundred collaborators still in prison in 1953.
51. The 1948 cost is quoted by Toribio Perez in ibid., vol. 3 no. 8 (4 February 1948), 84. The 1946 budget for the People's Court is in Republic Act No. 1 "An Act Appropriating Funds for the Operation of the Government of the Commonwealth of the Philippines Beginning July First, Nineteen Hundred and Forty-Six Until the General Appropriations Act For the Fiscal Year Nineteen Hundred and Forty-Seven Is Approved" http://www.lawphil.net/statutes/repacts/ra1946/

ra_1_1946.html (last accessed 28 November 2016). The 1947 revenue estimate is from "Message on the National Budget for the Fiscal Year 1947–1948" (11 February 1947) *Official Gazette* http://www.gov.ph/1947/02/11/message-of-president-roxas-on-the-national-budget-for-the-fiscal-year-1947-1948/ (last accessed 28 November 2016).

52. Reynaldo C. Ileto, "Orientalism and the Study of Philippine Politics." *Philippine Political Science Journal* 22, no. 45 (1 December 2001), 1–32.

Konrad M. Lawson has a broad interest in the aftermaths of modern war, and most of his research has been on the continuities and transformations of the 1940s transwar period. His first book manuscript explores the relationship between war crimes and treason in retribution against the military and police collaborators who helped maintain Japan's wartime occupations in East and Southeast Asia up until its defeat in 1945. Other topics of interest are the global history of political retribution, early post-WWII Scandinavia, decolonization in East and Southeast Asia, the colonial and postcolonial histories of Korea and Taiwan, Sino-Japanese cultural and political relations, and the transnational history of encounters and interactions with and within Asia.

Japanese Medical Atrocities and the Collaboration of the Scientific Elites: Postwar Perspectives

Arnaud Doglia

This chapter seeks to discuss the legacy in Japan of bacteriological/chemical warfare and medical atrocities after 1945.[1] The military elites of the Japanese Empire had plans to build a biological arsenal since 1917. Such weapons were developed in Japan and throughout the empire between 1919 and the end of World War II and used on several occasions on the continent, against both civilian populations and enemy troops. Numerous medical experiments, including vivisections of living human beings and frostbite experiments, were also performed throughout East Asia as part of an effort to develop both weapons of mass destruction and the means to improve the living conditions of Japanese troops on the battlefield.

It is in this context that, under the cover name "Epidemic Prevention and Water Purification Department of the Kwantung Army" (*Kantō gun bōeki kyūsui bu*), Unit 731 was set up and led starting in 1932 by Major Ishii Shirō. This secret corps, based in a military camp established in the village of Pingfan, twenty-four kilometers south of Harbin, was until the end of the war the core agent in a system of bacteriological and chemical

A. Doglia (✉)
Department of East Asian Studies, University of Geneva, Geneva, Switzerland
e-mail: arnaud.doglia@unige.ch

K. von Lingen (ed.), *Debating Collaboration and Complicity in War Crimes Trials in Asia, 1945–1956*, World Histories of Crime, Culture and Violence, DOI 10.1007/978-3-319-53141-0_7

warfare entities active throughout the puppet state of Manchukuo and China, as well as in Southeast Asia.[2] These units must be understood as a real network working within the Japanese Empire. They were responsible not only for the use of biological warfare in several areas of the continent but also for research on the effects of immunology in various climates.[3] The experiments conducted there can be broadly divided into five main categories: (1) surgery practice, (2) immunology experiments aimed at the discovery of unknown pathogen sources, (3) immunology experiments on the infectious capacity of pathogens, (4) experiments for the development of new therapies, and (5) experiments for the development of vaccines and drugs.[4]

However, these entities were not composed solely of army physicians. As the process of institutionalization grew in size, Ishii and others recruited in major universities throughout Japan. The scientific establishment provided lists containing the names of the most brilliant and promising researchers. Each year, Ishii delivered a series of lectures at universities in Japan to encourage students and researchers to enroll, for example in April 1943 at the University of Kanazawa, where he presented a "lecture on Japanese culture" (*Nihon bunka kōgi*) entitled "Epidemic Prevention on the Continent" (*Tairiku ni okeru bōeki nitsuite*).[5] In 1938, a first group of eight scientists from Kyoto Imperial University joined Unit 731, and as of 1939, total staff amounted to 10,045. In 1945, over 2,000 of them had civilian backgrounds.[6]

It is difficult to establish a precise number of the casualties caused by Japanese biological warfare, for several reasons. First of all, not all documents are available, and they probably never will be. Although there is ample evidence to attest to the existence of the crimes committed, the Japanese ordered the destruction of most material related to Unit 731 in 1945, and there is no certainty that what fell in the hands of the Soviet Union, China, and others has been made fully available to historians.[7] Some estimate that less than 0.1 percent of the remaining Imperial Japanese Army and Navy documents material ordered for destruction survived.[8]

The nature of the atrocities must equally be taken into account. Between 1940 and 1945, at least 3,000 human beings were killed in vivisections and experiments conducted in structures related to Unit 731.[9] But there is little clarity as to how many more died at the hands of the Japanese army in other camps, before 1940, and in the Chinese countryside. The events of the village of Songshan, in the Zhejiang province, are a case in point, among countless others that remain undocumented. In 1943, villagers who did not succumb to the plague were vivisected by the Japanese.[10]

Furthermore, if some cases of epidemics on the continent were the result of germ warfare organized by Unit 731 (such as the attack on the city of Ningpo on 10 September 1940), others are not proven and could have natural causes.[11] These parameters prevent a clear and precise estimate of the total number of victims. It has, however, generally been accepted by serious historians that "no less than 3,000" victims represents the least problematic figure.[12]

The formal entry of the Soviet Union into war with Japan on 8 August 1945 marked the beginning of the end for the imperial biological warfare program. On the same day, orders were given to destroy all evidence related to illegal activities near the Russian border. On 10 August, Tokyo ordered the Kwantung Army's chief of staff to dispose of all proofs of the use of biological weapons, to destroy the structures, and to evacuate the remaining 1,700 employees and their families.[13] Personnel were given cyanide in order to commit suicide in case of capture by Soviet troops. The remaining prisoners (an estimated 400 people) who were scheduled to be used in experiments were executed and their bodies cremated. On 16 August, instruction was received to burn all confidential documents in the boiler rooms of the Pingfan camp, a task never achieved owing to the large volume of material and bodies. The Soviet army reached Pingfan on the 17 August, earlier than expected, thereby gaining access to the remaining archives.

However, Ishii and the other leaders of the Japanese biological warfare program had already been evacuated (with their most important documents) on 9 August and arrived in Japan on the 26th. Ishii was put under house arrest in January 1946 by the Americans, who visited him no less than eight times in a couple of months.[14] Naitō Ryōichi, formerly head of Unit 9420, a research detachment in Singapore linked to Unit 731, was also detained at home. Wakamatsu Yūjirō, director of subsidiary Unit 100, in charge of animal research, was demobilized and repatriated. Kitano Masaji, formerly head of Unit 1644 in Nanjing, was arrested in Shanghai and put on board an American airplane in January 1946 to Tokyo, where he was interrogated by U.S. intelligence.[15]

Occupation authorities had no intention of indicting the elites of Unit 731. First, they were looking for criminals who could be punished with visibility. The International Tribunal for the Far East in Tokyo was to serve the same function of international justice as what had taken place in

Nuremberg. Second, both the political and the military leaders wished to punish the military clique, and not the scientific community, whose exact role remained unclear. The Allies needed generals and leaders responsible for obvious brutalities. A conspiracy to wage war, war crimes, or crimes against humanity reflected the narrative brought forward by the winner, according to which "militarism and militaristic institutions [...] have brought disaster on the Japanese."[16]

American suspicions that the Japanese army might have been using biological weapons had already emerged in 1941. Initially, those concerns were not given the utmost attention because "intelligence suggested a BW [biological weapons] threat that appeared limited and was not believed to be an immediate threat to military operations."[17] However, in 1945, Japanese bacteriological research had become invaluable in the eyes of Washington scientists: until then, it had been thought that such weapons were impossible to develop.[18] This line of thinking led American experts to push for the immunity from prosecution of war crimes of the main Japanese culprits and to bargain for their data in exchange for freedom and money.

The final report of Edwin V. Hill, the scientist who led the last of several missions to Japan in 1947 to gather several thousand pages of autopsy reports, clearly explains why none of the Japanese researchers were ever indicted during the Tokyo Trial:

> Evidence gathered in this investigation has greatly supplemented and amplified previous aspects of this field. It represents data which have been obtained by Japanese scientists at the expenditure of many millions of dollars and years of work. Information had accrued with respect to human susceptibility to those diseases as indicated by specific infectious doses of bacteria. Such information could not be obtained in our own laboratories because of scruples attached to human experimentation. These data were secured with a total outlay of ¥250,000 to date, a mere pittance by comparison with the actual cost of the studies.[19]

On 7 May 1947, Ishii started his collaboration with the United States. A few months later, "8,000 slides representing pathological sections derived from more than 200 human cases of disease caused by various B.W. agents" that had been "concealed in temples and buried in the mountains of southern Japan" were made available to American scientists. On 22 November, directive SCAPIN-1699 granted Ishii and all his colleagues complete immunity, as well as a sum of ¥250,000.[20]

Washington's interest in Japanese science did not stop there, and in 1946, occupation authorities set up Unit 406. This structure, originally dedicated to the improvement of sanitary conditions in occupied Japan, was quickly expanded throughout the country. In 1951, it was employing over a hundred Japanese physicians and technicians, including former Unit 731 members such as Kitano Masaji and Asanuma Kiyoshi.

The participation of Japanese scientists was inevitable, notably because, regardless of their crimes, only these men possessed the technical knowhow and expertise required to perform serious scientific research. Furthermore, from an institutional perspective, some of the activities of Unit 406 were handed down to the National Institute of Preventive Health (*Kokuritsu yobō eisei kenkyūjo*, currently *Kokuritsu kansenshō kenkyūjo*, the National Institute of Infectious Diseases). Between 1947 and 1983, seven of eight directors of this institution, as well as six of eight vice directors, were former collaborators of Ishii.[21]

The fact that none of these men were tried does not mean that there were no plans to indict them initially, although the idea was quickly abandoned. On 29 August 1946, during a discussion of the Nanjing Massacre at the International Tribunal for the Far East in Tokyo, Associate Prosecutor David Sutton mentioned the existence of Unit 1644 in Nanjing and the testing of poisonous serums on civilian prisoners.[22] Chief Judge William Webb asked for further evidence that Sutton could not provide, and the matter was dropped, the defense further claiming that it was part of a vaccination program for the Chinese population.

The material documenting the removal of evidence by the American administration is almost comical:

> 1. The subject documents were charged out to the Chinese Division on the 6th of November 1946 and have never been returned. 2. The Chinese Division say [*sic*] that these documents were turned over to the Philippine Division by them. 3. The Philippine Division claims that they turned the documents over to Mr. D. N. Sutton. 4. Mr. Sutton claims no knoledge [*sic*] of the documents what soever [*sic*]. 5. This matter is turned over to your office for action.[23]
>
> 1. It is true that these documents covering bacteriological warfare in China were once turned over to me after Chief of Counsel had asked me to make a study on it but later those documents were turned over to Mr. Sutton, then back to the Chinese Division. My last recollection of them is that Mr. Chu of the Chinese Division took the document to the Russian Division in order to sound the opinion of the Russian Associate Prosecutor

> whether two Japanese nationals who are in Russia could be made available for interrogation here.[24]

The American cover-up was not limited to bacteriological warfare but also concerned chemical warfare. For the United States, since both weapons had been employed interdependently on the battlefield, the prosecution of the use of both of them had to be abandoned and erased from public view. This was particularly obvious when American intelligence produced a report following research in China indicating that ultimate responsibility for the development and use of bacteriological and gas warfare was to be found at the highest level of government.

> This matter, as well as the poison gas episodes, assumes importance because of the obvious impossibility of developing such methods of warfare on the field of battle or through the resources of an army general in the field, and indicated that such prohibited methods of warfare were carried on by the Tokyo Government and not the field commanders.[25]

However, no further action was taken at the International Tribunal for the Far East. The author of the report, Thomas Morrow, resigned in August 1946 and returned to the United States. This episode marked the end of the cover-up at the Tokyo Trial, and, except for a few isolated cases, no further legal actions were initiated regarding Japanese biological warfare.[26] All these elements made it even easier for the scientific community to reintegrate the postwar medical establishment, some of these men posing as victims of the "irresponsible militarism" that had led them to commit atrocities.[27]

In the Soviet Union, things took a different turn. Moscow had known about Unit 731 since it entered the war (and Manchuria) in 1945. Soviet authorities started to build a case after accessing archives in Pingfan and capturing Japanese personnel. In 1946, the USSR was primarily interested in Ishii. A meeting with Soviet representatives was arranged in Tokyo, under American supervision, in spring 1947, but with little success. The demand for extradition submitted by Moscow obviously did not succeed either. However, the documents acquired in Manchuria and the testimonies of captured Japanese staff proved much more conclusive.

Between 25 and 30 December 1949, the Khabarovsk War Crimes Trials took place in the eponymous city of Khabarovsk, strategically located in the Soviet Far East and close to China (and Japan). Twelve former Japanese servicemen accused of having manufactured and used bacteriological warfare were put on trial, and their testimonies were corroborated by eleven more Japanese witnesses.[28] They were charged on four indictments: the organization of specific biological warfare units, criminal experiments on living human subjects, the use of bacteriological weapons against China, and preparation for the use of bacteriological weapons against the USSR.[29] The verdict was handed down on 30 December 1949. All twelve defendants were found guilty and sentenced to prison terms ranging from two to twenty-five years. In 1956, all those still alive and serving time were repatriated to Japan.

From abroad, the Khabarovsk Trial was immediately viewed as Soviet propaganda. The defense, the prosecution, and the judges, as well as the interpreters, were all Soviet citizens. Similarly, Moscow insisted on the ultimate culpability of the Japanese emperor and did not hesitate to glorify its own actions, claiming for instance that the "Soviet Union had saved mankind from the horrors of bacteriological warfare [...] and that the Japanese aggression only ended with the decisive defeat inflicted by the Soviet Army the Kwantung Army."[30] This certainly contributed to discrediting the impact of the trial overseas. The brevity of the event (especially when compared to the lengthy International Tribunal for the Far East) did not help either. At the same time, the trial heralded a period of growing rivalry between Washington and Moscow, with State Counsel for Prosecution in Khabarovsk Smirnov mentioning Associate Prosecutor David Sutton's comment during the Tokyo Trial and the subsequent cover-up in his plea. From Moscow's perspective, Khabarovsk was to be understood as justice vetted by the Soviet Union against the culprits, who had been granted immunity by the Americans.

In Japan, the reception of the Khabarovsk Trial and the discourses on medical and biological atrocities were not immediately obvious in the aftermath of the defeat, but they were not nonexistent either. In the first years of the occupation, General Headquarters (GHQ) was firmly in control. The Japanese government was very slow in providing information that the Americans had requested from them. The Allies had to wait until November 1946 to be given a single sheet of paper containing Ishii's name, date of birth, home address, and military records.[31]

However, the Japanese population proved to be a rather active source of information on Unit 731 in the years immediately following 1945. In the first weeks following the beginning of the occupation, hundreds of letters of denunciation landed on MacArthur's desk, and some of them openly mentioned medical atrocities. Some former servicemen even volunteered to secretly infiltrate Ishii's network to investigate.[32] Japanese expectations that justice would be served were high, especially from the Communist side. On 14 December 1945, two weeks after it was officially resurrected by the Allies, the Japanese Communist Party informed U.S. authorities of the existence of a network responsible for biological warfare and medical crimes.[33] This was the first of many steps taken by the Communists to pursue their hunt for war criminals in postwar Japan. Initially, these declarations were a helpful addition to the American search for the elites of the biological warfare program.

However, Communist enthusiasm was such that information started to leak out. In January 1946, the *New York Times* and the *Pacific Stars and Stripes* revealed the existence of a Japanese program of biological warfare.[34] Censorship was swiftly but discretely enforced in the public sphere in Japan and the United States, but it was also hoped that keeping the topic temporarily secret could help the Americans exert pressure on the main culprits, should they refuse to collaborate.

Censoring war atrocities (and more specifically medical crimes) was successful in the immediate postwar years. Japanese dailies seldom mentioned the topic, except for *Akahata*, the voice of the Communist Party. From December 1945 until summer 1946, the newspaper published a regular column entitled "Let's resolutely pursue war criminals" (*Sensō hanzai nin wo tekkei teki tsuikyū shiro*), asking potential witnesses throughout the country for help.[35] Originally, the emperor was the main focus of the hunt orchestrated by *Akahata*. Between December and March, several front-page articles accused Hirohito of war crimes.[36]

However, with the opening of the International Tribunal for the Far East on 3 May 1946, testimonies started to appear regularly in the newspaper. Anonymous letters detailed the crimes committed and revealed the names of the culprits, up to the involvement of the imperial family.[37]

> [. . .] During the present war, former Lt Gen ISHII, Shiro, an Army medical doctor, established a large scale human experimental station in the suburbs of HARBIN [. . .] and carried out brutal experiments on many Allied PsW. [. . .] The placing of his name on the war crimes suspect lists was inevitable, but lately, he has been using bribes to escape the consequences. [I am myself] a peaceful Japanese who respects the authority of the Allied Headquarters and request that the progress of the trial be made public [. . .].[38]

As embarrassing as they were for an administration trying to hide the crimes committed from the Japanese population, these confessions were precious to the men dispatched by Washington, culminating in the aforementioned report of Edwin V. Hill in 1947.

The minutes of the Khabarovsk War Crimes Trials, published by Moscow in 1950 in English, French, Chinese, and Japanese, were not widely accepted. It is difficult to estimate with precision their impact in Japan at the time. It is very likely that the minutes were brought into the country by the Communist Party in order to substantiate its hunt for war criminals. Nonetheless, two factors indicate that the outcome of Khabarovsk went relatively unnoticed worldwide, and more specifically in Japan.[39] First, the archipelago was still occupied by the Allies, who had secretly given Ishii and his colleagues immunity. Discussing the topic of biological warfare publicly was not an option if GHQ wanted to keep the deal they had just offered to the Japanese under wraps.

Second, in the growing context of the Cold War, American authorities feared that the result of the trial could benefit the public image of the Soviet Union internationally, especially in Japan. GHQ therefore decided to discredit the event further, not only by labeling it Soviet propaganda but also by depicting the trial as Moscow's strategy to hide more pressing issues, such as the situation of Japanese war prisoners in the Soviet Union, at the time estimated by Washington to be around 376,000 men. The Americans, with the help of the Japanese media, were usually successful in their endeavor. For example, on 22 November 1949, a large crowd gathered in front of the Soviet embassy in Tokyo demanding answers about the situation of war prisoners in Siberia. The final blow was delivered in the press a couple of days later:

> A spokesman for Gen. Douglas MacArthur's headquarters said today that the chemical section of this headquarters, in a "complete" search of its files, "did not find anything related to Japanese use of bacteriological warfare."[40]

The Japanese press temporarily paid attention to the start of the trial. On 27 December, the *Yomiuri Shimbun* published on its front page a Soviet press release announcing that the procedure had begun in Khabarovsk, with a figure of "3,000 victims" (*giseisha ha 3000 nin*).

However, the official narrative launched by GHQ had paid off. The press release was accompanied by another article, dedicated to U.S.–Soviet negotiations for the repatriation of Japanese prisoners of war.[41] The next day, Khabarovsk was relegated to the bottom of the page, in the form of a press release from Paris. Subsequent articles did not make the front page and were accompanied by news about Japanese prisoners and the Allied occupation. The same pattern applied to other newspapers. Throughout the duration of the trial, the *Asahi Shimbun* and the *Mainichi Shimbun* both published press releases regularly, systematically followed by American communiqués of flat denial. By 1 January 1950, the topic had disappeared from the media.

As could be expected, *Akahata* was the only one to devote regular front-page attention to Khabarovsk until February 1950. The names of the defendants and the details of the crimes committed were frequently printed, along with Ishii's name. This allowed readers to follow almost in real time the proceedings in the Soviet Union and to acknowledge the "repentance deep in the heart of each of the accused" (*Kaku hikoku kokoro kara no kaigo wo kataru*), as well as their "gratitude for the treatment by the Soviet Union" (*So dōmei no taigū ni kansha*).[42]

Articles on the topic continued to be published until late February. On 20 February, the links between Ishii and his colleagues in the academic world were exposed, along with the existence of a branch of Unit 731 in Niigata Prefecture.[43] This would be the last mention of the Japanese biological warfare program in the newspaper during the occupation. In June 1950, the Red Purge by GHQ led to the interruption of publication of *Akahata* and of any replacement newspaper. In the immediate postwar period, the Communist Party did not represent the majority of the Japanese population, which seemed to be satisfied with information provided under American guidance. However, the number of articles published by *Akahata* and elsewhere in the first five years following defeat indicates that the topic of the memories of medical atrocities had already been introduced to Japanese society.

The "unpursued" crimes of Unit 731 had become a hobbyhorse of the Japanese Communist Party in the media and occasionally in the world of politics. On 1 March 1950, a Communist Diet member remarked during a session:

> I would like to address the issue of war crimes linked to bacteriological weapons. This concerns mostly the Ministry of Justice, but the Ministry of Foreign Affairs has also been contacted, and we would like their answer. The issue was raised at the Khabarovsk War Crimes Trials [. . .] and evidence showed that [. . .] the Kwantung Army [. . .] conducted experiments on

> Chinese and Soviet citizens, as well as American POWs. Several thousand were used as human guinea pigs in this process. Furthermore, it seems that parts of this arsenal were used in China. [...] We would like to know if the government has further information on this issue.[44]

The Speaker replied:

> I am not aware of the details of the issue [...] you are raising. I can however tell you that this is a legal affair, and that the trials for war crimes related to the actions of the Japanese were conducted by the Allies, in accordance with the plans laid out by the Potsdam Declaration. Therefore, it seems that the question of bacteriological war crimes that you are currently raising does not fall within the competence of the government.[45]

A few months later, the Diet member was dismissed from the political sphere following the Red Purge. Despite censorship and the lack of visibility of the Khabarovsk Trial, these occurrences marked the beginning of a process whereby Unit 731 would gradually be discussed publicly in the coming decades.

In the general debate on war crimes and responsibilities in the 1960s and 1970s Japan, biological and medical atrocities committed by the Imperial Army did not hold a particular status. Communist interventions aside, such crimes were generally not addressed publicly. The idea expressed in the last citation, according to which justice had been administered by the winner(s), was commonly accepted. Nevertheless, beyond the narrative of "irresponsible militarism" set in place by the Allies, other reasons explained the absence of a debate on war atrocities, and more specifically on Unit 731.

First, the vast majority of the Japanese people were unaware of the existence of biological warfare, a very technical concept that only the scientific community was qualified enough to address. This perspective is especially obvious in popular media. In the aftermath of Hiroshima and Nagasaki, and amid the rising tensions of the Cold War, the subject of the discoveries of modern science being used to create weapons regularly made the news. Nuclear warfare represented the primary source of concern for the people, but on two separate occasions, the topic of biological weapons was introduced to readers.

In 1949, an article entitled "Bacteriological Weapons Are Fearful" (*Kowaru beki saikin heiki*) was published in *Sekai hōkoku*. The responsibilities of the Japanese and American governments were not discussed. Rather, these weapons were presented as a much more dangerous threat than what had happened in Hiroshima and Nagasaki, thereby comforting the population in their status of victim of the war: "an ounce was enough to kill 200 million people in a single attack." However, the development of biological weapons was also depicted as beneficial for Japan. A certain "Dr. Rosebery" explained that such means were currently being researched by the United States Navy and could potentially be used against the enemy. It would replace nuclear weapons, should World War III break out. [46] In 1952, another publication confirmed the general ignorance of the population. It stated that chemical weapons had been used during World War I, but "rarely" during World War II, because of the "humanism" that had characterized the last conflict. The use of bacteriological weapons was not even envisaged, not only because it had been forbidden by international conventions (The Hague in 1899, Geneva in 1925), but also because scientists did not possess sufficient knowledge to manufacture them. Bacteriological warfare was simply described as a "possibility" (*saikin sen no kanōsei*).[47]

Second, it is necessary to consider the human networks that survived the defeat of Japan. The scientists, physicians, and technicians who invented, manufactured, and performed experiments were still alive and had returned home. They reintegrated themselves into the scientific community, and the links they had established during (and before) the war were very much alive. In 1950, former head of Unit 9420 Naitō Ryōichi founded the first Japanese blood bank with two previous colleagues, Miyamoto Kōichi and Futagi Hideo. The former had been director in Harbin of a Japanese company that had secretly supplied equipment to the Japanese biological program, while the latter was an army physician who had served in Unit 731.[48] Kitano Masaji was later hired by Naitō to manage one of his factories in Tokyo.[49] Faced with the dire consequences of defeat, the technical knowhow of these men was seen as indispensable for Japan's reconstruction efforts. The establishment of the National Institute of Preventive Health and similar institutions devoted to the public health infrastructure of the country and the advancement of science attests to this.

The vast majority of members of the scientific community were therefore perfectly aware of the atrocities committed. These crimes had been perpetrated by themselves, their colleagues, students, or mentors, and some felt free to publish the results of their research after the war, openly mentioning their affiliation with Unit 731 or the details of experiments. In a 1963 publication in the *Japanese Medical Journal* (*Nihon iji shinpō*), Kitano circulated the results of his wartime Manchuria research, directly naming his colleagues and the existence of specific units.[50] The extent of the network was such that they were never under scrutiny: until historians began in the 1980s to expose publicly those former war criminals who had not passed away already, the general public did not understand or care about the details of these technical publications.

Third, those who wanted to publicly acknowledge their crimes were called liars and treated with contempt. In summer 1956, 1,017 Japanese war prisoners returned home. These men had been detained in Communist Chinese jails, and the "humane" treatment they had received pushed a portion of these men to take responsibility for the atrocities they had taken part in. A year later, some of these veterans formed an association to seek repentance and published *The Three All: Japanese Confessions of War Crimes in China*, a book detailing their deeds.[51] A first print run of 50,000 copies was bought up within three weeks. But the sensation caused by the vivid descriptions of atrocities caused disbelief in a society that was not yet ready to publicly face its past. The editor gave in to pressure and threats from right-wing lobbies and veterans and withdrew the book from circulation.[52]

All attempts by former members of the Japanese Imperial Army to set the record straight were regularly met with disbelief, and these men, misaligned in a society that in siding with the United States had forgotten the crimes committed on the continent, were labeled "brainwashed Communists." Until the normalization of relations with Communist China in the 1970s, World War II in Japan could only be remembered as a heroic act, centered on relations with the former Anglo-Saxon enemy.[53]

It was only through literature that the topic managed to surface in early postwar Japan. Early works were published using pseudonyms. The names of the protagonists were changed, and the novels sometimes included fictional elements. Ironically, these publications appeared sensationalist to the public, but the fact that they were labeled as "fiction" avoided confrontation with the narrative in place. Unlike *The Three All, Japanese Confessions of War Crimes in China*, testimonies of medical wartime atrocities transformed into literary accounts could be read in books and magazines available to all.[54]

In turn, these publications attracted the interest of historian Ienaga Saburō, who explicitly mentioned Unit 731 and other war atrocities in his history textbook. Starting in 1965, the ensuing lawsuits he initiated against the Japanese state garnered regular media attention.[55] In parallel, journalists, intrigued by the growing rumors of atrocities, published their findings as nonfiction works or televised documentaries featuring interviews with veterans.[56]

These documents prompted more reactions of veterans in Japanese society. Some threatened their authors, but a growing number offered their testimonies, triggering international collaboration between journalists in Japan and abroad. American reporter John Powell, who had accused Washington of using bacteriological warfare during the Korean War, worked together with Yoshinaga Haruko, amassing over 20,000 pages of classified documents.[57] By the 1980s, historians such as Tsuneishi Keiichi had entered the debate and unearthed documents to prove the existence of Unit 731. By the mid-1990s, lengthy lawsuits against the Japanese state were being conducted (either by individuals or associations of Chinese and Japanese citizens), demanding justice and compensation.[58] Japanese biological warfare had become an issue hotly debated in the public sphere.

The aim of this chapter was to present the reasons and context behind the absence of Allied war crimes trials regarding Unit 731. The memories of medical atrocities and biological warfare did not easily surface in postwar Japanese society. From a legal perspective, the issue was moribund from the start. It had been buried by the Americans, the Soviet Union only had a limited impact, and the existence of the Chinese victims had not yet been acknowledged.[59] From a scientific point of view, the official narrative was one of silent reconversion. By tacit mutual agreement, the medical and technical establishment turned a blind eye to the research that mentioned the atrocities. From a social angle, the authenticity of the veterans' confessions was too painful and realistic to be given any credit, and the commitment of the Communists was dismissed as propaganda.

Unit 731 was not the most pressing matter in Japan throughout the postwar decades. Nevertheless, the nonexistence of Allied justice did not signify that the issue had been entirely avoided. Rather, it remained a continuous narrative, uttered by very diverse groups, varying only in intensity over time, until it came to be recognized as another case of colonial violence.

Indeed, Japan used gas warfare for the first time during a colonial war. In the aftermath of the Wushe Incident of October 1930 in Taiwan, the Imperial Army air-dropped phosgene, yperite, and hydrogen cyanide to quash the revolt of the Seediq population, killing over 700. In 1932, Tokyo justified the use of certain types of gas, arguing that it was a case of colonial rebellion, strictly under Japanese sovereignty.[60] The same year, the Kwantung Army obtained from Tokyo the right to officially use tear gas in Manchukuo in the name of "internal police measures" (*kokunai keisatsu kōi*).[61] Lethal or not, the use of chemical weapons was institutionalized as an imperial strategy against colonial subjects and the Chinese enemy alike (starting in July 1937).

The same is true of bacteriological warfare. Such weapons were deployed for the first time during the war of Nomonhan against Soviet troops in 1939, followed a year later by massive campaigns until 1942, involving the contamination of wells and the spread of typhus and cholera, especially in Zhejiang Province, in order to crush the Communist guerrillas. These "research" programs were established to equip troops with these new weapons, and vivisections, as well as other experiments, were performed on non-Japanese human beings to improve the survivability of imperial troops on the battlefield.

However, Japanese medical and biological atrocities also need to be considered outside the prism of imperial violence. The experiments that led to the institutionalization of Unit 731 were mostly conducted by men who took the opportunity they had been given by the state to conduct large-scale trials outside of the theoretical framework of their laboratories. Altogether, over a hundred tests involving chemical weapons were conducted throughout Japan and in Taiwan (1928) and Korea (1930), for a total of forty-one times between 1925 and 1945. The order to deploy gas warfare in Taiwan in 1930 did not emanate from the general staff in Tokyo but from the army research central laboratory on colonial soil.[62]

Similarly, in Nomonhan, the use of bacteriological agents was above all a large-scale trial. Japanese scientists knew that the typhoid bacillus they spread would lose its infectivity when placed in water, and even though the war against Soviet troops was a military disaster for the Kwantung Army, announcing the crushing blow of August 1945, the operation was labeled a "success" because theoretical and laboratory conclusions matched outdoor testing results. To an extent, the biological weapons dropped on Chinese civilians (1940–1942) also represent large-scale field trials.[63] This is equally true of autopsy reports following the vivisection of living human beings, of central importance to Japanese physicians for analyzing the effects of germs on the body.

Ultimately, the responsibility of the scientific community is therefore just as important as that of its sponsor, the state, in a relation of mutual dependence. This is equally true of the "decolonization" process of Unit 731. Although the Japanese disposed of the victims' bodies, the rest of the process was incomplete. Not only did the Soviet Union acquire documents that could not be destroyed in a timely manner, but the structures also survived. Camps near the Soviet border were only partially dynamited by the Japanese and subsequently served as evidence. Buildings occupied by other units in urban China and Singapore were turned into hospitals after the war. As discussed earlier, prosecutions were minimal. The network of scientists was not dismantled but simply retransplanted back to Japan. In this way, the postwar dismemberment of the Japanese biological warfare program was very much left for other powers to carry out, if it was done at all.

The truth about Japanese war atrocities has long been established. However, the whys and wherefores of the topic still need to be considered today in the light of other judgments. Interpreting these crimes as a *fait accompli* relegated to the past prevents us from grasping the multiplicity of implications of the process of dissolution of the Japanese Empire.

Notes

1. For the purpose of this chapter, the word *biological* is used to mean both bacteriological and chemical warfare.
2. In 1938, Unit 1855 was established in Beijing. A year later, Units 8604 and 1644 were respectively set up in Guangzhou and Nanjing, and Unit 9420 was created in Singapore in 1942. Other institutions must also be taken into account, such as the Dairen production site or the island of Ōkunoshima (near Hiroshima), which welcomed the largest production site of chemical gas of the Japanese army. For details on the establishment of these units, see Tsuneishi Keiichi, *Nana san ichi butai, seibutsu heiki hanzai no jijitsu* (Tokyo: Kodansha, 1995), 28–9. Ōkunoshima is notably discussed in Tatsumi Tomoji, *Kakusareta Hiroshima* (Tokyo: Nihon hyōronsha, 1993).
3. *Materials on the Trial of Former Servicemen of the Japanese Army Charged with Manufacturing and Employing Bacteriological Weapons* (Moscow: Foreign Languages Publishing House, 1950), 50.
4. Tsuneishi, *Nana san ichi butai*, 105.
5. Yoshihata Tooru, "Nana san ichi butai chō Ishii Shirō no nihon bunka kōgi," *Hokuriku shigaku* 51 (2002): 77–8.

6. Tsuneishi Keiichi, "Unit 731 and the Japanese Imperial Army's Biological Warfare Program," in *Japan's Wartime Medical Atrocities: Comparative Inquiries in Science, History, and Ethics*, Nie Jing-Biao et al., eds. (London: Routledge, 2010), 25.
7. Sheldon H. Harris, *Factories of Death: Japanese Biological Warfare, 1932–1945, and the American Cover-Up* (London: Routledge, 1994), 314.
8. Yang Daqin, "Documentary Evidence and Studies of Japanese War Crimes: An Interim Assessment," in *Researching Japanese War Crimes Records, Introductory Essays*, Drea Edward et al., eds. (Washington: National Archives and Records Administration for the Nazi War Crimes and Japanese Imperial Government Records Interagency Working Group, 2006), 24.
9. *Materials on the Trial of Former Servicemen*, 118.
10. Ueda Makoto, *Pesuto to mura, 731 butai no saikin sen to higaisha no torauma* (Tokyo: Fūkyōsha, 2009), 16–7.
11. Imoto Kumao, *Shina jihen sakusen nisshi* (Tokyo: Fuyō Shobō, 1998), 75.
12. Matsumura Takao and Yano Hisashi, *Saiban to rekishi gaku, nana san ichi saikin sen butai wo hōtei kara miru* (Tokyo: Gendai Shokan, 2007), 12.
13. Guan Chenghe, *Nana san ichi butai ga yatte kita mura, Heibō no shakai shi* (Tokyo: Kōchi Shobō, 1997), 18.
14. Tabata Masanori, "Daughter's-Eye View of Lt. Gen. Ishii, Chief of 'Devil's Brigade'," *The Japan Times*, 29 August 1982, 12.
15. Tsuneishi Keiichi, *Hyōteki: Ishii, nana san ichi butai to beigun chōhō katsudō* (Tokyo: Ōtsuki Shoten, 1984), 216.
16. *Basic Initial Post Surrender Directive to Supreme Commander for the Allied Powers for the Occupation and Control of Japan (JCS1380/15)*, article 4e, 3 November 1945, published online at http://www.ndl.go.jp/constitution/e/shiryo/01/036/036tx.html (last accessed 6 May 2015).
17. William H. Cunliffe, ed., *Select Documents on Japanese War Crimes and Japanese Biological Warfare 1934–2006* (College Park: Interagency Working Group, 2006), 4.
18. It must be noted that U.S. interest in Japanese biological weapons was limited to bacteriological warfare and did not extend to chemical weapons. The Japanese army had only used tear gas, nausea gas, phosgene, mustard gas, lewisite, and hydrogen cyanide (one of the components of Zyklon B), which were all well known to the Great Powers after World War I and therefore had no great value. Yoshimi Yoshiaki, *Doku gasu sen to nihon gun* (Tokyo: Iwanami Shoten, 2004), 261–2.
19. Report of Edwin V. Hill, 12 December 1947, in Kondō Shōji, ed., *Nana san ichi butai, saikin sen shiryō shūsei 731* (Tokyo: Kashiwa Shobō, 2003), disc 6, 3.

20. *Brief Summary of New Information About Japanese B.W. Activities, point i.* 20 June 1947, in Cunliffe, *Select Documents*, 48. The details of which scientist received what part of the money is not specified.
21. Takemae Eiji, *The Allied Occupation of Japan* (New York: Continuum, 1983), 427.
22. *International Military Tribunal for the Far East*, 29 August 1946, in Kondō, *Nana san ichi butai*, disc 3, 4546–52.
23. *Central Files Unit to Chief, Document Division*, 2 April 1947, in Kondō, *Nana san ichi butai*, disc 3.
24. *Memorandum for Lt. Ohberg, Acting Chief of Document Division, from Mr. Lopez*, 3 April 1947, in Kondō, *Nana san ichi butai*, disc 3.
25. Col. Thomas H. Morrow to Joseph B. Keenan, *Sino-Japanese War*, 2 March 1946, 12, in Kondō, *Nana san ichi butai*, disc 3.
26. During the War Crime Trials in Hong Kong (1946–48), Australian military authorities condemned two Japanese army officers to death for their role in hydrogen cyanide experiments. A third was absolved. *A471/1*, National Archives of Australia, ACT Regional Office, Canberra, Yoshimi, *Doku gasu sen*, 271. Trials were also conducted in Shenyang and Taiyuan by the Chinese Communist government, after 969 Japanese prisoners were given by the Soviet Union in the name of goodwill, following the signing of the Sino-Soviet Treaty of February 1950. At least nine of these men were linked to Unit 731 or performed vivisections. Although they were all treated with leniency, they denied personal responsibility. For more details and other occurrences, see Suzy Wang, "Medicine-related war crimes trials and post-war politics and ethics," in *Japan's Wartime Medical Atrocities: Comparative Inquiries in Science, History, and Ethics*, Nie Jing-Biao et al., eds. (London: Routledge, 2010), 36–41.
27. *Potsdam Declaration, Proclamation Defining Terms for Japanese Surrender* (Potsdam: 26 July 1945), article 6.
28. *Materials on the Trial of Former Servicemen*, 3, 36–7. According to the chief Russian-Japanese interpreter at the trial, the original date of the event was rushed because Stalin was about to re-introduce the death penalty in early 1950 (abolished in 1947). Since the trial was used as a showcase of "Soviet humanism," the accused had to be treated with leniency. Suzy Wang, "Medicine-Related War Crimes Trials," 41.
29. Boris G. Yudin, "Research on Humans at the Khabarovsk War Crime Trial," in *Japan's Wartime Medical Atrocities: Comparative Inquiries in Science, History, and Ethics*, Nie Jing-Biao et al., eds. (London: Routledge, 2010), 64.
30. *Materials on the Trial of Former Servicemen*, 8, 97, 104, 463. The need to accuse Hirohito (and Japanese capitalism) was obvious in the plea offered by the defense. The political and social system of Japan was to

blame for what had happened, rather than the servicemen themselves, 486–538.

31. Harris, *Factories of Death*, 252.
32. "Japanese War Crimes Records at the National Archives: Research Starting Points," in *Researching Japanese War Crimes Records, Introductory Essays*, Drea Edward et al., eds. (Washington: National Archives and Records Administration for the Nazi War Crimes and Japanese Imperial Government Records Interagency Working Group, 2006), 96.
33. Harris, *Factories of Death*, 260.
34. Harris, *Factories of Death*, 243. GHQ reports available in Kondō, *Nana san ichi butai*, disc 3.
35. "Sensō hanzai nin wo tekkei teki tsuikyū shiro," *Akahata*, December (Day unavailable), 1945, 1.
36. For example, 19 December, 18 February, 16 March.
37. Harris, *Factories of Death*, 251. The direct cousin of Hirohito, Prince Takeda, was a colonel under Ishii's direct orders. After the war, he became president of the Japan Skating Federation. Tsuneishi Keiichi, *Kieta saikin sen butai, Kantō gun dai nana san ichi butai* (Tokyo: Chikuma Shobō, 1981), 116.
38. *Digest of letter from Ueki Hiroshi to General MacArthur*, 11 October 1946, in Cunliffe, *Select Documents on Japanese War Crimes*, 36.
39. In the 1990s, the historian Hata Ikuhiko remembered finding in a second-hand bookshop in the Kanda area in Tokyo a copy of the minutes of the Khabarovsk War Crimes Trials in 1952. This would confirm that the subject had quickly become a thing of the past, or that it was too marginal to be on the shelves of sellers of new books. Hata Ikuhiko, *Shōwa shi no nazo wo ou, jōkan* (Tokyo: Bungei Shunjū, 1999), 361.
40. *Associated Press dispatches from London and Tokyo*, 24 December 1949, Harris, *Factories of Death*, 320.
41. "Giseisha ha 3000 nin," *Yomiuri Shimbun*, 29 December 1949, 1.
42. "So dōmei no taigū ni kansha," *Akahata*, 5 January 1950, 1.
43. "Niigata ni mo atta," *Akahata*, 20 February 1950, 2.
44. "Gun i gakkō sekichi de hakken sareta jinkotsu mondai wo kyūmei suru kai," http://www.geocities.co.jp/Technopolis/9073/index.html (last accessed 25 July 2011).
45. "Gun i gakkō sekichi de hakken sareta jinkotsu mondai wo kyūmei suru kai." This was not the only time that Unit 731 was brought up in the political sphere. The issue was originally addressed on 23 December 1949. Until 2003, the topic has been mentioned 206 times (thirty-seven times between 1949 and 1965). Kojima Toshirō, *Sengo shi no naka no saikin sen to nana san ichi butai* (Nagaoka: Nagaoka Daigaku Shōgai Gakushū Senta, 2004), 73–4, 87–8.

46. "Kowaru beki saikin heiki," *Sekai hōkoku* 21, 1949, 88.
47. Sugi Yasusaburō, "Dokugasu sen to saikin sen," *Shōsetsu kōen*, December 1952, 90.
48. Yoshinaga Haruko, *Nana san ichi: tsuigeki, sonotoki kanbutachi ha...* (Tokyo: Chikuma Shobō, 2001), 250.
49. Aoki Fukiko, *731: Ishii Shirō to saikin sen butai no yami wo abaku* (Tokyo: Shinchō Bunko, 2005), 55–6.
50. Kitano Masaji, "Ryūkō sei shukketsu netsu oosaka shinai ni hassei," *Nihon iji shinpō* 2021 (1963): 19. For more details on this specific topic, see in particular Tsuneishi, *Kieta saikin sen butai.*
51. *Sankō, Nihonjin no Chūgoku ni okeru sensō hanzai no kokuhaku*, Kanki Haruo, ed. (Tokyo: Kōbunsha, 1957).
52. Kasahara Tokushi, *Nankin jiken to sankō sakusen* (Tokyo: Ōtsuki shoten, 1999), 82.
53. This phenomenon is especially obvious in the dramatic increase of war chronicles (*senki mono*) in Japan. In 1945, there was only one such publication, but already thirty-two in 1952 and sixty in 1956. Yoshida Yutaka, *Nihonjin no sensō kan, sengo shi no naka no henyō* (Tokyo: Iwanami Bunko, 2005), 95.
54. Akiyama Hiroshi, "Saikin sen ha junbi sareteita!," *Bungei shunjū*, August 1955, presented the autobiographical testimony of a teenager drafted by Unit 731 and sent to work in Manchuria. It was republished a year later as a book, Akiyama Hiroshi, *Tokushu butai nana san ichi* (Kyoto: San Ichi Shobō, 1956). See also Yoshimura Akira, *Nomi to bakudan* (Tokyo: Bunshun Bunko, 1975), first published in 1970 under the title "Saikin" in the magazine *Gendai.*
55. A detailed account of the lawsuits can be found in Hein Laura and Mark Selden, eds., *Censoring History: Citizenship and Memory in Japan, Germany, and the United States* (Armonk: M.E. Sharpe, 2000).
56. Yoshinaga Haruko directed a series of three documentaries of one hour each, broadcast on TBS (Tōkyō Broadcasting System) between August 1975 and November 1976. The most famous example of written nonfiction is Morimura Sei'ichi, *Akuma no hōshoku* (Tokyo: Kadokawa Bunko, 1983), first serialized in *Akahata* in July 1981.
57. Williams Peter and David Wallace, *Unit 731, Japan's Secret Biological Warfare in World War II* (New York, The Free Press, 1989), 250. His findings were first published in John W. Powell, "Japan's Germ Warfare: The US Cover-up of a War Crime," *Bulletin of Concerned Asian Scholars*, 12,4 (1980).
58. For a detailed account of the involvment of civil society in Japan and of the trials,see Arnaud Doglia,*L'arme biologique japonaise, 1880–2011: réalités historiques et anatomie de la mémoire* (Bern: Peter Lang, 2016), 280–90.

59. Researchers agree today that the fact that the Khabarovsk trial was ideologically biased does not mean the evidence it presented was invalid. Until the 1980s, the minutes were one of the only sources of information on the functioning of the Japanese biological warfare program. Nie Jing-Bao, "The West's Dismissal of the Khabarovsk Trial as 'Communist Propaganda': Ideology, Evidence and International Bioethics,"*Journal of Bioethical Inquiry*, 1,1 (2004): 32.
60. Matsuno Seiya, *Nihon gun no doku gasu heiki* (Tokyo: Gaifūsha, 2005), 139.
61. *Kan san ichi denki, dai nana nana kyū go hen* (unsigned government directive), printed in: Yoshimi Yoshiaki and Matsuno Seiya, eds., *Doku gasu sen kankei shiryō* (Tokyo: Fuji Shuppan, 1997).
62. Yoshimi, *Doku gasu sen*, 29.
63. Tsuneishi, "Unit 731," 26–27.

Arnaud Doglia is currently a postdoctoral research fellow in the Department of East Asian Studies at the University of Geneva, Switzerland. He is interested in contemporary Japan and East Asia. He received his MA (East Asian studies) and his PhD (Japanese studies) from the University of Geneva. His first book, published by Peter Lang, is entitled *Japanese Biological Warfare, 1880–2011: Historical Realities and the Anatomy of Memory* (2016). His current research, Japanese Medical Atrocities: Narratives of Reconversion of Former War Criminals in Postwar Japan, seeks to analyze in depth the network of scientists and physicians who participated in medical experiments up to 1945, equally discussing their profile, reconversion, and responsibility. Other topics of interest include the birth of bioethics in Japan, Japanese war crimes and their memories in East Asia, World War II and Cold War atrocities, and social history and popular culture during the Allied occupation and in postwar Japan. *The research leading to these results has received funding from the European Research Council under the European Union's Seventh Framework Programme (FP7/2007–2013) /ERC grant agreement n° [313382].This chapter was published in the context of Project 100011_169861 (Le Japon et l'Asie de l'Est face à la Seconde Guerre mondiale), funded by the Swiss National Science Foundation.*

The Question of Complicity: Japan's Early Postures toward War Crimes and War Responsibility in the Aftermath of the Second World War

Barak Kushner

Currently, in the UK there is a popular comedian, Henning Wehn who, tongue-in-cheek, labels himself "Germany's comedy ambassador" and gains big laughs for such a pronouncement. Along with his excellent mockery of British self-loathing, Wehn starts out by critiquing the UK housing market but links it to World War II (WWII): "I mean you British, why do you all want to be owned by a house . . . I am sorry, why do you all want to own a house?" His routine then goes on to disparage the poor standards of the housing market in London and the UK in general. "Basically all you get is 3,000 old bricks held together with moldy wall paper and it costs an absolute fortune. I am pleased that in Germany we

---

The research leading to these results has received funding from the European Research Council under the European Union's Seventh Framework Program (FP7/2007-2013) / ERC grant agreement n° 313382.

B. Kushner (✉)
Modern Japanese History, Department of East Asian Studies/ Faculty of Asian and Middle Eastern Studies, University of Cambridge, Cambridge, UK
e-mail: bk284@cam.ac.uk

K. von Lingen (ed.), *Debating Collaboration and Complicity in War Crimes Trials in Asia, 1945–1956*, World Histories of Crime, Culture and Violence, DOI 10.1007/978-3-319-53141-0_8

lost World War II. You flattened all our cities and we rebuilt them properly after the war. [Audience laughs.] And if that had not been the case we would be living in shitholes like you do," he ends, pointing to the British audience and getting further laughs. "So, Al Murray," turning upstage to the British master of ceremonies for the evening, "Who won the war now?" (ending his short opening gambit with big laughs again).[1]

This routine, but more importantly Wehn's ability to tweak the British historical view of WWII, is entertaining but also historically puzzling. The British audience loves it – a bit of truth in that housing in the UK is substandard and overpriced. But no one in the audience throws things at the stage and Wehn does not receive death threats. Why is it that the British can accept his sarcastic snub about their victory in WWII but economic loss in the postwar period, while a similar joke would be impossible if not dangerous for a Japanese comedian in China? Is it only because the UK was victorious in WWII, or is culturally more open to satire? China was also, in theory, part of the victorious Allies who defeated Japan. Certainly, the UK was never invaded and experienced no Nanjing Massacre, as occurred on the Chinese mainland, but the UK did fight a very brutal war in Europe and the Nazis continually bombed Britain's urban centers, with London receiving the brunt of the attacks. Some readers may feel that even posing this question borders on the absurd or overly naïve. To be sure, Henning is not performing this joke in France, which has laws about publishing tracts that contravene the state's definition of "proper" historical memory, nor is he doing such routines in Poland, directly vanquished by the Third Reich and which shares a less lengthy and healthy postwar relationship with Germany than does the UK.[2] Regardless, this issue should give us pause to consider the differences in cultural attitudes toward WWII between Europe and Asia, and why some societies can turn the war into a form of memory that offers release, or at least mock it in a socially constructive manner, instead of one that fans the flames of continued antagonism.

It may be this idea of "just deserts" or flipping UK victory in the war on its head for public amusement that entices British audiences because, in part, the German comedian acts out this routine with a glint in his eye, demonstrating that he and his audience share a common knowledge that they both realize WWII was fundamentally wrong and that Germany lost. Is there some accepted consensus about WWII in a common European memory that differs greatly from the situation in East Asia that allows for this mutual release of tension through humor?[3] Moreover, is it that a sense of justice has been attained in Europe that supposedly bolsters these shared UK–German emotions, and does this seemingly shared historical consensus feed the evolution of historical memory in Western Europe? Or does this commonality emanate from Germany's own more dogged pursuit of war crimes that somehow seemingly failed to reach its objectives in East Asia?[4]

In Japan, memory and history compete against each other, unlike in Germany, where they coexist in relative harmony. The American occupation, in both its censorship and democratization efforts, partly shaped early postwar Japanese domestic debates about WWII, informing the Japanese about the truth of the Pacific War history, and these ideas were further disseminated as news about the Tokyo War Crimes Trial. The results solidified the idea that Japan's military was responsible for the war. Censored Japanese media, controlled and massaged, in part, by the Americans, were mainly responsible for creating this historical view. In contrast, the public had a hard time accepting this imposed view. Herein lies a major factor in Japan's postwar history-versus-memory gap. Instead of moving forward by themselves to confirm or disprove the occupier's view of the war in Asia and against the Allies, Japanese mainly responded by saying they did not believe it. Second, as Ariyama Teruo notes, this American view did not correspond to many of the personal experiences the Japanese had undergone during the war – sending loved ones off to battle, evacuating the cities, experiencing air raids – so it was doubly difficult to align what the Japanese were hearing from outsiders with what they believed about the war.[5] Consequently, Japanese war memories quickly became divorced from a master narrative that was being offered up in the occupied media in the early years of the postwar.

Under these circumstances, Japanese efforts did not focus on investigating their own war crimes but rather centered on the issue of Japan's defeat and debating reasons for the loss of the war in general, encapsulated in the vague Japanese term "war responsibility" (*sensō sekinin*).[6] War responsibility was the hot topic in the immediate postwar period and mostly had to do with trying to figure out who was responsible for starting the war or who was responsible for the defeat. War responsibility also touched on the issue of war crimes, but in a different way than how it evolved in Europe and in a manner that suggested the Japanese had their own internal hierarchies about deciding the meaning of responsibility and justice in the postwar period. My chapter will briefly seek to broadly set out the contours of these early international debates on war crimes, focusing mainly on China and

Great Britain and then delving into how the Japanese responded. Within Japan, four main groups competed to control how the war crimes trials were viewed: the Japanese media, the imperial household, the imperial military, and the civilian government. The fact that each group maintained a competing ideology on how to manage or respond to the Allied calls for war crimes trials demonstrates the fractured nature of authority and rule both in wartime and then immediate postwar Japan. Each political and civilian entity wished to mitigate its own losses, minimize its own responsibility for the war in the eyes of others, and press for its own continued privileges.

War Crimes Trials in China Did Not Bring About Introspection

Discussions of war responsibility, the pursuit of justice, and the search for the meaning of WWII are far from mere historical baggage; they resonate with the everyday fabric of political life in East Asia today. In fact, given Japan's 2015 conservative government push to revise its constitution and China's efforts to strengthen its dominance in the region, these debates will not abate for the foreseeable future.[7] How both Japan and China view their history is pregnant with political significance, as has been the case since late 1945. In 2014, the *Asahi Shimbun* revealed letters of support Prime Minister Abe Shinzo sent to a regional memorial ceremony honoring Class A and other war criminals, hailing those executed by the Allied powers as having "sacrificed their souls to become the foundation of the fatherland."[8] The wording of the commemoration made clear the tendentious Japanese reasoning: "America's indiscriminate bombing of Japan's cities, the dropping of the atomic bomb, the Soviet Union's contravention of its treaty with Japan and the illegal detention of prisoners of war (POWs) are all war crimes. In short, the BC class war crimes trials of Japan and the Japanese were based on hatred and revenge, they were nothing more than that."[9]

This division between Japanese memory and history is more salient than ever and demonstrates that memory in Japan is not just in conflict with US-imposed occupation-era historical narratives but the greater narrative of the Chinese as well. In response to Japan's ripostes, the mainland Chinese Communist government continues to dredge up the history of its immediate postwar benevolence toward Japan as evidence of Japan's inability to correctly accept the past. The Chinese remain flummoxed about official Japanese obstinacy to acknowledge the Class A war crimes that were prosecuted at the Tokyo Trial, and the lesser war crimes known as Class B and C war crimes trials, which were pursued in forty-nine venues around postwar East and Southeast Asia from 1945–1951.

The Chinese Communist Party then held its own trials in 1956, after the Chinese Nationalists under Chiang Kai-shek had already conducted theirs from 1946–1949, trying to demonstrate to the world and to Japan that the Communists were *even more* benevolent than their Chinese Nationalist competitor. The Communists released the vast majority of the slightly more than 1,000 Japanese prisoners, executing no one, and prosecuting only forty-five of the higher-ranking former military and Manchukuo officials.[10] These men had already been incarcerated from 1945 to 1950 in the Soviet Union, and then again in China from 1950 to 1956, when they were tried in two courts – in Taiyuan, Shanxi Province, and Shenyang, Liaoning Province.[11] During their imprisonment these Japanese military officers and civilian officials penned extensive self-criticisms, and these confessions were later submitted to the Chinese courts as evidence of Japanese war crimes. Many of these Japanese men also published their own versions and diaries when they were eventually repatriated to Japan.[12] Toward the end of the 1980s and early 2000s Chinese translations of these confessions were published, and several reproductions were issued again for both domestic and international consumption.[13] In the lead-up to the 70th Anniversary of the end of WWII, Beijing was interested in playing this political card again with the online re-release of these Japanese war criminals' "self-confessions" as a way to remind the Japanese government of a past Beijing regards as manufactured and not accurate.[14]

On the one hand, the Chinese government has gained the lion's share of international support in the war of words surrounding wartime responsibility and the fact that Japan is not facing its own history, even though Beijing frequently shows its own distaste for "historical facts" by not publicly discussing sensitive moments within post-1949 Chinese mainland history, for example, episodes such as the Great Leap Forward (1958–1961) or the impact of Mao's disastrous Cultural Revolution (1966–1976).[15] Fang Lizhi, the late Chinese physicist who defected in 1990 after months of hiding in Beijing's U.S. embassy, remarked that history in China was equal measures creating and ignoring. This is what Perry Link, famed scholar of China, also described as the process of "forgetting history," which is "an important device of [CCP] rule," forcing "the whole of society to forget its history, and especially the true history of the Chinese Communist Party itself."[16] Link has grown even more critical lately, suggesting that this absence of historical understanding is leading to a lack of moral focus in China. He does not mince words when he suggests that China's struggle to build its own modernity and identity after the slow downturn of the Qing Dynasty from the mid-nineteenth century has not been easy. "For nearly two centuries, the great ancient civilization of China has been looking for a way to reinvent itself for the modern era. This process has involved fits, starts, and reversals; it has caused trauma and led to at least 70 million unnatural deaths."[17]

Certainly, the Chinese have rightly not forgotten Japanese imperial atrocities, but at what cost to a balanced sense of their own national history? Has this preoccupation overshadowed everything else or pushed the Japanese themselves precariously close to teetering off the balancing board, instead of encouraging them to remain focused on a sterner regime of self-examination? The rampant increase of rebellions against such ideas within more conservative or right-wing circles in Japan, regarded by them as "masochistic history" (*jigyakushi*), has arguably reached a climax in recent years. Much ink has been spilled in considering this Chinese over-emphasis on the idea of the century of humiliation, in which the Chinese people idealize their own suffering, most dramatically in regard to Japan, as a process that has forged its national identity.[18] However, one must start asking whether this emotional tendency on both sides, China and Japan, is helping to lead to any sense of reconciliation or whether it is serving more limited ends.

The March Toward War Crimes Trials After WWII

In considering the evolution toward war crimes trials of the Japanese at the dawn of the postwar, I was struck by the writings of Louis Allen.[19] Allen was an Englishman recruited into Japanese language learning at the start of WWII who found himself in Burma at the end of the war interrogating Japanese POWs for further investigation as war criminals. At one point in the process he stumbled upon one hapless former Japanese soldier and reflected on the new paradigm Japanese soldiers faced as a vanquished military in the wake of their August 1945 surrender:

> Now and then, the human reality of the war crimes issue became more real than nominal roles and indecipherable names. On one occasion, I was asked to interrogate a number of Japanese who were suspected of being involved in ill-treatment of POWs aboard ship. One of them, as he came before me

> and sat down, was literally quaking. He could not keep still, and as he sat and sweated, I looked at him and felt the hideous uncontrollable fear inside him. I did not necessarily take it to be a sign of guilt. The situation alone could have produced it. But, although his name seemed to fit a name on my list, I found I could not go on. I was suddenly struck by the thought – something which never happened with the Kempei [military police] – that I had no right whatever to be in a position to reduce another human being to this state of almost animal terror. I told him to go.

In the end, Allen adds that his decision may have been incorrect and that "it may more probably have been a moral weakness on my part...."[20] Such an attitude should give us pause to think about the sudden and broad powers the Allies were given with respect to the Japanese, who were until a moment before in complete control of those lands. As with the Chinese Communist trials mentioned earlier, war crimes trials and the pursuit of justice were not always about retribution. British tribunals abroad were theoretically conducted in accordance with the war office in London, with political instructions issued by the judge advocate general, but often fell into disagreement with the Foreign Office when officials grasped the potential impact on foreign policy. Ernest Bevin, UK Minister of Foreign Affairs in the early postwar period, believed that putting German military generals through trials would not be productive longer term for UK interests. In the end, as Kerstin von Lingen notes, even though the British and Germans had been enemies, "the military solidarity with former foes was remarkable."[21] We see this phenomenon in East Asia as well in the course of the Chinese Nationalists' treatment of certain Japanese war criminals, who were more useful to Chiang Kai-shek as allies against their common foe – the Chinese Communists. Chiang, thus, pressured a Kuomintang (KMT) military tribunal to find the last Japanese army general who led the imperial forces in China, Okamura Yasuji, "not guilty," arguably in exchange for Okamura's assistance later to form a group of former Japanese military officers to return to Taiwan. The Chinese Nationalists had fled there in 1949 and wanted the Japanese military officers to teach them strategy and Japanese "martial spirit" to implement the Nationalist plan to retake the Chinese mainland.[22]

Some British leaders were equally reticent about taking harsh measures in war crimes trials, even though Prime Minister Winston Churchill initially felt that the Nazis should merely be shot as a way of meting out justice.

However, his thoughts concerning justice in East Asia, on the fringes of the destabilized British Empire, were slightly more nuanced given the British need for assistance in rebuilding.[23] Ironically, even given their antipathy toward the Japanese military, the British needed such troops to stay in command and control so that their former European colonial holdings could be regained with a minimum of disruption and discomfort.[24] Maurice Pascal Alers Hankey, more commonly known as Lord Hankey, was perhaps one of the more vocal and far from convinced about making blanket war crimes charges against the Japanese. Hankey, who served in various capacities for many years in the colonial defense establishment, essentially retiring just before WWII erupted, opposed the Allied plan to hold war crimes trials and was a lifelong supporter of convicted Class A war criminal Japanese Foreign Minister Shigemitsu Mamoru.[25] Hankey took the somewhat unpopular position at that time that the threat of such trials encouraged the Axis powers to take desperate measures to prolong the war, and he dismissed the effort as empty propaganda that did nothing for the victims but only impeded the peace process. For Hankey, Foreign Minister Shigemitsu Mamoru's guilt by association with Japan's wartime cabinet and subsequent punishment (avoiding death by hanging by the merest of judicial margins, he believed) were not in the spirit of modern diplomacy and law. The Dutch Judge at the Tokyo War Crimes Trial, Bert Roling, later agreed with Hankey's assessment, and the two corresponded on this topic.[26] Obviously, this idea, along with the long dissent of the Indian Judge, Radhabinod Pal, helped to gird Japanese moral and legal discontent with war crimes tribunals in general, and not just the Class A trial. Hankey was aware of Churchill's pragmatic attitude toward war criminals, and this demonstrates some of the issues postwar leaders had to balance – a sense of justice with the realistic policy goal of pushing to rebuild and restabilize a region wrecked by decades of war.

> He [Churchill] has strong feelings about the prosecution of war crimes in Japan, notably the case of Prime Minister Tojo. He points out that Americans are going to need Japanese co-operation in the years ahead, and at this juncture, three years after the end of the war, to hang prominent people in that country seems to him stupid... No ruler of a country can control the actions of his troops. On the same theory, noth [sic] Roosevelt and himself would have been executed of [sic] the Allies had lost the war.[27]

Hankey might not be representative of the overall British or Allied position toward Japanese maneuvers to avoid postwar justice, but his stalwart opinion demonstrates that, regardless of political orientation, both the Allies and the Japanese continually maintained a schizophrenic approach toward the future, keeping one eye facing forward but weighing that progress against the need to investigate responsibility for the past.

History and Justice – the Japanese Way

The international frameworks that were developing in Europe and in China, outlined earlier, demonstrate the divide in the world concerning how best to pressure Japan from the outside to deal with its war crimes, but what about domestically? We should not forget that the construction of a legal basis for pursuing postwar justice was never predestined. In East Asia, the adjudication of war crimes trials based on the idea of international law was nothing short of an epic shift in legal attitudes and witnessed entirely new ways of managing the notion of justice. Even with 5,700 individuals indicted in 2,244 official trials across Asia, representing Class B and C war crimes, the scope of "justice" in European indictments numerically dwarfed what happened in East Asia.[28] This imbalance matters for two reasons. First, as evidenced in the current Japanese and Chinese media that I mentioned at the start of this chapter, the war of words about war crimes and their conflict with Japan's stated goal of the war as the "liberation of Asia" is a battle that has never waned in East Asia. Many still also believe a more utopian version of justice was achieved "over there in Europe," a situation that supposedly remains elusive in the Far East. This refrain, that Germany has atoned for its past while Japan has not, disregards the situation elsewhere in Europe. France continues to delay a full examination of its history regarding transporting Jews to concentration camps, the war of decolonization in Indochina, and the war in Algeria. More importantly, Italy, Spain, and many Eastern European countries have also shown rather weak efforts to come to terms with similar issues within their national history and the legacies of WWII.[29] Germany may actually be the outlier in terms of apology politics or confronting its own historical demons, but that is also partly because the Nazi emphasis on genocide was so extreme to begin with. If we start to compare Japan with the rest of the world, does the shadow that its imperial behavior casts change shape in any meaningful way?[30] Such a historical investigation does not, of course, deny Japanese atrocities and imperial aggression; the Japanese were far from passive actors on the world stage. But for comparative purposes we may wish to look to alternatives outside of Germany when examining war crimes outside of Japan. Regardless, what research does demonstrate is that the belief held by many Japanese that they were victims on the sharp end of receiving postwar justice is a process that began immediately as the war was ending and did not merely emanate from domestic dissatisfaction with the occupation. Japan's social response to war crimes was initially led by military officers (both demobilized and repatriated) and government officials, many of whom had held elite positions during the war.

After surrendering, the Japanese immediately took their own unilateral moves to mediate, stall, and deflect occupation-era attempts to investigate responsibility for imperial behavior during the war. Far from inertly accepting the terms of the July 1945 Potsdam Declaration, which stipulated that the Japanese would be subjected to war crimes trials, the Japanese initiated many active policies that reverberate to this day. What has become clear is the extensive Japanese internal efforts, both military and civilian, from 1945 until today to collect war crimes trial documentation with a goal of shaping a defense for Japan but not with the aim of revealing the true extent of the damage Japan's empire caused or to necessarily follow the course of "justice." However, even then we cannot really corral all the machinations and policies toward war crimes trials in Japan into one group – they were too numerous and so we can highlight their divisions and goals in what follows.

Japanese Media and Imperial Household Stances

The initial moments of the postwar period marked the early contours of the Japanese debate on war crimes. On 15 September 1945, Japanese statesman Hatoyama Ichiro remarked in the *Asahi Shimbun* that the Japanese people were concerned with the unfair sense of "dual justice," that only Japan was being judged for its wartime behavior and not the Allies.[31] His comments predated the Tokyo War Crimes Trial, which did not begin until the spring of 1946, and raised the issue of the inhumanity of the United States dropping the atomic bomb on two Japanese urban centers. Hatoyama was able to seize on such a topic, in part, because news in Japan about the new form of bomb was slow and few domestic Japanese inhabitants really understood how it was any different from regular bombing campaigns.[32] On 21 September 1945, the *Asahi Shimbun* published an article entitled "Judging War Criminals, Starting the Effort on Our Own: a Plea to Join International Trade and Rebuild the Nation."[33] The article stated that the imperial army and navy had initiated their own efforts to investigate responsibility for the war but underscored that the emperor was blameless.

The public clamor to limit the areas placed under judicial scrutiny concerning war responsibility soon led to a larger portion of society being forgiven when Emperor Hirohito on 3 November 1946, the day of the announcement of Japan's new postwar constitution, offered amnesty to all sorts of Japanese criminals. In addition to announcing his "deep pleasure" for a constitution that would serve as the "cornerstone to building a peaceful nation," Hirohito went further in his imperial rescript. It was a fascinating edict in that it was announced as a "great amnesty," but in actuality it ended prison for many charged with crimes during the war, such as those convicted of lèse-majesté, thought crimes, and political crimes. At the same time the imperial fiat also granted amnesty to soldiers who had gone AWOL, those who had been convicted in courts martial, those who had not followed orders of a superior officer during the war, and, more importantly, members of the imperial navy and army who had committed crimes against POWs or other crimes abroad.[34] In what the *Asahi Shimbun* labeled an "unprecedented scope," the imperial measure also contained a clause stipulating that such amnesty was not applicable to those who had committed crimes "against the goals of the occupation."[35] In some ways, Hirohito's imperial pronouncement offered blanket immunity for the very type of war crimes the Allies were starting to pursue against the Japanese, though it remains unclear whether the edict had any legal impact. Regardless, it certainly set the moral contours for the internal debate on war crimes soon after Japan's surrender.

This imperial announcement was followed by a government directive offering a complex web of bureaucratic rules to potentially assuage those who had judgments rendered against them previously in courts now considered "foreign" – those in Okinawa, Karafuto, Korea, Taiwan, Kwantung Leased Territory (Liaodong Peninsula in China), or in the South Pacific Islands (referring to the Marianas and Marshal Islands). Such formerly sentenced individuals could give this directive to the prosecutor in their home jurisdiction, and it would explain that their rights had been restored with this amnesty.[36] Interestingly, the emperor could only offer such amnesty according to Japanese law, which had essentially been defanged by the terms of the occupation. The war was over, and it was time to rebuild, at least that was the Japanese argument, an opinion that failed to take into account a full settlement of accounts regarding the extent of the havoc and damage the even brief Japanese rule in East Asia had caused. Japanese newspapers wrote of seven types of crime being pardoned, which led to amnesty for 330,000 individuals, the paper wrote.[37] The fact that this amnesty covered both improper wartime laws that had terrorized Japanese liberals and mixed it with laws that related to war crimes and crimes against non-Japanese would increasingly dampen Japanese postwar enthusiasm about the need to address the legacy of war crimes because the emperor had essentially delivered the verdicts that he had already dealt with it.

The Imperial Military Response to Calls for War Crimes Trials

It was not just the emperor and Japanese media that ultimately cordoned off a more robust form of assessing war responsibility. Internal circles within the former Japanese imperial armed forces also took pains to deal with their straitened situations immediately following the surrender. Former naval Captain Toyota Kumao, who headed a new group internal to the Second Bureau of Demobilization (formerly the Ministry of the Navy), was charged with keeping naval officers out of legal trouble, defending them to the best extent possible, and collecting trial records or whatever evidence was necessary as a means to offering a later defense or gain clemency. Two days after surrender the imperial navy had set up a committee to deal with the end of the war and quickly established a "Naval End of War Committee" (*Kaigun shusen iinkai*), with seven subcommittees, one of which was designed to deal with war criminals.[38]

The Tokyo War Crimes Trial (1946–1949) educated the Japanese public and the world about the cruelty that the imperial Japanese army had visited upon other Asians and POWs, if not also the Japanese people. This was in deep opposition to how the Japanese navy wished to appear, winning support for its supposed altruistic *bushido* behavior during the long war. In many ways, the former imperial navy was very successful in the venture to prove itself more civilized – far fewer naval officers were pursued for Class A war crimes than their army counterparts.[39] This was not merely a coincidence but a specific goal. Toyota's group, established in secrecy, was told to prevent war crimes trials of naval officers. He, like many other Japanese in official positions, believed that the Allied pursuit of war crimes was unlawful because "war is a national action and no individual responsibility on the level of international law can be prosecuted. If such a clause existed it was an ex-post facto law, a law created after the fact."[40] (This was not necessarily a new idea; at the Versailles Peace Treaty talks decades earlier, following the close of WWI, Japanese leaders had voiced a similar opinion that individuals should not be held responsible for state crimes, even though the delegation eventually went along with the Allied consensus to pursue the German Kaiser.)[41] Toyota's group worked long hours to help former naval officers to obscure the truth in Allied court proceedings and assisted them in their testimony. Occupation forces were probably ignorant of these preparations.[42]

Toyota seemingly developed a deep opposition to the Allied pursuit of justice, perhaps because he did not repatriate directly to Japan at the end of the war. Like many Japanese who spent the war connected to the apparatus of empire, he found himself in Europe at the end of the war. Recall that Germany surrendered in May 1945, which left the Japanese diplomatic corps remaining there rather exposed. Toyota had been posted for several years to Berlin as a military attaché in the Japanese embassy. Japanese Ambassador to Germany Oshima Hiroshi had fled but not in time, and he was eventually caught and later brought up on charges as a Class A war criminal, but first Toyota Kumao was taken with him to the United States as a prisoner at the end of the war in Europe.[43] Oshima and many of his retinue were initially sent to Fort Hunt in Alexandria, Virginia (which Toyota wrote was "on the banks of the Potomac in Washington, DC").[44] The area is now a national park, but at the time Fort Hunt was a secret American facility used to debrief and interrogate Nazi scientists and also set up to interrogate the small group of Japanese officials who were picked up along with them in Europe.[45] It appears that Toyota was detained at Fort Hunt, and that is where he learned the painful news from the U.S. media that Japan had lost the war. He recalls "observing the American people united together in denigrating behavior toward the Japanese. This was painful to the extent that words cannot describe it...."[46] The surrender unnerved him, and Toyota says he thought to himself, "What can I do now?" At this point he decided that the salvaging of Japan's dignity was best achieved by preventing humiliating and one-sided war crimes trials. And with that mental determination, after a series of other bureaucratic posts, once Toyota repatriated in December 1945, he first went to work for the Temporary Cabinet Investigation Section from early 1946 and later in some capacity or other engaged with analyzing Japan's war crimes trials for about ten years. After that he was placed in charge of efforts to amass records from all over the world while working directly under the auspices of the Ministry of Justice for eight years.

In total, Toyota spent eighteen years engaged in these tasks. He collected everything from defendants, interpreters, memos, clergy, and others – whoever might have had anything. He and his team interviewed 700 people and aimed to use that information as the basis for Japan's proposed countermeasures to release, grant clemency, or prove the innocence of Japan's war criminals.[47] In a postwar naval ministry veterans magazine, Toyota wrote that he dedicated his efforts to the spirits of 1,000 fallen comrades "as victims of the defeat" and whose conviction at trials abroad met with an "untimely end."[48] Close to 1,000 Japanese had been executed in the Class B and C war crimes trials in East and Southeast Asia. Toyota Kumao's group continued to work until 1970 (within the Ministry of Justice), gathering information and data on the war crimes trials, largely for the purpose of promoting the idea of Japanese war criminals as victims. Sandra Wilson has written extensively about former veterans groups and related associations that were established outside of and within the main prison that housed the war criminals, Sugamo Prison, which were also effective in creating this postwar sense of victimization.[49]

It is worth remembering that through these efforts the former imperial navy succeeded in shunting much of the blame and burden of and for the war onto both civilian members of the government and the imperial army, for example leaders such as Tojo Hideki, while helping to draw the emperor and other naval officials away from the prying eyes of Allied scrutiny. There was a battle of blame between the occupiers and the Japanese, but also a struggle among the Japanese to push responsibility away from some sectors and heap more of it on the shoulders of the army and a few secondary leaders.

Was Justice Served by War Crimes Trials?

While the imperial navy was taking its first steps toward vitiating the defeat, it was not clear whether that examination considered the reasons behind the defeat as a military exercise or as a moral failure. The Japanese term for war responsibility, *senso sekinin*, was fluid and employed differently by different groups to mean, among other things, the search for why Japan lost or why Japan started the war. The term also signified who was precisely responsible for the defeat. For the Japanese, the term "responsible" rarely covered the legal terrain of where responsibility lay in order to prosecute war crimes. In Japan's case, many of the individuals responsible for such a disaster stayed on in government and the administration in the postwar. Some of these men were arrested but never tried, some were never even arrested, and others were convicted as war criminals but later released and regained their prominent positions. Kishi Nobusuke (arrested as a war criminal but never indicted) was later a postwar prime minister and may be the best-known example. There was also Shigemitsu Mamoru, who later became foreign minister after being convicted as a Class A war criminal (the one Lord Hankey felt was unduly pursued), and Kaya Okinori, who after the war served as minister of justice but was also convicted as a Class A war criminal as minister of finance. There was also the well-known shadowy figure Kodama Yoshio (a fixer in the parlance of the day), who was arrested but never indicted and ultimately slipped through the Allied net. One could not prosecute all responsible, to be sure.

Just how confused and precarious the Japanese government's own position was in the early moments as the war ended becomes clearer through the example of Okazaki Katsuo's experience flying to Manila a few days after surrender. Okazaki was ordered to take a plane as a representative of the foreign ministry to Manila, to determine how the end of the war should be handled in negotiations with the Americans. It was made clear to him that at the end of the war no one was certain what was going to happen, and he almost lost his life bringing back surrender instructions from the Philippines because his team was unsure how the rest of the Japanese military would respond if the precious cargo were lost.[50] Since the dawn of its modern era Japan had never suffered a defeat, so Okazaki reasoned that there was little certainty regarding how both civilian and military Japanese officials would react if the parameters of the surrender were not clearly laid out. Japanese attitudes about how to react to the end of the war, and to responsibility for the war, were still being aggressively argued about within Japanese circles as the occupation began, and how that would play out was open to wide interpretation.[51]

The Japanese Civilian Government Response

The Japanese government had also established its own series of committees to deal with analyzing war responsibility. These are detailed in a fascinating summary, "Fundamental Direction and Attitude Japanese Government Should Take Toward War Crimes Trials," written on stationery from the Second Bureau of Demobilization. The report revealed the history of early postwar Japanese plans for dealing with the war crimes issue. And that is precisely the point: the aim was to "deal with" the imposition of such trials, not actually dig into, investigate, or pursue them. Rather, the Japanese goal was effectively to mediate efforts to the extent possible during the occupation.

The report states that Japan agreed to provide for a smooth transition at the close of the war and immediately established an End of War Administrative Bureau (Shusen jimukyoku).[52] However, the idea was floated to deal with war criminals under the leadership of the foreign ministry's Nakamura Toyoichi. Following the 11 September 1945 announcement of the first arrests of "war criminal suspects," the report notes that the numbers arrested and incarcerated slowly began to increase, so Japan felt a pressing need to set up a special office to manage issues specifically related to war crimes, to liaise with the Americans, and to provide information as well as carry out processing duties. The Japanese were not quite fully prepared for the scale of what they faced, nor did they really grasp the central issues at stake. (While the Japanese government was aware of the contents of the Potsdam Declaration, which mentioned that the abuse of Allied POWs would be prosecuted, it was not clear how this process would be implemented.) With all deliberate speed, Japan made moves to put forward a plan that made clear its position, though perhaps forgetting it had no real authority to do that. On the morning of 12 September 1945, the prime minister, foreign minister, minister of the army, minister of the navy, chief of staff, Minister of State Konoe Fumimaro, the minister of justice, and several others gathered to discuss these terms at a meeting convened to determine the end of war strategy. The decision at this meeting was that even if the Allies were to pursue such trials unilaterally, Japan should make the first move and push investigations into war crimes, pursue responsibility of individuals, and hand those results over to General Headquarters. The reason for doing this was to avoid letting the process be biased by Allied one-sidedness and because the Japanese state should have sympathy for such individuals. After the meeting, Kido Koichi, home minister at the time, presented this decision as a memorial to the emperor. In response, the emperor essentially remarked that he was saddened that his imperial subjects would be charged with crimes, having fought the war bravely in his name. At night on the 12th, the same meeting reconvened and Kido informed members of the emperor's comments. They continued their deliberations, found their decision to be sound, and at night the cabinet made it a formal decision to hold their own war crimes trials.[53] Ultimately, this effort was short lived, but the strategy was clear – try to block Allied efforts where possible.

Of course, there was the problem with Class A war criminals that in looking at their culpability the issue would ultimately touch on the emperor's role, so three major policies were laid out with respect to any matter dealing with war crimes:

1. Do not touch on anything related to the emperor's responsibility.
2. Protect the nation.
3. Within the framework of the first two points and to the extent possible, defend individuals.[54]

The Imperial Legacy Lives On

As soon as it was legally feasible, the Japanese government actually conducted an about-face regarding its understanding of the 1952 San Francisco Peace Treaty when it accepted the judgments of Allied war crimes tribunals. In August 1953, the government passed new measures that essentially granted released Japanese war criminals amnesty and allowed them back into mainstream society to receive welfare benefits or pensions or permitted their families to receive some portion of financial assistance. Moreover, these regulations were amended numerous times over the ensuing decades. In the words of Japanese historian Hattori Ryuji, this created an environment in which the government gave the impression that war crimes trials on the level of domestic law neither carried a stigma nor were any longer considered an actual crime since they did not prohibit individuals from receiving government benefits, as was previously illegal during the occupation.[55]

Decades after WWII had ended, in 1981, Iwanaga Kenji, a former Japanese imperial naval officer, wrote in an imperial Japanese navy veterans magazine that what Japan needed but lacked was the patriotism to defend itself. A high Gross National Product is insignificant, he wrote, if one does not love one's country. Why is it that all other countries have patriotic fervor except for Japan? Iwanami asked. It is due to the Pacific War (1941–1945), he wrote specifically and tellingly, not mentioning the much longer and larger war that began in China in

1937. Or maybe it is due to the fact that people believe that Japan was the sole *hanzaikoku*, "criminal country," he suggested. Iwanaga insisted, as did many of his generation, that the United States was responsible for WWII, having backed Japan into a corner, and that Japan needed to teach this set of facts to its younger generations. (Sadly, this belief seemingly ignores the devastation that the imperial military brought about within Japan itself, but that is a much longer digression.) The former naval officer argued that Japan's postwar constitution had been imposed on the nation from the outside, but he failed to appreciate how much Japan had actually benefitted from this postwar situation, developing into a rich and wealthy country in the interim. Paradoxically, Japan was wealthy and stable precisely because it lost the war. For former imperial military men, such as Iwanaga, the postwar era meant nothing because it was connected to a Japan that completely denigrated its militarist and imperial past.[56]

The fact of the matter is that, even years after the war, some Japanese military groups were still arguing among themselves, not about whether what they did was right or wrong, but rather how right they were and that it was deleterious for younger Japanese and the nation at large not to realize this. Given all the effort that went into the Allied production of war crimes trials, how did such an antithetical mindset develop? I posit that part of the framework for calling into doubt the verdicts of the war crimes trials was not merely due to legal inadequacies and often had little connection with the trial processes themselves. The initial backlash against this postwar pursuit of justice came from within Japanese military and civilian circles in the early stages of the postwar period and helped to shape successive Japanese generations to avoid looking harshly at the sort of war Japan waged in Asia and the Pacific. This frame of mind also helped to configure how the pursuit of justice was seen as merely another step in the process of victimizing the Japanese.

Recall that in the 1950s China's policy toward Japan was precisely the policy that Churchill espoused for Europe – pragmatism over emotion. (And here I think a Euro-Asia comparison of war crimes issues may be more fruitful than looking constantly at the American examples.) Churchill said, "Revenge is, of all satisfactions, the most costly and long drawn out; retributive persecution is, of all policies, the most pernicious. Our policy, subject to the exceptional cases I have mentioned, should henceforward be to draw the sponge across the crime and horrors of the past – hard as that may be – and look, for the sake of our salvation, toward the future. There can be no revival of Europe without the active and loyal aid of all the German tribes."[57] China also wished for the revival of an economically vibrant Japan, not because it was just, but because it served Chinese interests as well.[58]

Conclusion

To end wars, as to begin them, societies need to be mobilized, and that requires propaganda. To win "hearts and minds," governments require information on the enemy or the ability to set out new social goals that will galvanize the population into action. We need to constantly question what sort of intersection we have here between the pursuit of postwar justice and the force of propaganda that aimed to "resocialize" Japan at the end of the war. Was the Allied need for closure and finding the locus of responsibility the means to that end?

Several years ago in London I delivered a talk concerning how postwar Japanese society viewed the war crimes debate and how it had evolved since 1945. I specifically avoided talking about the United States, instead focusing all my remarks on Japan's war in China and Japanese war crimes on the Chinese mainland. I did so for two reasons. The first reason was selfish – many excellent scholars are looking into this area and the specific U.S.–Japan postwar relationship, so I feel I have little extra to add. The second reason was more strategic: by avoiding getting entangled in the debate on the morality of the American decision to drop two atomic bombs, I aimed to focus on what I thought was a less debatable set of issues. I laid out my case carefully cordoning off U.S. involvement and said, "Let's just focus on Japanese military actions in the process of colonizing China during the war." And yet, in the end, an elderly Japanese woman came up to me, someone who has lived for over thirty years in the UK, and reprimanded me for daring to talk about Japanese war crimes without talking about the horror of the atomic bomb – as if the two are equated and we are not free to hold the Japanese responsible until we have adjudicated American actions. I reminded her, as I do others, that a *tu quoque* defense is never valid, and yet this refrain is a mantra for many. The mindset created by the Japanese government and military seventy years ago remains firm for many Japanese today, and this underscores a deeper problem. Why did a consensus about justice served, that seemingly allows the British to laugh at German jokes about the war, never develop in East Asia or even within Japan itself? Part of the reason must be the lack of this shared consensus about the roots of the war and the war itself, not merely the lack of transitional justice following surrender.

In 1952, just after the end of the occupation, the Japanese Federation of Bar Associations announced the start of a movement to release war criminals and called for the government to respond. The group even published a book in the same year detailing their position, under the title *The Legal Baselessness of the Tokyo Trial*.[59]

The volume of work in this genre has never abated in Japan, but many memoirs and books have also been published that suggest that Chinese ideas about its notion of justice were probably very different than they are now. It is telling to consider that perhaps at one moment in the past, there was actually a time when the Chinese and the Japanese might have developed a shared consensus, something along contemporary UK–German lines. Former Japanese military delegates that went to China on numerous visits during the 1950s and early 1960s quote Mao as saying that he did not hate former imperial Japanese soldiers. On the contrary, he wanted to engage them in dialogue and get them to visit China more. As Mao acknowledged, "I don't want visitors from Japan that already agree with me; we want to invite those who don't."[60] Though I have never been a big fan of quoting Mao to reveal some gem of truth, in this instance his approach may have been the best model at the time to have actually achieved that very consensus on postwar justice that currently seems so elusive.

Notes

1. From Henning Wehn's show, https://www.youtube.com/watch?v=L6az6J38–I (last access for all links given in this paper, unless otherwise stated, is 25 May 2015).
2. For a simple overview see Raffi Wartanian, "Memory laws in France and their implications: Institutionalizing social harmony," http://www.humanityinaction.org/knowledgebase/117-memory-laws-in-france-and-their-implications-institutionalizing-social-harmony (last accessed 28 November 2016). For a provocative discussion of history and memory in France concerning similar issues see Henry Rousso, *La dernière catastrophe: L'histoire, le présent, le contemporain* (Paris: Collection NRF Essais, Gallimard, 2012).
3. There certainly is comedy about the war in Japan and some examples in China. For example, the Japanese film *Warai no daigaku* (*University of Laughs*), focuses on the witty repartee between a wartime comedic script writer and the censor who vexes him. *Winds of God* is a provocative comedy that was first produced as a stage play about two twentieth-century Japanese

comedians who find themselves transported in time to a kamikaze training camp in wartime Japan and attempt to come to terms with the meaning of life and death. The Chinese film *Guizi lai le* (*Devils on the Doorstep*) followed a similar trajectory, even though it was at first banned in China, but to date there have not been interactive comedic exchanges, such as the one Wehn attempts, in any mainstream or popularly recognized attempts. For a larger view of the image of Japan and the Japanese in postwar Chinese humor, see Barak Kushner, "Unwarranted attention: the image of Japan in twentieth century Chinese humour," in Jessica Davis and Jocelyn Chey, eds., *Humour in Chinese Life and Culture: Resistance and Control in Modern Times* (Hong Kong: Hong Kong University Press 2013), 47–80.

4. While Germany has pursued its own domestic war crimes, these did not come immediately, as is often assumed. See Kerstin von Lingen, "Germany as a role model? Coming to terms with Nazi War Deeds, 1945–2015," in Barak Kushner and Sherzod Muminov, eds., *The End of Empire and Japan's Search for Postwar Legitimacy*, (London: Routledge, 2017), 299–315.
5. Ariyama Teruo, "Sengo nihon ni okeru rekishi kioku media," *Mediashi kenkyukai*, April, 2003, 6–8.
6. On postwar Japanese former military efforts to stymie the war crimes process see Barak Kushner, *Men to Devils, Devils to Men: Japanese War Crimes and Chinese Justice* (Cambridge, MA: Harvard University Press, 2015), 54–56.
7. *Yomiuri Shimbun*, 3 May 2015, Tokyo morning edition.
8. "Abe Praised Class-A War Criminals for Being 'foundation' of Japan's Prosperity," *New York Times*, 28.8.2014, http://www.nytimes.com/2014/08/28/world/asia/japan-says-premier-supported-ceremony-honoring-war-criminals.html?_r=0 (last accessed 6 December 2016).
9. Japanese website describing war criminals as "martyrs"; see at http://www.syowajyunnansya.jp/pro3.htm (last accessed 6 December 2016).
10. Barak Kushner, *Men to Devils, Devils to Men: Japanese War Crimes and Chinese Justice* (Cambridge, MA: Harvard University Press, 2015), 281–2.
11. Shanxisheng renmin jianchayuan, ed., *Zhenxun riben zhanfan jishi (taiyuan): 1952–1956* (Beijing: Xinhua Chubanshe, 1995); Guo Xiaoye, *Riben youling—wentu duizhao—erzhan qijian qinhua zhanfan shenpan jishi* (Beijing: Dangdai shijie chubanshe, 2004); and Guo Zhangjian et al., eds., *Riben zhanfan de zaisheng zhidi—zhongguo fushun zhanfan guanlisuo* (Japanese translation) (Beijing:Wuzhou Zhuanbo Chubanshe, 2005). There is an identical book with a dual English translation and the subtitle "Place of Rebirth."
12. For example, those from officials of a fairly high standing, and thus representative of elite views, would be Jono Hiroshi, *Sansei dokuritsu senki—shusen yonnenkan mo chugoku de tatakatta nihonjin no kiroku* (Sekkasha, 1967);

Furumi Tadayuki, *Wasureenu manshukoku* (Keizai oraisha, 1978); and Kaeriyama Noriyuki, *Ikite iru senpan—Kanei Sadanao no ninzai* (Fuyō shobo shuppan, 2009). Unless otherwise noted, all Japanese books are published in Tokyo.

13. Yuan Qiubai and Yang Guizhen, *Zuie de zigongzhuang: xin zhongguo dui riben zhanfan de lishi shenpan* (Beijing: Jiefang Chubanshe, 2001).
14. Chinese website detailing the confessions of the war crimianls tried by the Chinese communists at http://61.135.203.68/rbzf/index.htm (last accessed 6 December 2016).
15. Books about these "sensitive" topics are usually produced in Hong Kong though often authored by mainland or foreign scholars. For the famine resulting from the Great Leap Forward see Frank Dikotter, *Mao's Great Famine: The History of China's Most Devastating Catastrophe, 1958–62* (London: Bloomsbury, 2011).
16. Fang Lizhi, translated by Perry Link, "The Chinese Amnesia", http://www.nybooks.com/articles/archives/1990/sep/27/the-chinese-amnesia/ (last accessed 28 November 2016).
17. Perry Link, "What It Means to Be Chinese-Nationalism and Identity in Xi's China," *Foreign Affairs*, 20 April 2015 (https://www.foreignaffairs.com/articles/china/2015-04-20/what-it-means-be-chinese?cid=rss-all-what_it_means_to_be_chinese-000000) (last accessed 28 November 2016).
18. William A. Callahan, "History, Identity and Security: Producing and Consuming Nationalism in China," *Critical Asian Studies*, 38:2 (2006), 179–208.
19. For an overview of Chinese trials of the Japanese, see Barak Kushner, *Men to Devils, Devils to Men: Japanese War Crimes and Chinese Justice* (Cambridge, MA: Harvard University Press, 2015). For a larger discussion concerning these trials in memory and history within Sino–Japanese relations, see Iko Toshiya, *Senso wa do kioku sareruno ka: nitchu ryokoku no kyomei to sokoku* (Kashiwa Shobo, 2015).
20. Louis Allen, "Autobiographical: Innocents Abroad: Investigating War Crimes in South-East Asia," in Ian Nish and Mark Allen, eds., *War, Conflict and Security: Japan and Asia-Pacific, 1941–1952, The Writings of Louis Allen* (Leiden: Global Oriental, 2011), xxxvi.
21. Kerstin von Lingen, *Kesselring's Last Battle: War Crimes Trials and Cold War Politics, 1945–1960* (Lawrence: University of Kansas, 2009), 78–9. For an overall treatment of the British war crimes trials of the Japanese see Hayashi Hirofumi, *Sabakareta senso hanzai – igirisu no tainichi senpan saiban*, (Iwanami Shoten, 1998).
22. The most recent comprehensive book on this in Japanese is Nojima Tsuyoshi, *Rasuto batarion: Sho kaiseki to nihon gunjintachi* (Kodansha, 2014); in English, see Barak Kushner, "Ghosts of the Japanese Imperial

Army: The 'White Group' (Baituan) and Early Post-war Sino-Japanese Relations," *Past and Present*, 218, suppl 8 (Transnationalism and Contemporary Global History), (2013), 117–50. Chinese oral history about the training that these Chinese Nationalist officers received from the Japanese and the extent of the KMT plan to wrest the Chinese mainland from Communist domination can be found in Guofangbu Shizhenbianyishi, ed., *Chenfeng de zuozhan jihua, guoguangjihua koushu lishi* (Taipei, Taiwan: Guofangbu Shizhenbianyishi, 2005).

23. "Ian Buruma in conversation with Prospect," online *Prospect Magazine*, 25 October 2013. Buruma quotes Churchill as having said that the Allies should take the Nazis, "put them up against the wall and shoot the bastards."
24. I discuss one example of this in Barak Kushner, *Men to Devils, Devils to Men: Japanese War Crimes and Chinese Justice* (Cambridge, MA: Harvard University Press, 2015), 138.
25. In his memoirs, Shigemitsu describes Hankey as a friend of Japan whose actions at the Paris Peace Conference after WWI left a deep impression on the Japanese diplomatic mission and that he was one who made tireless efforts to try and save the Anglo–Japan alliance from being nullified in 1923. Shigemitsu Mamoru, *Gaiko kaisoroku* (Chuko Koron Shinsha, 2011), 380.
26. Hankey Papers in the Churchill Archives, Churchill College, University of Cambridge, UK. HKNY/20/1.
27. In the Hankey Papers in the Churchill Archives, Churchill College, University of Cambridge, UK.; HKNY/20/1, notes from the *Forrestal Diaries*, "Trial of War Criminals," 12 November 1948. See also Maurice Pascal Alers Hankey, *Politics, Trials, and Errors* (Oxford: Pen-in-Hand, 1950).
28. Yuma Totani provides the most up-to-date list and details in *Justice in Asia and the Pacific Region, 1945–1952* (Cambridge, UK: Cambridge University Press, 2015), 9–10.
29. One rather telling mode of scholarship in this vein would be Jan Gross' revealing works about Polish history: *Neighbors: The Destruction of the Jewish Community in Jedwabne, Poland* (Princeton: Princeton University Press, 2001), and *Fear: Anti-Semitism in Poland After Auschwitz* (New York: Random House, 2006).
30. Thomas Berger cogently discusses the less understood aspects of a Japan–Germany comparison in *War, Guilt, and World Politics after World War II* (Cambridge, UK: Cambridge University Press, 2012).
31. Asahi shimbun kensho showa hodo shuzaihan, eds., *Shimbun to showa* (Asahi Shimbun Shuppansha, 2010), 222.
32. Asahi Shimbun Company, *Media, Propaganda and Politics in 20th-Century Japan*, trans. Barak Kushner (London: Bloomsbury Publishers, 2015), 91–2, 96–7. News outside the country was ironically a bit easier to come by. Takasaki

Tatsunosuke, who was soon to head the Japanese Association of Those Left Behind in Manchuria, learned from Red Cross official Marcel Junod on 7 August 1945 that the bomb dropped on Hiroshima the day before was a new form of weapon, an atomic bomb. See Mayumi Itoh, *Pioneers of Sino-Japanese Relations: Liao and Takasaki* (New York: Palgrave Macmillan, 2012), 29–30. Junod was the first Western doctor to directly witness the extent of Hiroshima's extinction as a city in early September 1945.

33. *Asahi Shimbun*, 21 September 1945 (morning edition).
34. Full text of *Chokurei*, number 511, November 3, 1946.
35. The edict is reprinted in full in *Kanpo*, November 3, 1946.
36. R. John Pritchard, "The gift of clemency following British War crimes trials in the Far East, 1946–1948," *Criminal Law Forum*, 15 (1996): 22–4.
37. "Sanjusanmannin ni onsharei taishanado nana shurui no kohani ni wataru," *Yomiuri Shimbun*, 3 November 1946 (morning edition).
38. Toyota Kumao, *Senso saiban yoroku* (Taiseisha, 1986), 49–50.
39. A fascinating reappraisal of bushido and how it is an invented tradition is analyzed in Oleg Benesch, *Inventing the Way of the Samurai: Nationalism, Internationalism, and Bushidō in Modern Japan* (Oxford: Oxford University Press, 2014).
40. *NHK Supesharu: nihonkaigun, 400 jikan no shogen, dai sankai, senspan saiban, dai ni no senso* (NHK, 2012) (DVD); NHK supesharu shuzai-han, *Nihon kaigun yonhyakujikan no shogen: gunreibu sanbôtachi ga katatta haisen* (Shinchosha, 2011), 295; Toyota Kumao, "BCkyu senpan saiban no shinso," in Shinjinbutsu oraisha, ed., *Senso saiban shokeisha issen*, Bessatsu rekishi dokuhon, dai 15go (Shinjinbutsu oraisha, 1993), 32–7.
41. Yokoshima Koji shows that, even though the Japanese mission to the Versailles Peace Talks eventually acceded to pursuing war crimes against the Germans, it was never an idea that gained traction in elite Japanese circles. See "Kaiza sotsui mondai o meguru minkangawa no ninshiki," *Shien*, vol. 71, no. 2 (March 2011): 15–26.
42. I offer more detail on this process in Barak Kushner, *Men to Devils, Devils to Men: Japanese War Crimes and Chinese Justice* (Cambridge, MA: Harvard University Press, 2015), 55–7.
43. Carl Boyd, *Hitler's Japanese Confidant: General Oshima Hiroshi and MAGIC Intelligence, 1941–1945* (Lawrence: Kansas University Press, 1993), 176–7.
44. Toyota Kumao, "Senso saiban no atoshimatsu ni tsuite," *Suiko* (July 1973), 22.
45. No new information has been uncovered about the interrogations of the Japanese there, but the German interrogations have been analyzed in Soenke Neitzel and Harald Welzer, *Soldaten: On Fighting, Killing, and*

Dying: The Secret World War II Transcripts of German POWs (New York: Knopf, 2012).

46. Toyota Kumao, "Senso saiban no atoshimatsu ni tsuite," *Suiko* (July 1973), 22.
47. Some of these materials have started to be declassified in the National Archives in Tokyo, but the process is slow, and I have only just gained access to new files.
48. Toyota Kumao, "Senso saiban no atoshimatsu ni tsuite," *Suiko* (July 1973), 24.
49. Sandra Wilson, "After the trials: Class B and C Japanese war criminals and the postwar world," *Japanese Studies* 31,2 (2011):141–9; "Prisoners in Sugamo and their campaign for release, 1952–1953," *Japanese Studies* 31,2 (2011): 171–90; "War, Soldier and Nation in 1950s Japan," *International Journal of Asian Studies* 5,2 (2008), 187–218.
50. Okazaki Katsuo, *Sengo nijunen no henreki*, in the series: Shirizu sengoshi no shogen – senryo to kowa, 6 (Chuo Koronsha, 1999), 19–22.
51. Eto Jun, ed., *Senryo shiroku*, vols. 1 and 2 (new edition) (Kodansha gakujutsu bunko, 1995) details the extensive negotiations required for Japan to surrender in all venues across the empire and numerous initial conversations with Allied officials concerning how the end of empire and beginning of the occupation would take shape.
52. Yasukuni Shrine Archives, 61023, 393.4, Inoue shiryo, Senso saiban ni taisuru nihon seifu no kihon taido narabi ni hoshin. This is written on "Daini fukuinkyoku zanmu shoribu" stationery, no pagination.
53. Toyota Kumao, *Senso saiban yoroku* (Taiseisha, 1986), 51, says it is suspected that this cabinet decision was never publicly released, and I have not been able to locate the contents elsewhere.
54. Yasukuni Shrine Archives, 61023, 393.4, Inoue shiryo, Senso saiban ni taisuru nihon seifu no kihon taido narabi ni hoshin. This is written on "Daini fukuinkyoku zanmu shoribu" stationery, no pagination. See also Toyota Kumao, *Senso saiban yoroku* (Taiseisha, 1986), 48–62; Higurashi Yoshinobu, *Tokyo saiban* (Kodansha 2008), 147–50.
55. Hattori Ryuji, *Gaiko dokumento rekishi ninshiki* (Iwanami Shinsho, 2015), 6.
56. Iwanaga Kenji, "Taiheiyo senso no sekinin to aikokushin," *Suiko* (July 1981), 20–2.
57. Hankey Papers in the Churchill Archives, Churchill College, University of Cambridge, UK, HKNY/20/2, Clemency for War Criminals in Germany, Notes by Lord Hankey.
58. Amy King details this economic relationship in Amy King, "Imperialism, industrialisation and war: The role of ideas in China's Japan Policy, 1949–1965" (PhD diss. Oxford, 2012); and Amy King, "Reconstructing China: Japanese technicians and industrialization in the early years of the PRC," *Modern Asian Studies*, 50,1, (2016), 141–74.

59. Fukasaku Teiji, ed., *Hoteki konkyo o kaku tokyo saiban: ippan senpan himen no undo o isso sokushin suru tame no katsudo* (Nihon bengoshikai, 1952).
60. As quoted in Shiroyama Hidemi, "'Moto gunji hochudan' to Motakuto gaiko no senryakusei – chugoku gaiko toan kara miru gunkokushugi no seisan" *Soshio saiensu* 19 (March 2013), 76–92.

Barak Kushner teaches modern Japanese history in the Faculty of Asian & Middle Eastern Studies at Cambridge University. He was awarded a 2012–2013 British Academy Mid-Career Fellowship which he used to complete his third book entitled *Men to Devils, Devils to Men: Japanese War Crimes and Chinese Justice* (Harvard University Press, 2015). In 2013 he launched a 5-year European Research Council funded project, "The Dissolution of the Japanese Empire and the Struggle for Legitimacy in Postwar East Asia, 1945–1965." Kushner's second book, *Slurp! A culinary and social history of ramen – Japan's favorite noodle soup* (Brill, 2012), analyzed food and history within Sino-Japan relations and was awarded the 2013 Sophie Coe Prize for Food History. *The Thought War – Japanese Imperial Propaganda* (Hawaii 2006), Kushner's first book, delved into the history of wartime Japanese propaganda. He was a 2008 Abe Fellow and conducted research concerning "Cold War Propaganda in East Asia and Historical Memory." Previously, Kushner worked in the US Department of State as a political officer in East Asian affairs and taught Chinese and Japanese history at Davidson College in North Carolina, USA. As a scholar he has written on wartime Japanese and Chinese propaganda, Japanese media, Sino-Japanese relations, Asian comedy, food history, BC class war crimes, and the Cold War. (For more see www.barakkushner.net)

Erratum to: Oaths of Allegiance in the Singapore Trials

CHEAH Wui Ling

Erratum to:
Chapter 4 in: K. von Lingen (ed.), *Debating Collaboration and Complicity in War Crimes Trials in Asia, 1945–1956*,
https://doi.org/10.1007/978-3-319-53141-0_4

The original version of Chapter 4 was inadvertently published with incorrect author name "C. Wui Ling" instead of "CHEAH W.L.". The chapter has been updated.

The updated online version for this chapter can be found at
https://doi.org/10.1007/978-3-319-53141-0_4

K. von Lingen (ed.), *Debating Collaboration and Complicity in War Crimes Trials in Asia, 1945–1956*, World Histories of Crime, Culture and Violence, DOI 10.1007/978-3-319-53141-0_9

Index

K. von Lingen (ed.), *Debating Collaboration and Complicity in War Crimes Trials in Asia, 1945–1956*, World Histories of Crime, Culture and Violence, DOI 10.1007/978-3-319-53141-0

The manufacturer's authorised representative in the EU is Springer Nature Customer Service Centre GmbH, Europaplatz 3, 69115 Heidelberg, Germany. If you have any concerns regarding our products, please contact ProductSafety@springernature.com

Printed and bound by CPI Group (UK) Ltd, Croydon, CR0 4YY
25/09/2026
02222854-0001